T0048689

What is Sexual History?

What is History? series

John H. Arnold, *What is Medieval History?*

Peter Burke, *What is Cultural History?* 2nd edition

Peter Burke, *What is the History of Knowledge?*

John C. Burnham, *What is Medical History?*

Pamela Kyle Crossley, *What is Global History?*

Pero Gaglo Dagbovie, *What is African American History?*

Shane Ewen, *What is Urban History?*

Christiane Harzig and Dirk Hoerder, with Donna Gabaccia, *What is Migration History?*

J. Donald Hughes, *What is Environmental History?*

Andrew Leach, *What is Architectural History?*

Stephen Morillo with Michael F. Pavkovic, *What is Military History?* 2nd edition

Sonya O. Rose, *What is Gender History?*

Brenda E. Stevenson, *What is Slavery?*

Jeffrey Weeks, *What is Sexual History?*

Richard Whatmore, *What is Intellectual History?*

What is Sexual History?

Jeffrey Weeks

polity

First published in 2016 by Polity Press

Polity Press
65 Bridge Street
Cambridge CB2 1UR, UK

Polity Press
350 Main Street
Malden, MA 02148, USA

ISBN-13: 978-0-7456-8024-8
ISBN-13: 978-0-7456-8025-5 (pb)

A catalogue record for this book is available from the British Library.

Library of Congress Cataloging-in-Publication Data

Names: Weeks, Jeffrey, 1945– author.
Title: What is sexual history? / Jeffrey Weeks.
Description: Cambridge, UK ; Malden, MA : Polity Press, 2016. |
Series: What is history? | Includes bibliographical references and index.
Identifiers: LCCN 2015036001| ISBN 9780745680248 (hardcover : alk.
paper) |
    ISBN 0745680240 (hardcover : alk. paper) | ISBN 9780745680255 (pbk. :
alk.
    paper) | ISBN 0745680259 (pbk. : alk. paper)
Subjects: LCSH: Sex–History. | Sexual ethics–History.
Classification: LCC HQ12 .W443 2016 | DDC 176/.4–dc23 LC record
    available at http://lccn.loc.gov/2015036001

Typeset in 10.5 on 12 pt Sabon by Toppan Best-set Premedia Limited
Printed and bound in the UK by CPI Group (UK) Ltd, Croydon, CR0 4YY

For further information on Polity, visit our website: politybooks.com

In loving memory of my parents

Raymond Hugh Weeks (1924–1976)

and

Eiddwen Weeks (1921–2014)

Contents

Preface and Acknowledgements   ix

An Introduction   1
    What is a History of Sexuality a History of?   1
    Narratives   5
    Summary of the Book   9

1   Framing Sexual History   11
    Towards a Critical Sexual History   11
    Theoretical Detours   13
    Bodies   15
    Subjectivities and Affect   17
    Generations   19
    Times Present, Times Past, Times Future   20

2   The Invention of Sexual History   23
    The Magic of Words   23
    The Natural History of Sexuality   26
    The New History   31
    The Emergence of Social Constructionism   33

3   Querying and Queering Same-Sex History   38
    What is Homosexual History?   38
    Recovering the Lesbian and Gay Past and
       Historic Present   40
    Deconstructing and Reconstructing
       the Homosexual   43

The Queer Challenge	48
Beyond the Binary	50
Making Connections	54
4 Gender, Sexuality and Power	57
Dangers and Pleasures	57
Sexual Violence and Sexual History	58
Historicizing Female Sexuality	61
Sexuality and the Theory Wars	64
Rethinking Power	66
Intersections	68
On Manliness, Masculinity and Men	72
5 Mainstreaming Sexual History	75
Into the Mainstream	75
The Birth of Modern Sexuality?	77
The Normalization of Heterosexuality	81
The Great Transition	84
AIDS and the Burdens of History	88
Same-Sex Marriage and New Patterns of Intimacy	91
6 The Globalization of Sexual History	96
Globalizing Sexual History	96
Historians and Transnational Sexual History	98
Patterns of Sexual History	101
The Colonial Legacy and the Postcolonial Critique	104
Sexual Regimes, Sexual Lives	107
History and Human Sexual Rights	112
7 Memory, Community, Voice	116
Unofficial Knowledges and Counter-History	116
Memory and Community	119
The Sexual Archive	120
Voice	125
Living Sexual History	129
Suggestions for Further Reading	131
Notes	147
Index	175

Preface and Acknowledgements

My interest in the history of sexuality began as I was researching the history of political and social ideas in late nineteenth-century Britain. It was difficult to avoid the realization (though generations of historians had managed to do so) that the radical and socialist writers of the period I was reading about had also been intensely interested in sexuality, and were heavily influenced by the feminist ideas of the period, by the first stirrings of a new homosexual consciousness, and by the early days of sexology, the new science of desire. It's not surprising, then, that throughout my writing career I have been intensely interested in how ideas of sexuality, and the very idea of sexuality itself, emerged at the end of the nineteenth century and began to shape social and political thinking.

This book in a sense continues that interest. It is in part about the idea of a sexual history, how it emerged, a little shyly, perhaps, in the nineteenth century, had a quiet, even covert existence for the first half of the twentieth century, and only began to stretch its limbs and transform itself from the 1960s and 1970s, in the wake of the cultural and social upheavals of the period. But sexual history is not just about ideas. It is a highly practical enterprise, involving a range of skills and practices, from archive searching to building new archives, from interpreting obscure texts to creating new knowledge, from trying to uncover traces of the past to writing histories of the present, from producing distinguished tomes to building a website and making documentary films. Sexual history today embraces both high theory and community histories, ivory-tower specialisms and democratic practices. It has become a major presence in the wider practice of history, and a historical presence in the practice of sexual politics.

Which means it is impossible to be fully comprehensive in a brief overview of sexual history in a short book. I have therefore focused on several key themes: the 'invention' of the subject and the development of a critical sexual history; the historicizing of homosexuality and sexual and gender dissidence; the relationship between gender and power, and their intersection with various dimensions of oppression and resistance; the mainstreaming of sexual history, and the emergence of 'modern sexuality'; the globalization of sexual history; and the significance of community history. I hope that in exploring these themes the reader will gain insight into the wider adventures of doing sexual history.

Writing is by its nature a lonely business, but doing history is necessarily a collaborative one, because we build on the work of many others. I have expressed my debt to friends, colleagues and collaborators in my previous books and I won't repeat all their names here. I will, though, repeat my warmest thanks to them for all they have contributed in different ways over many years. Some individuals, however, have given particular support in writing this book, through ideas, references, intellectual stimulation, invitations to give papers or write articles, critical appraisal, administrative support and emotional sustenance. It's a pleasure to thank Peter Aggleton, Dennis Altman, Sue Bruley, Mariela Castro Espin, Matt Cook, Daniel Defert, Mary Evans, Robert French, Brian Heaphy, Clare Hemmings, Janet Holland, Jonathan Ned Katz, Brian Lewis, Karin Lutzen, Daniel Marshall, Rommel Mendes-Leite, Henrietta Moore, Ken Plummer, Paula Sequiera, Frederic Simon, Carol Smart, Marc Stein and Graham Willett. I must also thank the anonymous readers of the book for their positive and constructive comments. I have tried to accommodate their suggestions, but I alone, of course, remain responsible for the final product.

My partner, Mark McNestry, has as always given indispensable support. Without him, there would be no book.

My mother died when I was writing this book, thirty-eight years after my father. I miss them both, respect them deeply, and thank them for making everything possible. I dedicate this book to their memory with love.

An Introduction

What is a History of Sexuality a History of?

When I began writing about the history of sexuality in the 1970s it was like venturing into an unexplored territory. It was sparsely populated. There were few prominent features, and no reliable maps. Hardly anyone visited.[1] Today sexual history is flourishing: the territory is well cultivated, the population is highly vocal, and there are plentiful guides, with highly developed global links. It has made great strides from the margins to the mainstream. In this book I hope to show how this happened, and what its implications are for thinking about, and living, that complex historical phenomenon we know as sexuality.

For most of the twentieth century histories of sexuality were relatively rare, and were overwhelmingly shaped by the self-declared 'scientific' paradigms established at the end of the nineteenth century following the emergence of sexology as the 'science of sex'. Pioneering sexologists were conscious of the historical significance of what they were setting out to do – nothing less than to put the study of sexuality on a scientific basis by understanding the laws of sexuality and their impact on individual and social life (see chapter 2). The aim was to contribute to the achievement of sexual justice through the application of reason and scientific knowledge – 'Through Science to Justice', as Magnus Hirschfeld, the

German pioneer of sexology, sexual reform and homosexual rights, proclaimed as his watchword. In this task pioneering sexologists advocated an increasing historical understanding of sexuality, and especially of the truth of the sexual categorizations and sexual and gender types their writings and clinical practice had 'discovered'. In turn, their sexual science became the taken-for-granted framework for would-be historians in succeeding generations, until at least the 1970s.

Despite these ambitions, early sexual historians remained marginal to the practice of history as a profession, rarely touching the mainstream let alone trespassing long in the wary groves of academe. When a new generation in the 1970s began challenging both the hegemony of sexology and the practice of history, in the name of alternative theories and knowledge, under the influence of new social movements and identities, they too at first experienced an academic coolness, especially in history departments. It is noticeable how many of the early writers on sexual history in the 1970s and 1980s were research students, junior faculty, independent scholars and activists in the women's or gay movements, far from the ivory towers of academic prestige.

Much has changed. Many of the pioneers have become senior professors. The subject is taught at undergraduate and postgraduate levels in most universities in the global North and increasing numbers in the global South. Publishers' lists groan with books on sexuality in general and histories of sexuality in particular. Mainstream and specialist journals pour out articles, in a scholarly production line. There are countless archives, physical and virtual; and websites, blogs, vlogs, listservs, online discussion groups and social network pages devoted to sexual history. There are national and international conferences, seminars, workshops and (often jet-setting) transnational communities of scholars. There is a creative grassroots history embodying the promise of pioneers in the 1970s to develop a new democratic history. Every year thousands of people in North America, Britain and Australasia attend events to celebrate LGBT History Month or equivalents. And there is a growing recognition of the global resonance of sexual history, with a new concern with transnational history and the construction of local, regional and national sexual histories in the global South (see chapter

6). Writing about sexuality has become a vital part of the historical endeavour, whilst also feeding into and being fertilized by a range of other disciplines, from sociology, social anthropology, literature, philosophy, politics, legal studies and cultural geography, to more recent hybrids such as cultural, postcolonial, gender, race/ethnic, LGBT and queer studies.

But in all this effort, amongst all the sound and fury, there is a nagging question: what is a history of sexuality actually a history of? Sexual history sometimes feels like a feverish activity without a clear or fixed referent. Sexual historians have been preoccupied with identities, and with non-identities, with homosexuality, queerness, paraphilias, perversion, transgression, subversion and resistance, as much as, sometimes more than, heterosexuality, respectability, the normative, the average, the ordinary. They engage with fertility, reproduction, birth control, abortion, but also with celibacy, masturbation, fantasy, erotica, pornography and purity. They cover transactional sex work as well as marriage (same-sex and other-sex), singleness as well as partnerships (couple and polyamorous), cohabitation and living apart, casual sex, abstinence and asexuality. Historians of sexuality explore the organization and cultures of families, traditional, extended, nuclear or chosen, as well as networks, friendships and subcultures, on the ground, in the mind or in cyberspace. They are concerned with the porous and ever-shifting boundaries of private and public life, secrets and lies and the closet, as well as public declarations and displays, and coming out. And they are concerned with sexual health and sexual ill-health: sexually transmitted infections, HIV/AIDS, 'sexual addiction' and the historic use of contraceptives or potency drugs.

The history of sexuality is inextricably intertwined with structures of power. You cannot really think sexuality without gender: masculinity, femininity, cisgender, transgender, inter-sex, hermaphrodite, bi-gender, all configuring sexual possibilities and meanings. Sexualities, and their histories, intersect with histories of race, class, age, religion, and with geographies, urban and rural spaces, and increasingly cyberspace. The history of the sexual needs a grasp of the languages that give sense to, order and discipline inchoate passions, but also has to deal with the emotions and affect that people are particularly sensitive and prone to: love and desire, hope and pride, pain and terror, shame and insult, triumph and humiliation, trauma, panic, sexism, homophobia, biphobia, transphobia, racial fear and horror of the Other, nationalism and fundamentalism. Emotions get locked into structures or assemblages which have their own histories, as fear of homosexuality is locked into heteronormative structures, or misogyny locked into gendered oppression. Historical sexualities are local, national, transnational, cosmopolitan, global. There are sexual cultures which have complex histories, histories of bodies and bodily reconstructions. There are histories of movements, campaigns – for and against lesbian, gay, bisexual, transgender and queer (LGBTQ) rights, for and against reproductive rights, against sexual violence, the sex trade, to protect children, religious, socially conservative and fundamentalist groupings – and histories of NGOs, and governmental, cross-national and international organizations, all of which have their own trajectories, intricately intertwined with other sexual histories. There are patterns of domination, hierarchy, regulation, and multiple subjectivities and forms of agency – individual and collective. Which is why sexuality, and its history, are always necessarily political, even if the politics are often nicely obscured in the name of scholarly objectivity.

And a key to the new history from the 1970s: there are histories of 'sexuality' itself, not as the sum total of all of the above, but as a concept, a set of discourses, an embodiment of truths.

No single history, let alone one short book, can cover this vast and ever-growing continent of knowledge. I focus instead on the ways in which an emerging and developing sexual history has created the possibility of thinking of the erotic in new ways, putting sexual concepts, beliefs and practices into more carefully delineated historical contexts. My purpose is to demonstrate the significance of a *critical* sexual history which avoids the naturalism/essentialism/biological determinism which has bedevilled efforts to understand the sexual past and present, and opens the ways to an understanding of the history of sexuality as fundamentally social and human, that is fully historical. Through this we can, I suggest, encourage a creative and meaningful dialogue between past and present.

Narratives

Analysis of the past is mediated through our current preconceptions and perceptions, but the past also continues to live in the present. The present in all its complexity and confusions is deeply historical. We live and breathe a living history in our everyday lives, shadowed and shaded by meanings, categories, laws, structures, institutions, beliefs, prejudices, discriminations, phobias, oppressions, struggles, embodiments and memories that are part of the deep consciousness and unconscious of our cultures. We may accept these historic burdens, resist them, reject them, ignore them or try to transform them, but it is difficult to forget them entirely. We make our own histories, but rarely in circumstances of our own choosing. People may have freedom of will, but they are never entirely free agents.

Sexuality is particularly freighted by a living past because it is so intimately connected with our sense of who we are, where we came from and where we are positioned, by identities, gender and social recognition, as well as our deepest feelings and current ways of being in the world. It is also profoundly contested. Sexuality and intimacy are the focus for critical value debates: about conflicts between the traditional and the new, faith and the secular, the majority and minorities; about relations between men and women, men and men, women and women, the family and personal desires, adults and children, the old, the able and less or differently abled; on the meanings and implications of sexual, gender and ethnic/racial diversity; around reproductive rights and new reproductive technologies, representation and new digital forms of communication and connectivity, and so on. These value debates translate into political conflict, and to an unprecedented degree sexual issues have moved to the centre of the political stage in an increasingly globalized and networked world. So those who are engaged in attempting to understand change in historical and intimate life as people live it today are inevitably doing more than simply record the truth of the past. By their interventions they are inevitably asserting a particular set of value-laden narratives about the present too.

Narratives provide examples of the ways in which 'reality' is constituted and structured through sets of beliefs, assumptions and the appropriate selection of evidence. They are powerful because they carry the unconscious assumption that what is being elaborated for the reader is a 'true history'. But the very act of selection can obscure a complex and more contested history. Strong narratives of sexual change have been particularly powerful in shaping recent scholarship, and understanding their often hidden assumptions can help us see what is missing.[2]

The progressive story is rooted in the optimism of the late nineteenth-century and early twentieth-century pioneering sexologists and sex reformers, that sexual change would come as a result of good will and rational thought. A more muted and cautious story of sexual modernization arose in the 1950s and 1960s, which strongly influenced the liberalizing currents that battled for sexual reform in many parts of the West. By the late 1960s a stronger liberationist story emerged, which directly linked sexual freedom with social revolution. The spirit of this liberationist politics was quite different from the cautious liberalism that proclaimed sexual modernity, but there were important links. They both shared a theoretical assumption that sexuality was a powerful force for good that the social repressed. The major problem with the narrative is the assumption of inevitability and determination that lies behind it. There is, of course, a lot to be said for a story of progressive advance, at least if you live in large parts of the prosperous West, for there has been dramatic and on the whole beneficial change in everyday life for millions of people. But to say that does not mean that change is either automatic or inevitable, or that it is neutral, It can lead to intensified regulation as well as greater freedoms. And in many parts of the world radical changes in intimate life have barely begun, or have been subjected to severe repression.

The mirror image of the progressive narrative is the declinist story. Its characteristic note is a lament for the awful state of the present – the broken families, the high rate of divorce, the sexualization of young people, the incidence of mindless sexual promiscuity, the commercialization of love, the porni-graphication of society, the over-visibility of homosexuality, the explicitness of sex education and the media, the weaken-ing of values, the collapse of social capital, the rise of sexual diseases, dramatized by the AIDS epidemic – and a compari-son of that with some golden age of faith, stability and family values. If the progressive mind-set assumes that the erotic in itself is a positive force for good, if only liberated from igno-rance, prejudice or capitalist exploitation, the declinist or socially conservative view (a social conservatism that goes far beyond and transcends traditional party-political commit-ments) assumes that it is not so much bad as potentially dangerous, unless framed in traditional frameworks of family and (heterosexual) marriage.

A third great narrative tends to present a history where, despite deceptive shifts, nothing has really fundamentally changed at all. This is a story of continuity in terms of the underlying structures of power, despite apparently striking epiphenomenal changes. There is a powerful account which uses the work of Michel Foucault to suggest the all-embracing nature of power in modern societies, and has invested in concepts of governmentality to theorize the resilience of con-temporary societies against meaningful change.[3] Similarly, theorists of formalization and informalization[4] have empha-sized the 'controlled decontrolling' of emotions that has become dominant in Western societies since the 1950s.

There is a radical feminist version of this continuist story, which acknowledges some changes, but stresses the continu-ities, especially in terms of the relations of power between men and women. We will see its impact in the development of feminist sexual history (chapter 4). A 'queer' subset of the story does recognize that there have been great changes in attitudes towards homosexuality and sexual diversity, but wonders how much has fundamentally changed in a hetero-normative culture. Isn't a gay identity little more than a pseudo-ethnic identity that is easily accommodated by late capitalist societies? Isn't same-sex marriage simply an assimi-lation into heterosexual values (see chapter 3)?

The queer critique of the present often overlaps with a neo-Marxist, anti-capitalist, anti-globalization subset of this story, which focuses on the impact of neoliberal restructuring of the global economy and its unsettling and resetting of everyday life. New rights for women have to be balanced against the continuing exploitation of women on a global scale, economic as well as sexual. The structural readjustment policies of the IMF and World Bank have trapped millions in poverty that inhibits the development of sexual freedoms and intimate life. This subset recognizes the power of individualizing tendencies, but sees them as accommodating to the necessities of the latest phase of capitalist development. Indeed, the legal reforms and institutional achievements of LGBTQ people that many have welcomed as the signs of greater toleration are seen as fully complicit with the strategic need of neoliberalism.[5]

There are elements in all these positions which are at least plausible, which is why they resonate with historians. They all, however, suffer from crucial lacunae. The progressive story too readily forgets the contingencies of history, the tortuous and uneven routes that have brought us to the present. The declinist story celebrates a golden age that never was. The continuist versions want to stress the strength of hidden structures of power, and embody an implicit determinism, suggesting that sexuality is a direct product of determining forces ('patriarchy', 'capitalism', 'neoliberalism', 'heteronormativity', to name but the most popular), but in doing this they minimize the host of social, legislative and cultural changes that have dismantled the traditional moral order in many parts of the world, and the real changes that individuals have been able to make in their everyday lives.

To my mind, a critical sexual history should go beyond these narrative closures that limit so much sexual history. It is reluctant to offer a single story, but stresses the existence of multiple narratives. It recognizes that sexuality is inevitably and always enmeshed in the coils of power relations, but rejects overarching determinants, and stresses the vivacity of collective and personal agency. It seeks to understand the *longue durée* of deep structures and embedded and embodied traditions, while grasping the significance of conjunctures, critical moments when the kaleidoscope is shaken and new patterns emerge. Above all, it advances a pluralistic history that stresses the profound historicity of sexuality. There is no master-key to unlock the secrets of the past, but a critical sexual history can help us understand the many different ways in which we humans make sexualities.

Summary of the Book

Chapter 1, 'Framing Sexual History', explores the elements that have contributed to the development of new and critical histories of sexuality since the 1970s, from theoretical advances to the materiality of bodies, their subjectivities and emotions, from generational sexualities to the complexities of time. Chapter 2, 'The Invention of Sexual History', traces the evolution of sexual history from the nineteenth century to the 1970s and 1980s. In this chapter I argue that there was a fundamental shift in focus then, from a historical approach rooted in scientific (that is, biological or psychological) concepts of the sexual, to a social and cultural reconceptualization, opening the way to what became known as a constructionist approach. This is usually associated with the writings of Michel Foucault, but I suggest that this downplays other critical contributions, not least the alternative knowledges being shaped by the feminist and gay and lesbian movements. Chapter 3, 'Querying and Queering Same-Sex History', explores the growth of what became known as lesbian and gay history, and the theoretical challenge offered to it by the shift towards queer history from the 1990s. I suggest that in some ways the distinction between these phases is a false one, especially as the historicizing of the concepts of the homosexual, the gay or lesbian was already well established. What the queering of this new history really achieved was to go beyond the categories as they exist, focusing not only on the emergence and conditions of existence of familiar concepts, but also on what it meant to live before and beyond these categories. Chapter 4, 'Gender, Sexuality and Power', begins with the debates within second-wave feminism about the meanings of sexual history in a gendered world. Historical debates were at the heart of what became known as the 'sex wars', underlining fundamental political and cultural divides which ultimately fractured the idea of a single women's movement. The different understandings of power were central to these controversies, and to historical understanding of sexual domination and subordination of women, and the potentialities of resistance. The chapter goes on to explore the intersectional nature of sexuality, and especially the significance of race and class in shaping sexual and gendered meanings and identities. It concludes with an exploration of the significance of these new approaches to the historical understanding of masculinity and male sexualities.

Chapter 5, 'Mainstreaming Sexual History', focuses on five key moments in the creation of modern Western notions of sexuality: the eighteenth-century emergence of 'modern sexuality'; the 'heterosexualization' of the culture; the 'sexual revolution' of the 1960s and beyond; the AIDS crisis from the early 1980s; and finally the profound shifts in the meanings of intimate life at the turn of the new millennium, of which the rise and rise of same-sex marriage was a dramatic symbol.

In chapter 6, 'The Globalization of Sexual History', I begin with the 'transnational turn' in writings about sexuality, and go on to explore the colonial history of sexuality and gender which continues to shape attitudes towards and in the global South, and the emergence of challenging new sexual histories from within the postcolonial world. Attitudes to same-sex practices here as earlier in the West have played a key role in sexual discourse, entwined with state-sponsored homophobia in many countries. These issues have become closely linked with the development of human sexual rights as a global discourse, with LGBTQ rights particularly arousing enormous controversy. The chapter concludes with a reflection on the contested meanings of what it is to be human, and how this impacts on the meanings of human rights and sexual justice. Finally, chapter 7, 'Memory, Community, Voice', shifts the focus back to one of the roots of the new social history of the 1970s and 1980s, the emphasis on the importance of historical knowledge rooted in the community and in democratic historical practices. The chapter argues that memory is a critical element in community practices, and is created and nourished through the establishment of sexual archives and giving voice to those denied it in the past.

1

Framing Sexual History

Towards a Critical Sexual History

At the heart of a critical sexual history is the belief that sexuality is a fundamentally social, and therefore historical, structure. It challenges the traditional view that the erotic is a natural phenomenon to which society has to react. In its place historians have increasingly emphasized the ways in which what we have conventionally seen as a biological truth is shaped by culture into a complex unity of plural and diverse identities, subjectivities, beliefs, behaviour, ideologies and erotic practices. It is a historical not a natural unity.

Historians began to argue from the 1970s that sexuality was 'socially constructed'. This modest idea, increasingly familiar to sociologists and social anthropologists of the time, proved explosive amongst historians. The tortured and often fevered debates that followed in the so-called 'constructionist–essentialist' controversy will be explored more fully in chapters 2 and 3. My point here is not to argue a case but to map a critical landscape. Social constructionism, like any other historical concept, had a birth, life and death, and then an afterlife, like an echo of the big bang. This new approach posed two mighty challenges which lingered long after the concept became 'unfashionable', at least in the slightly mechanistic sense suggested by the phrase. First, it questioned and problematized the very categories and concepts that had provided the basis for writing about sexuality since the late nineteenth century. Concepts such as homosexuality and heterosexuality, bisexuality, transvestism, perversion, masturbation and a host of sexual variations were shown to have distinctive histories. Ideas of masculinity and femininity as both antagonistic and complementary had specific conditions of emergence. Gender was a powerful but unstable category with shifting meanings. And above all, the master concept of sexuality itself was no longer seen as a fixed feature of thinking about the body and its possibilities and pleasures. It was a 'historical invention'. Secondly, it followed that if these concepts and ideas had specific histories then it was impossible to believe in a single history of sexuality. There were many histories, each with its own genealogy, conditions of emergence, and effectivity; and indeed many sexualities. The concept of sexuality, as it was found in scientific texts and in common-sense usage, far from being a universal, was culturally specific, and the task of the historian was to tease out the specific meanings, to question the taken-for-granted, and to try to understand discontinuities as much as continuities. Such an approach was in one sense not really new. Historians generally had grown used to analysing the changing meanings of apparently fixed categories like class, nation, race or ethnicity. Why should gender and sexuality alone have the status of eternal verities?

Such challenges unsettled many, however, especially those committed to the identities they had so painfully forged, and were now being told by the more provocative historians were 'fictions', even if 'necessary fictions'.[1] Many lesbian and gay activists were outraged at this apparent denial of their history, and many historians agreed, producing alternative interpretations based on the fixity and permanence across time of homosexual identities. A similar impulse can be found in feminist historiography based on the essential difference of men and women: was patriarchy an ahistorical reality, a particular organization of sexual possibilities, or too general to be useful? All that needs to be said at this stage is that historians influenced by constructionist ideas were just as committed to sexual justice as their colleagues, but did not believe that the road to this was through reifying minority identities or imagining transhistorical structures. More crucially, there was a recognition that the categories they were problematizing were not neutral descriptions. They had emerged and had effects in specific configurations and hier- archies of power, around religion, medicine, the psychologi- cal professions, the state, gender, racial or ethnic groups, and the like, which had given rise to intricate forms of domina- tion, governance and regulation, or resistance, transgression, subversion and agency. Sexuality and power were inextrica- bly linked, with the erotic as a critical vector for the opera- tion of domination. But the forms of power, as of sexuality, took different shapes in different societies, and required sen- sitive understanding of cultural difference.

Given such perplexities, it is perhaps not surprising that some recent historians of sexuality have stressed the 'radical unknowability' of a past where it is hazardous to assume we can know how people saw their erotic beings in other times.[2] This clearly poses questions about the viability of the whole historical enterprise: if we cannot really know the past, is it really worth trying to do sexual history? In practice, histori- ans have emphasized the ways in which the very act of his- torical research and writing constructs forms of evidence to represent and illuminate the complex ways in which past and present are contingently intertwined: we construct our own sexual archives in the process of making history.[3] From this perspective, sexual history is as much a history of representa- tions of sexuality as an account of who did what to whom, where and when in other places at other times. This is a position I am sympathetic to, because it stresses the impor- tance of attempting to tease out the meanings and effectivity of ideas, concepts and practices as they existed in specific cultures and historic periods rather than imposing modern (Western) interpretations on them. But that should not mean that any sort of coherent history is impossible. We can still give a structure and pattern to the past, as long as we accept that it is always provisional.

Theoretical Detours

As the late Stuart Hall reminded us, 'Theory is always a detour on the way to something more important.'[4] It sometimes feels that the history of sexuality is burdened with a surfeit of theory. Yet as the complexities of these issues show, we cannot escape theory, much as some might wish to. Whatever the risks, theoretical engagement has been central to the recent writings on sexual history. If sexual knowledge is itself constructed in different ways in different cultures, it is crucial to understand how forms of knowledge shape what we understand as the sexual in particular circumstances. A major reason why the introductory volume of Michel Foucault's *The History of Sexuality* became so central to the early elaboration of the new sexual history in the 1970s and 1980s, especially in the Anglophone world, is that his work seemed to offer theoretical insights into the ways in which sexual knowledge was created in defined historical circumstances. Sexuality is lived in particular organizations of meaning, discourses and narratives that shape the inchoate possibilities of the body.

This engagement with a particular theoretical orientation, itself complex and variegated, risks obscuring or marginalizing other major contributions to contemporary sexual theory: studies of urban sexual subcultures and of human sexual behaviour, post-Kinsey sociology and social psychology in the USA, the pioneering sociologies of homosexual roles and sexual stigma in Britain, histories of 'formalization' and 'informalization' in the 'civilizing process' from the Netherlands and Germany, and a host of theoretically sensitive feminist, and lesbian and gay, writers who in the decades since the 1970s have illuminated history as well as sexual theory.[5]

A striking feature of these intellectual developments has been their multidisciplinary and cross-disciplinary nature. Pioneering feminist and lesbian and gay historians in the 1970s sought theoretical insights from sociology and social anthropology. Later, new preoccupations from within the unlikely quarter of cultural geography helped shape historical work – on the 'geography of perversions', the spatial organization of sexuality, the pleasures and dangers of city life, the urban/rural divide, the configuration of sexual cultures. Not surprisingly, spatial metaphors abound in sexual history: boundaries, borders, frontiers, closets, performance spaces, the global, cyberspace.

Most unexpected of all, perhaps, has been the influence of literary and related humanities studies. The most widely quoted critique of social constructionism in its early form came not from a historian wedded to essentialist thinking but from the poet and literary theorist Eve Kosofsky Sedgwick. Another poet, Adrienne Rich, offered the early outline of a theory of 'compulsory heterosexuality', which paved the way for later theories of 'heteronormativity'.[6] Few of the most influential contributors to queer theory from the 1990s had backgrounds as trained historians, even as they contributed to queer history: they came from the disciplines of philosophy, classics and above all literature.

This might explain the exotic range of 'turns' which have been claimed for sexual theory, and sexual history. A quick scan through assorted key texts reveals amongst others: a cultural turn, a linguistic turn, a psychoanalytical turn, a Foucauldian turn, a poststructuralist turn, a queer turn, an affective turn, a materialist turn, a historicist turn, a transnational turn, a posthumanist turn *and* a humanist turn, a Deleuzian turn, an ethical turn and an anti-social turn. At worse these point to a very unhistorical chasing after the latest theoretical fashion. At best, they hint at the vivacious theoretical engagements and intellectual eclecticism which have helped shape sexual history.

Given this theoretical bent, it is not surprising that the anthropologist Carol Vance once declared that the most important sexual organ was between the ears.[7] How we think about the sexual inevitably shapes how it is lived, ordered, regulated, resisted – and written about. But sexuality is about many things besides theory. It is also about bodies and emotions, and historians of sexuality have increasingly invested in better understanding of how these are framed in specific socio-historical contexts.

Bodies

Since the 1970s there has been an explosion of interest in the social meanings of and investments in the body. The idea of women's right to control their own bodies, so central to second-wave feminism, indicated the politically and culturally charged significance of bodies and what Grosz called 'female corporeality'.[8] More recently, the emergence of transgender as a critical challenge to gender absolutism has brought to the fore the disjuncture between bodies and meanings, and the potential mutability of the body. Michel Foucault famously saw the regulation of the body as the key to the shift in modes of governance and control in modern societies, giving rise to what he termed 'biopower'. Technologies of power pressed the flesh into the service of social organization through the disciplining effects of discourse. The 'docile body' was the focus for the production and regulation of human individuals and the control of populations, producing social beings who were simultaneously subjects and subjected.

Modern technologies have ensured that bodies can be constantly engineered and re-engineered in a multiplicity of ways, through diet, consumption, advertising, clothes, fashion and uniforms, cosmetic surgery, reproductive technology, 'sex change', sport and physical exercise, and medicine. The digital revolution, far from liberating bodies from their earthly roots, continues to entwine them. Are we already cyborgs, half human and half machine, increasingly moulded by the interactions of cyberspace as Donna Haraway suggested at the beginning of the digital era?[9]

Yet the body is more than a passive surface for the operation of power. The body is also the site of strong resistances. Many body transformations may be expressions of individuality and personal empowerment. People with disabilities have resisted marginalization and affirmed their sexual being, moving towards what Kafer called 'crip' liberation.[10] Forms of surgical intervention to 'change sex' have been vital for many trans individuals in achieving a sense of harmony between body and gender identity. Phenomena such as hysteria, especially in the nineteenth century, and anorexia nervosa more recently, classically seen as female maladies (though large numbers of men have always suffered from them), can be read as struggles over contradictory demands on a woman and her body, partially if temporarily resolved by a transformation of the body. The body has never been less docile, Anthony Giddens has suggested.[11]

As the Australian sociologist Raewyn Connell argued, 'bodies are addressed by social process and drawn into history, without ceasing to be bodies'.[12] Embodiment describes an active process in which the body is shaped and changed by historical practices, through which gender, sexual desires and sexual identities are forged, drawing on the multiple possibilities of the body but transforming them into active elements of individual lives, social worlds and historical understanding.

Subjectivities and Affect

If material bodies provide the potential on which sexuality draws, subjectivities and emotions are the vectors through which sexuality is lived. Feelings, emotions and affects have been a crucial part of the thinking on sexuality since the nineteenth century. Psychology was a constitutive part of the origins of sexology, and psychoanalytic theories recur in twentieth-century sexual histories. Nor was emotion missing from the new sexual scholarship that emerged in the 1970s. The pioneering sociology of sexuality from writers such as John Gagnon, William Simon and Ken Plummer, with its emphasis on sexual scripts, was underpinned by an interactionist social psychology derived from George Mead.[13] Like many others, I found myself battling with the Lacanian 'recovery' of Freud as a way of understanding sexual identities and subjectivities in the 1970s, and even flirted with the work on desire of Gilles Deleuze and Félix Guattari, long before they became fashionable for social theorists after the millennium.[14] For pioneering sexologists sexuality was on the borderline of biology and psychology, with biology generally winning. If a simple biologism is rejected, as it generally has been since the 1970s, as an all-embracing explanation for the complex, wilful, contradictory feelings that are inevitably and invariably evoked by sexuality, then a dialogue if not an accommodation between history, the psycho-social and emotions is both necessary and desirable.

The question of subjectivity has been central to this dialogue. The concern with same-sex and female sexual identities in the new sexual history inevitably posed the question of what constitutes the subjective and especially what the relationship was between social structures, concepts, discourses and sets of belief on the one hand, and the individual sense of self and identity and the feelings attached to them on the other. Discourses, located in the realm of language, may work to address and constitute the subject, but they cannot guarantee how the subject will identify with and take up different subject positions. In relation to both gender and sexual identities the individual subject is never wholly captured by a unitary model of who and what they are. In the multiplicities of desires and possible identifications lies the possibility of refusing identity.[15] As Heather Love has written, 'the analysis of uncodified subjective experiences is an important supplement to the study of the history of formal laws, practices and ideologies'.[16]

Increasingly historians of sexuality have become interested in what the Welsh social theorist Raymond Williams called 'structures of feeling', the patterning of emotions and ways of seeing that shape distinct ways of doing things. Other concepts such as 'habitus' (after Norbert Elias and Pierre Bourdieu), 'desiring machines' (after Gilles Deleuze and Félix Guattari) or 'assemblages' (popularized by Jasbir Puar) are similarly concerned with the structuring of swirling emotions into distinct patterns that become psycho-social realities. Another key figure in the reorientation towards affect was Eve Kosofsky Sedgwick. She became heavily influenced by the work of the American psychologist Silvan Tomkins, when she was looking, as she wrote, 'for some usable ideas on the topic of shame'.[17] Shame was to become a key theme for queer theorists, and to influence historical work, both in the USA and in France, less so in Britain. Sedgwick's psychology carried its own universalizing tendencies, but it propelled new explorations of the complexity of feelings around the sexuality–gender matrix, in the present and in the past. This became more imperative as the optimism that pushed the agenda of feminism and gay politics in the 1970s gave rise to a sense of impasse: the divisions within feminism as revealed in the so-called sex wars, the apparently irresistible rise of social conservatism, especially in the USA, and the impact of the HIV/AIDS epidemic contributed to a much darker mood in sexualities work by the 1990s, and a growing interest in emotions and affect in history. Memory, loss, trauma, insult, mourning, abjection, melancholia, as well as shame became topics that some felt urgently needed historical attention.

Generations

Issues such as embodiment and affect were closely associated with a new generation of feminist and queer activists and theorists in the 1990s, reorienting historical practice away from identity towards heightened concerns with diversity, intersectional issues, especially the intricacies of race and class, and affect. Ken Plummer has written about 'generational narratives' through which perspectives and standpoints derived from changing social worlds give rise to different stories about the past and present.[18] The earliest manifestations of sexual history were inspired by the first generation of sexologists, formed in the wake of the scientific breakthroughs and intellectual developments of the late nineteenth century, and especially the Darwinian revolution. The renewal of sexual history from the 1970s was carried through largely by baby-boomers, born in the wake of World War II, growing up in the increasingly affluent 1950s, university educated in the 1960s, radicalized by the cultural revolution of that decade, and politically inspired by civil rights, anti-war agitations, and the new social movements that burgeoned in the 1970s. This generation was sceptical of the overbearing claims of science, resistant to rigid inscriptions of gender and sexuality, and a carrier of major transformations of sexual manners and mores in the following fifty years. It sought legitimation through the truth of its experiences, desires, memories and aspirations.

The baby-boom generation has been both praised and blamed for the widespread social liberalization of these years, but it is important to remember that this generation was itself sharply divided. Many of the leading lights in the powerful waves of social conservatism that fought against family and sexual change in the name of traditional values were of the same age-cohort as feminists and gay liberationists, shaped by the same experiences, but ending up with radically different responses – just as the sexual theorists and reformers active from the 1880s and 1890s were very much of a small minority in their generation, defining themselves against Victorian morality. Not only are there divisions amongst those of the same chronological generation, but different sexual generations co-exist, so that today conservative traditionalists of all ages, radicals now growing old (and less radical?), the AIDS generation marked by sexual fear and backlash, young erotic explorers, libertarians, dissidents, liberals and fundamentalists jumble together in uneasy co-existence. Each generation, and each fragment of a generation, brings different understandings to the complex and shifting world of sexuality.

Theories themselves tend to have a limited lifespan as the inexorable flux of ideas (or 'turns') floods on. The ideas of the earliest, largely European sexologists were under sustained challenge by the 1940s, from new waves of largely American sexual experts, led by Alfred Kinsey. From the 1970s social constructionists rejected the 'essentialism' of their immediate precursors. It seems to be a prime feature of each generation to reject vehemently the values and ideas of its predecessor. Sexologists found themselves challenging, almost as they were inventing, Victorian ideals. Gay liberationists in the 1970s dismissed their less militant predecessors in the 1950s and 1960s, even though they had paved the way for new forms of knowledge, a new politics – and a new history. Queer theorists have rejected gay liberationists.[19] So the story goes on. In the perspective of history the differences may seem minuscule and the continuities more important. For those living in and through a particular generation, discontinuities and the triumph of the new may seem more fundamental in defining who and what you are.

Times Present, Times Past, Times Future

Critical sexual history, with its emphasis on the historical, culturally shaped nature of those categories we take for granted, has been preoccupied with questioning and problematizing the time-bound nature of the ideas we have in the present, and their limitations in understanding the past. It was not so much that we had buried or forgotten our sexual past, but that that past was possibly radically different from our present. As the distinguished historian of psychiatry Arnold Davidson observes, 'We perpetually look for precursors to our categories of sexuality in essentially different domains, producing anachronisms at best and unintelligibility at worse.'[20]

Avoiding anachronisms but finding intelligibility has been a fundamental challenge to sexual historians. For Michel Foucault an effective history was a history of the present. History is a practice undertaken in a particular present and for particular reasons linked to that present.[21] What many sexual historians have taken from this is a way of understanding this deeply historical present, not as the logical culmination of the past, but as a shifting configuration of traces of the past in a complex and living present, providing a survey of the battleground rather than a story of progress, a critical history rather than a conventional history. Such an approach stresses the otherness and openness of the past, and the discontinuities between past and present, but at the same time the strangeness of the past illumines the contingencies of the present, and its multiple time frames.

Human temporality, Plummer has argued, is a narrative. We live sexual lives in a particular place, and at a particular time, alongside others living in different temporalities. At any particular time there is a multiplicity of temporalities, delicately intertwined, which can have profound implications for thinking about different sexual histories.[22] For example, Judith/Jack Halberstam has famously defined a 'queer time' developed in part in opposition to the times shaped by reproduction, the family and normative heterosexuality, subject to different rhythms, logics, necessities and identifications. Queer time emerged most spectacularly, she argues, at the end of the twentieth century, as the shadow of the AIDS epidemic seemed to suggest a diminishing future and a new emphasis on the here and now.[23]

The emphasis on the co-existence of different temporalities is important for indicating how our positioning towards the past is shaped as much by our deepest feelings and commitments as by theoretical inclinations and 'truth'. One example of this is a pervasive nostalgia that echoes through much recent sexual history, shaped by those declinists who see a golden age fast receding into the mists of time (as golden ages always must), but also by those who regret passing time. It is there in writers who lament the fading of a more transgressive sexual radicalism, and resurrect utopian hopes with little likelihood of realization. It is implicit in a sub-Foucauldian view which regrets the onset of a defining, categorizing sexual culture that seeks the truth of one's being in one's sex, and compares it with a less rigidly defined sexual culture (in the pre-gay 1950s, or the pre-homosexual eighteenth century, or the pre-sodomite classical world). It is there in liberal analyses which looks back to a culture less dominated by knowingness and sexual consumerism, and vehemently there with those social conservatives who lament the passing of the normative family, gender and sexual values of an earlier age. It is difficult to avoid the feeling that an aching nostalgia tells us more about the discontents of the present than the lives of the past.

But nostalgia as a particular example illustrates my wider point: that we engage with the past with emotion as much as reason. The historian cannot avoid this. The best we can do is acknowledge it as one aspect of doing sexual history, not seeking the causes of our present, or blindly pushing contemporary beliefs and preconceptions into the past, but trying as best we can to make contact across time and place with other lives and other values. We need to acknowledge that we are different, and yet can still find moments of identification, that highlight our common human aspirations across the chasm of time – making the connection, the human gesture, across time and space.

2
The Invention of Sexual History

The Magic of Words

Words and magic, Sigmund Freud observed, were once the same thing, and words have retained much of their magical power even today.[1] Words can excite us, direct us, pain and punish us, give us hope and fill us with fear. They can place us, and shape who and what we are and want to be. And they provide critical markers of historical shifts in ideas and values. Without words as concepts 'one sees nothing; and, as should be even more evident, without concepts one says nothing'.[2] Which is why I am beginning this chapter with words and concepts. They provide a mighty insight into the history of sexuality, and the history of that history.

The early sexologists were avid creators of words and new meanings. From the pens of these pioneers flowed a dazzling array of neologisms, categories, taxonomies and concepts that revolutionized the twentieth-century languages of sexuality. The word 'sexuality' itself had emerged in English early in the nineteenth century, meaning the quality of being sexual, that is, relating to being masculine or feminine. The sense of sexuality as referring to an identity – his or her sexuality, implying orientation, preference or practices – was largely a creation of the twentieth century, indicating new preoccupations with the sexual self.

Other key terms, 'homosexuality' and 'heterosexuality', which have demarcated the dominant binary divisions for the past century and more, were invented, by the Hungarian Karl-Maria Kertbeny (also known as Karoly-Maria Benkert), in the 1860s. Alternative terms for 'the homosexual' circulated, with subtly different meanings: 'invert', 'urning', 'third-sexer', 'intermediate type'.[3] Other neologisms proliferated, from the 'antipathic sexual instinct' and 'bisexuality' to 'zoophilia', taking in 'coprolagnia' and 'urolagnia', 'fetishism' and 'kleptomania', 'exhibitionism' and 'sadomasochism', 'frottage' and 'chronic satyriasis', 'eonism' or 'transvestism', and many others, as the erotic world of sexuality was redefined in new forms of discourse. Such terms were much more than new paint for old truths. They represented a transforming shift in the ways in which sexuality was thought, and how people saw themselves and others, based on new perceptions of truth.

Sexology was a major vehicle for this transformation. The self-declared scientific study of sexuality and desire was developed in the last decades of the nineteenth century with striking ambitions. The first major sexologist, the Viennese forensic psychiatrist Richard von Krafft-Ebing, wrote in *Psychopathia Sexualis* that his task was no less than to reduce the manifestations of erotic life to their 'lawful condition'. Just as contemporary sociology in the hands of Karl Marx, Emile Durkheim and Max Weber was seeking to lay bare the laws of society, so sexology set itself the task of uncovering, describing and analysing the laws of nature.[4]

We can trace the earliest manifestations of a new would-be scientific zeal in relation to sexuality to the theorists of masturbation in the eighteenth century. Samuel Tissot's fulminations against onanism marked a crucial transition: what you did was now something more than an infringement of divine law; it told the world what sort of person you were.[5] Other formative works followed: on prostitution, childhood sexuality, hysteria and the sexual aberrations. Karl Heinrich Ulrichs published twelve volumes on the third sex between 1864 and 1879, which influenced Carl Westphal's 'discovery' of the 'contrary sexual impulse' in 1870, and Krafft-Ebing's work on the sexual perversions. It was the last of these who pulled together the scattered trails into a new approach.[6] A host of investigators of the highways and byways of the erotic soon followed, aided by the new prestige of the biological sciences following the publication of Charles Darwin's work on the origins of species and sexual selection. In his *Three Essays on the Theory of Sexuality* (originally 1905), which was itself a major influence on the course of sexology, Sigmund Freud acknowledged the particular influence of nine writers, including Krafft-Ebing, the British Havelock Ellis and the German Magnus Hirschfeld. There were many others, drawn from penology, law, psychiatry, psychology, anthropology and medicine.[7]

The new self-declared science of sexuality was based on a conviction that underlying the diversity of individual experience was a complex natural process – the 'sexual instinct' – the understanding of which would enable a more enlightened insight into the key problems of the contemporary world. This involved a theoretical break with older theories of moral insanity or degeneration, replacing them with a mixture of biological and psychological explanations. In the process, sexuality was emerging as a distinct continent of knowledge. All the sexologists accepted that the ultimate purpose of the sexual instinct was reproduction, with gender and sexuality locked together as a biological imperative. But to an extraordinary degree the early work of these pioneers was concerned with the variations or, less benignly, the perversions of the sexual instinct. This involved a major effort of classifying and defining sexual pathologies, which gave rise to the new definitions and sexual taxonomies which were to prove so influential. This concentration on the perversions cast new light, of course, on the 'normal'. Freud was to show that the path to normality was prolonged and hazard-strewn. The perversions were not so much byways as keys to understanding the new domain of sexuality. In particular, they opened the way to specifying a person by defining his or her sexuality. As Krafft-Ebing put it, 'upon the nature of sexual sensibility the mental individuality in greater part depends'.[8] To know a person's sexual nature was to know that person. Sex was coming to be seen by sexology, and in the wider society, as 'the truth of our being'.

Sexologists saw themselves as discovering what had long been there, but obscured by ignorance. Historians today are more likely to see sexology as in large part constitutive of this new continent, not so much discovering sexual types as helping to conceptualize or 'invent' them in new ways. In the next chapter I will explore this issue in more detail in relation to the history of homosexuality. Here I want to emphasize that sexologists such as Krafft-Ebing, Havelock Ellis and Magnus Hirschfeld did not conjure sexual types out of thin air. As historians have shown, their accounts developed in dialogue with their patients and clients, who provided the subjects of the ever-expanding case studies that brought to life the sometimes arcane and often Latinized aetiologies and classifications deployed in the textbooks.[9] The invert, the masochist, the sadist or the transvestite already existed in a living history. But what sexologists did do was to provide much of the language and discursive forms through which meanings and emergent sexual identities were articulated, and to place them within a new hierarchy. Often they became advocates of better understanding of those that society had execrated as wicked, sinful, sick or mentally inadequate. The leading sexologists saw themselves as having a dual role: exponents of a more scientific approach to understanding sexuality; and, through scientific understanding, advocates for more humane ways of dealing with the personal and social problems to which sexuality gave rise.

There were manifest ambiguities in these early efforts to achieve 'sexual justice'. Many sexologists and reformers not only called for more liberal laws and tolerant attitudes, but also lent their weight to normalizing institutions, to defences of 'cures', especially of homosexuality, to biological theories of female sexual passivity, to racist assumptions about cultural difference, and to eugenic solutions to the 'problems' of overpopulation and the proliferation of the 'feeble-minded', which more recent historians have been disinterring in detail.

The Natural History of Sexuality

Historians had not entirely ignored sexuality prior to the emergence of the science of sexuality.[10] Sexual dissipation had famously been presented by Edward Gibbon as a factor explaining the decline and fall of the Roman Empire, and the early studies of major social concerns such as prostitution or masturbation made regular historical references, where they were available. Anglophone countries were much less advanced in this than French- or German-speaking countries, and characteristically discussed sexuality without quite mentioning it. Just prior to the emergence of early sexology, the Irish historian W. E. H. Lecky published in two volumes *A History of European Morals from Augustus to Charlemagne* (1869), which became a blueprint for later studies in Britain, focusing on changing attitudes towards morality without explicitly referencing sexuality. His work is full of references to sin, corruption, shame, passion, moral dignity and redemption without directly broaching the subject itself. It made morals a legitimate area of historical scholarship, but assumed that patterns of sexual behaviour were timeless. As late as the 1950s this was still a characteristic approach, even in such a key essay as Keith Thomas's classic study of 'the double standard' of morality, which helped spark a new interest in the history of sexuality in Britain.[11] Morals become a marker for sexual practices at a time when writing about sexuality made you morally dubious.

But for sexologists there was an imperative for people to write more directly about sexuality in history. Their elaboration of the sexual instinct and its aberrations or variations was for them a key theoretical breakthrough, and it was necessary to demonstrate that these were not products of sin, weakness of will or modern corruption but manifestations of a biological and psychological reality through history. This involved in the first place emphasizing the power of sexuality in history: an overpowering, instinctual force in the individual that shaped not only the personal but the social life as well. It was a basically male drive. It was also a firmly heterosexual drive, defined ultimately by reproduction.

But secondly, the 'stepchildren of nature', so recently described in glorious detail, were now retrospectively seen through the prism of history. Iwan Bloch, often credited as the inventor of the term 'sexology' (at least in its German form of *sexualwissenschaft*), was praised by Freud for moving from pathological to anthropological interpretations of inversion/homosexuality. Bloch's compendium, *The Sexual Life of Our Time*,[12] was an exhaustive cataloguing of sexual aberrations in all periods, cultures and races, and in doing this, like Freud, Bloch suggested the common nature rather than the peculiarity of the perversions. In essence, he presented a naturalistic approach, taking for granted the sexological categories and typologies whilst recognizing that attitudes towards them were products of particular cultures. This had already been pioneered by early documenters of homosexuality or inversion in history, such as Kertbeny, Karl Heinrich Ulrichs, Magnus Hirschfeld, Havelock Ellis, John Addington Symonds and Edward Carpenter.

Havelock Ellis began his majestic *Studies in the Psychology of Sex* with a study of sexual inversion co-authored with Symonds. This combined the latest biological and psychological theories with case studies and detailed historical examples, which in turn formed the raw material for a great detail of later historical explorations of homosexuality in history: many of the new historians of the 1970s began by mining this volume for evidence and references, especially in the heavily revised subsequent editions following its disastrous first publication and prosecution.[13] The approach adopted by Ellis in the first volume characterized all subsequent volumes of the *Studies*. They were basically histories of reactions to sexuality, rather than attempts to explain why and how sexuality shaped human societies. But they had a potentiality that went beyond these limitations, for they also, in varying degrees, provided evidence for the obvious but obscured truth, that the ways sexuality was thought, regulated, feared and lived in the metropolitan nations of Europe and North America were not the only or inevitable ways in which sexuality could exist. Sexology was confirming in would-be scientific detail that there were many ways of doing sexuality.

Writings such as Bloch's and Ellis's were a powerful influence on the development of comparative work on sexuality, particularly in relation to sociology and anthropology, as in the work of the Finnish-born Edvard Westermarck. David Halperin has credited him with one of the earliest deployments of the term 'homosexual love', and in seeing ancient Greek pederasty as a historical phenomenon rather than a simple example of Greek peculiarity.[14] 'Greek love' was of particular interest to a number of historians because here was a phenomenon that had apparently been at the heart of classic civilization, with a high degree of social acceptance. J. A. Symonds had lauded it in an early, privately circulated booklet, *A Problem in Greek Ethics*, which had been incorporated into his work on sexual inversion with Ellis. Hans Licht's *Sexual Life in Ancient Greece* was a more extended study that demonstrated that a whole range of sexual perversions were rampant in that society, with no apparent harm to its civilization, with homosexuality widely practised, acceptable and culturally rich. Kenneth Dover's famous study of Greek homosexuality followed this approach, especially in one particular regard, by making a crucial distinction that sexology had sought to clarify, between perversion and perversity: the former could be seen as a variation of the sexual instinct, the latter as a matter of situational behaviour, with the implication that what was natural and inborn should be treated with greater toleration than what was a product of manners and vice.[15]

Sexual history thus had a purpose. It allowed reformers to justify claims in the present for change by showing the problems or wrongs of the past. Writers on homosexuality, birth control or prostitution were happy to deploy historical knowledge to this end. Max Hodann's *History of Modern Morals*, written by a German exile from Nazi Germany, who had worked with Magnus Hirschfeld, was translated in 1937 by the British socialist and feminist birth control campaigner Stella Browne, who was an active supporter of sex reform, birth control and abortion.[16] Such books were grist to the mill for reformers.

In historical writings such as these there was an easy naturalism which married science, reform and history as essential components of a progressive agenda. This became the dominant approach, but there were other, if closely related theoretical trajectories, notably attempting, a little uneasily, to marry Marx and Freud. Already in Germany by the end of the nineteenth century key members of the Marxist Social Democratic Party – Hirschfeld himself was a supporter – were heavily engaged with sexology, making, for example, an attempt to understand the Oscar Wilde homosexual scandal as a problem for historical materialism: why was an apparently natural phenomenon subject to such hostility from the ruling class?[17] Freud distanced himself from Marxism, but offered profound historical insights, if on a grand scale, through his analysis of civilization and its discontents.

From the 1920s serious attempts were made to marry the Marxist and Freudian traditions, with varying degrees of success, and in the most famous products of this endeavour, the writings of Wilhelm Reich and Herbert Marcuse, sexuality emerged as a major historical player. The difficulty was that by and large theoretical constructs took precedence over mere historical evidence. The dangers of such an approach could be seen later in the popular historian Gordon Rattray Taylor's neo-Freudian interpretation of *Sex in History*: 'The history of civilization is the history of a long warfare between the dangerous and powerful drives and the systems of taboos and inhibitions which man has erected to control them.'[18] He accounted for changing attitudes in terms of obscure alternations between 'matrist' and 'patrist' cultures, leaving us with a grand but rather abstract cyclical theory of social change.

The famous study by the literary historian Steven Marcus, *The Other Victorians*, which Michel Foucault was to play with when critiquing the 'repressive hypothesis' in the introduction to his own (anti-Freudian) *The History of Sexuality*, relied on a similar Freudian explanation, and heavily influenced some later historians. Marcus quoted Freud to the effect that 'perhaps we must make up our minds to the idea that altogether it is not possible for the claims of the sexual instincts to be reconciled with the demands of culture'.[19] What for Freud was a statement of the tragic human dilemma, that civilization requires the repression of human possibilities, became a catch-all explanation of contingent historical shifts. So Marcus's explanation of nineteenth-century pornography, for instance, was in terms of this conflict between the overpowering demands of the sexual drive and a social fabric disrupted by massive change.

When the great social historian Lawrence Stone turned his scholarly attention to sexual behaviour we can see a similar cyclical explanation in his own work on *The Family, Sex and Marriage*, published in 1977: 'In terms of both sexual attitudes and power relationships, one can dimly begin to discern huge, mysterious, secular swings from repression to permissiveness and back again.'[20] The explanation for these swings unfortunately remained obscure.

The New History

Works such as Marcus's and Stone's, whatever their weaknesses, signalled the growth of a new interest in sexuality in history in the 1960s and 1970s, and in underpinning that with greater theoretical explanation, though one clearly rooted in the sexological tradition. In part, this growing interest reflected the new preoccupation with sexuality in public discourse. The 'great transition' in sexual behaviour and attitudes that began in the 1950s, and was carried forward by the post-war baby-boom generation, unsettled traditional patterns of family and intimate life, and opened new possibilities, and even a largely conservative historical profession began to broaden its agenda (see chapter 5). The idea of searching for early 'sexual revolutions', for example, can be traced via the analysis of demographic change in Edward Shorter's study, *The Making of the Modern Family*, though now located in the late eighteenth century.[21]

Demographic-based history was to prove a key entrée into what Peter Laslett described as the 'world we have lost', of not only kin and family forms and households but reproductive patterns, marriage, 'illicit love', illegitimacy and birth rates.[22] Many of these studies provided important insights into patterns of sexual life, even as the ostensible subject of the scholarship lay elsewhere. The emphasis on the long, slow evolution of family patterns (and hence of sexual behaviour) was an important one, which clearly owed something to the influence of the French *Annales* school, offering a deep history over the *longue durée*, but there was also a strong awareness of the complex intermingling of continuity and change, such as in the impact of proletarianization, urbanization and industrialization on intimate life. Reconstituting family patterns over extended periods showed that dramatic shifts, as in the rates of illegitimacy, were initially at least a product of traditional patterns confronted by disruptive change.

Such studies were part of a much wider turn towards social history from the late 1960s, challenging the narrowness of a history that focused overwhelmingly on the machinations of a political elite and largely ignored social and cultural experiences. The *Journal of Social History* first appeared in 1966, *Radical History Review* in 1973, *History Workshop Journal* and *Social History* in 1976. The new history sought to rescue ordinary people from what E. P. Thompson, in his classic *The Making of the English Working Class*, labelled the 'condescension' of history, and of historians.[23] It explored class struggle, work, the poor, crime, witchcraft, prostitution, migrations, slavery and racial histories, as well as households and family. The History Workshop movement, inspired by Raphael Samuel, put a new emphasis on a 'history from below' (see chapter 7). With the rise of second-wave feminism and gay liberation from the late 1960s, the emphasis on those marginalized and hidden by History with a capital H opened the way to new forms of sexual history, usually from young scholars heavily influenced by the new movements. With it came a willingness to challenge the naturalistic meanings of sexuality itself.

As Robert A. Padgug put it, in introducing a special edition of *Radical History Review* devoted to 'Sexuality in History' in 1979 (one of the first journals to attempt this), 'In any approach that takes as predetermined and universal the categories of sexuality, real history disappears.'[24] In trying to work through the dilemmas that this approach threw up, a number of younger historians were being drawn to wider debates in the social science about sexuality, and especially those sociologists, social psychologists and anthropologists that were developing a critique of what came to be known in the 1970s and 1980s as an 'essentialist' view of sexuality directly inherited from sexology. In their book *Sexual Conduct*, John H. Gagnon and William Simon challenged the 'drive reduction' model that they saw as central to the sexological tradition, the idea of a 'basic biological mandate' that pressed on, and so must be firmly controlled by the cultural and social matrix. The developing critique opened the way to a more social and historical understanding of sexuality, what became known as social constructionism. Could it be the case, Gagnon and Simon innocently asked, that there might have been a need, at some unspecified time in history, to invent an importance for sexuality?[25] Here was a challenge and an invitation that many of a new generation of historians found hard to resist.

The Emergence of Social Constructionism

Social constructionism has at its heart a preoccupation with the complex and multiple ways in which emotions, desires and relationships are shaped by the different cultures we inhabit. It is concerned with the historical and social organization of the erotic.

This theoretical stance had many roots. From sociological and social-psychological approaches such as symbolical interactionism, ethnomethodology and dramaturgy came an emphasis on the importance of social interaction, language and performance in shaping symbolic meanings, and what Peter Berger called the 'social construction of reality'. From social anthropology came an awareness of the variety and relativity of sexual cultures, both cross-nationally and in the burgeoning cities. Post-war sex research, especially that of Alfred Kinsey and his successors, revealed the huge dimensions of sexual variability and the wide prevalence of 'deviance'. Subsequently, poststructuralist and deconstructionist theories destabilized and problematized fixed meanings and structures.[26]

As this suggests, there were many potential constructionisms. They have cohered around a number of common assumptions. First, we should no longer set 'sex' against 'society' as if they were separate domains. Like Gagnon and Simon, Ken Plummer had argued that sexuality, far from being the very definition of 'the natural', was subject to socio-cultural shaping to an extraordinary degree. It is only because sexual activities are embedded in sexual scripts that the physical acts themselves become important.[27] Secondly, there is an emphasis on the social variability of sexual forms, beliefs, ideologies, identities and practices, and of the existence of different sexual cultures. There are indeed sexualities rather than a single sexuality. Thirdly, we must abandon the idea that we can fruitfully understand sexual history in terms of a dichotomy of pressure and release, repression and libera-tion. Sexualities are a result of diverse social practices that give meaning to human activities, of social definitions and self-definitions, of struggles between those who have power to define and regulate, and those who resist. Critics like John Boswell complained that social constructionists were' nomi-nalists', concerned with words and concepts rather than 'reality'.[28] Against that, constructionists would argue that we can only understand sexuality by understanding the web of meanings in which it is entwined and which shape what we think of as sexual at any particular time. 'Sexuality' is not a given, it is a product of social meanings and negotiation, power and struggle, regulation and human agency.

Social constructionist approaches were initially developed in relation to homosexuality. The classic starting point is widely seen as an essay on 'The Homosexual Role' by the British sociologist Mary McIntosh, first published in 1968, whose influence can be traced in a range of historical studies from the mid-1970s.[29] What is important about the work is that it asks what was at the time a new question: not, as had been traditional from the late nineteenth century, what are the *causes* of homosexuality, but rather, why are we so con-cerned with seeing homosexuality as a condition that has causes? And in tackling that new question, McIntosh pro-posed an approach which opened up a new research agenda: seeing homosexuals as a social category, rather than a medical or psychiatric one. McIntosh makes a critical distinction between homosexual behaviour and 'the homosexual role'. Homosexual behaviour is widespread; but distinctive roles have developed only in some historic cultures, and do not necessarily encompass all forms of homosexual activity. The creation of a specialized, despised and punished role or cat-egory of homosexual was a form of social control designed to minoritize the experience, and protect and sustain social order and traditional sexual patterns, in a very particular history (her historical examples largely come from London in the eighteenth century).

These insights were eagerly taken up by some young his-torians of sexuality.[30] But by the late 1970s a new theoretical element came into play, that represented by the work of Michel Foucault.[31] Foucault's essay on *The History of*

Sexuality is often seen, misleadingly, as the starting point of constructionist approaches, but there can be no doubt of the subsequent impact of what was planned as an introduction to a multi-volume study. Like Gagnon and Simon, Foucault appeared to be arguing that 'sexuality' was a 'historical invention', emerging in the eighteenth century but assuming a strong meaning from the nineteenth century. Like McIntosh, he saw the emergence of the concept of a distinctive homosexual personage as a historical process, but with the late nineteenth century as the key moment. Like McIntosh, he suggested that psychologists and psychiatrists had not been objective scientists of desire, as the sexological tradition proclaimed, but had on the contrary been diagnostic agents in the process of social labelling. For Foucault they were key players in the shaping of sexual discourses that created new subjects and subjectivities in the nineteenth and twentieth centuries: the hysterical woman, the sexualized child, the heterosexual couple busily controlling births, and the invert or homosexual. Each of these was an axis of power-knowledge, and the focal point of new forms of biopower and governmentality, regulating individuals and populations. The task of Foucault's history was not to sketch a grand master plan (Marxist, Freudian, liberal or even conservative) that would offer a single explanation, but to trace the genealogies of these new forms of knowledge and power. Far from sexuality being the focus of a politics of liberation, he was suggesting, it was more realistically the locus of discipline and subjection. But at the same time, his suggestion that people do not react passively to social categorization – 'where there is power, there is resistance' – left open the question of the subversion of these categories, and the possibilities of sexual identities and subjectivities that were oppositional to dominant hierarchies.

These new approaches, however, were fiercely contested. Many influenced by gay liberation saw in the historicization of the homosexual category a way of explaining the stigma that homosexuality carried, and the possibilities of challenging it. What was made in history could be changed in history. Others, however, believed firmly that homosexuality was intrinsic to their sense of self and social identity, essential to their nature, and sharply contested any idea that 'the homosexual' was an historical invention. This was at the heart of the so-called social constructionist–essentialist controversy in the 1970s and 1980s (see chapter 3).

There were other problems. Social constructionism, Vance noted, had initially paid little attention to the construction of heterosexuality.[32] In fact, the work of lesbian and gay historians was to throw considerable new light on the making of the binary divide that had constructed homosexuality as the Other of a silent norm. One of the early attractions of the first volume of Foucault's *History* was precisely that it both offered an account of the birth of the modern homosexual, and put that into a broader historical framework: by postulating the invention of sexuality as a category in Western thought, and in delineating the shifting relationships between men and women, adults and children, the normal and the perverse, as constituent elements in this process. Foucault himself was criticized for putting insufficient emphasis on the gendered nature of this process, but this was more than compensated for by the developing feminist critique of heterosexuality as an institution and structure, with its own complex history (see chapter 4).

Although the constructionist debates began within the disciplines of sociology and history, later developments, taking forward both theoretical and political (especially feminist) interventions, owed a great deal to poststructuralist and deconstructionist literary studies, and to the emergence of queer studies. Whereas history and sociology had characteristically attempted to produce order and pattern out of the chaos of events, the main feature of these approaches is to show the binary conflicts represented and reshaped in literary texts. The texts are read as sites of gender and sexual contestation, and therefore of power and resistance. Eve Sedgwick's work, and that of the American philosopher Judith Butler, were in part attempts to move away from the essentialist/constructionist binaries by emphasizing the 'performative' nature of sex and gender (though performativity and performance were in fact already present in symbolic interactionism and the work of Erving Goffman). For queer theorists, the perverse is the worm at the centre of the normal, giving rise to sexual and cultural dissidence and a transgressive ethic, which constantly works to unsettle binarism and to suggest alternatives.[33]

Much of the debate about the homosexual/heterosexual binary divide was based on the perceived Western experience, and was located in some sense of a historical development. Yet from the beginning, comparisons with non-Western sexual patterns were implicit in constructionist perspectives. Foucault controversially compared the Western 'science of sex' with the non-Western 'erotic arts'. It was the very fact of different patterns of 'institutionalized homosexuality' across cultures that formed the starting point of McIntosh's essay. So it is not surprising that constructionist approaches have fed into studies of sexuality in general, and homosexualites in particular, in other cultures, tribal, Islamic, Southern, global (see chapter 6). And this comparative framework has increasingly been deployed within contemporary Western societies themselves to uncover the co-existence of different if overlapping sexual cultures, notably in Europe.[34]

Historical and social constructionism has advanced and changed rapidly since the 1970s. The 'category' that early scholars were anxious to deconstruct has become 'categories' which proliferate in contemporary societies. 'Roles', neat slots into which people could be expected to fit as a response to the bidding of the agents of social control, have become 'performances' or 'necessary fictions', whose contingencies demand exploration. 'Identities', which once seemed fixed and determined, are increasingly seen as fluid, relational, hybrid: people are bundles of possibilities, not quite today what they were yesterday, or will be tomorrow. Identities have come to be seen as built around personal 'narratives', sexual stories people tell each other in the various interpretive communities to which they belong. Sexual orientation may, or may not, be a product of genetics, psycho-social structuring or environmental pressures. For those influenced by social and cultural approaches to sexuality, however, other questions were central: not what *causes* the variety of sexual desires, preferences or orientations that have existed in various societies at different times, but how different histories shape different meanings of sexuality, and the effects these have had on individual subjectivities and ways of life.

3
Querying and Queering Same-Sex History

What is Homosexual History?

Homosexuality has long been central to sexual history. Establishing the historical legitimacy of same-sex love was a prime aim of pioneering writers on same-sex practices from Ulrichs and Kertbeny through Symonds, Carpenter and Hirschfeld to 'Xavier Mayne', who published the first comprehensive history in 1907. From the very first page of the French novelist André Gide's *Corydon*, his classic defence of same-sex love published in the 1920s, Didier Eribon has observed, we are plunged into the history of homosexuality.[1]

After World War II, the immersion in history continued to gather pace. For pioneering homophile organizations such as the Mattachine Society and the Daughters of Bilitis in the USA, the Homosexual Law Reform Society in Britain, COC in the Netherlands and Arcadie in France, anchoring an emerging consciousness in a forgotten or obscured history was an essential moral and political task. There was, in Christopher Nealon's graphic phrase, a 'foundling relationship' to history, involving a sense of exile from sanctioned experiences on the one hand, and a sense of identification with others who redeem the exile on the other.[2]

The characteristic approach at first focused on legitimizing homosexuality by demonstrating a lineage of great figures of the past. Popular homosexual history was overwhelmingly concerned with great homosexuals of history, from Julius Caesar to Shakespeare, from Jesus to Oscar Wilde, from Sappho to Queen Christina of Sweden.[3] What such work lacked was a sense of shifting meanings, historical context, complex identities, or changing taboos or stigmas. At the core was a fixed view of *the* homosexual, usually male, whose central characteristics barely shifted through time, culture or place. Yet more frustrating for those who wanted a new history of homosexuality was the apologetic tone of even the most sympathetic of contemporary liberals in the 1950s and 1960s when confronting homosexuality in past and present.

In retrospect, the radical generation of the 1970s was perhaps a little harsh in its critique of this post-war work. Much of it was indeed largely a recycling of increasingly familiar material, but it had significantly contributed to the social science literature from the 1940s to 1960s, which helped transform the public image of the homosexual from a pathologized biological or psychological anomaly into a recognized 'social being'.[4] The description of homosexuals as constituting 'a sexual minority' with a distinctive way of life and a definable history fed into emerging new categorizations and individual and collective identities.

But as a new and more radical gay consciousness dramatically emerged from the late 1960s, so did an increasingly sophisticated and complex historical project that both affirmed lesbian and gay identities and helped transform the field of sexual history more broadly. As Laura Doan has noted, the history of homosexuality has been the field's 'gravitational centre'. Between 2002 and 2008, over half the articles published in the new discipline-defining *Journal of the History of Sexuality* were on homosexuality, while only one article addressed heterosexuality as such.[5]

There were no doubt many reasons for this – the urgent sense of political commitment that propelled it, the enthusiasm and growing depth of the scholarship, and the broad range of periods, countries and problems that could be explored. But the various attempts at a history of homosexuality also offered a test bed for investigating what was to become the most contested and difficult question: what exactly was a history of homosexuality? If sexuality was a concept without a precise referent, how much more so was this true of homosexuality, with its baggage of religious taboos, moral revulsion, psychological stigmatization, social oppression and popular prejudice, and highly distinctive and varied social and historical forms.

Same-sex relations between women immediately posed questions about the broad meaning of homosexuality. Despite considerable debate about lesbianism in the medical literature, it tended to have a muted role in public debate for most of the twentieth century.[6] This was largely because the focus was overwhelmingly on legal controls on homosexuality, which, with rare national exceptions such as Austria, tended to affect men rather than women. Could the interests of homosexual men and women ever be the same? This was a marker of more profound problems about the idea of a unitary concept of homosexuality. If the term had only existed since the 1860s, and most of the language that became familiar in the twentieth century had been invented in the last decades of the nineteenth century, were contemporary words or concepts of any use for earlier periods? If 'gay' was already being challenged in the heated politics of the 1970s by lesbians and transgender people as not inclusive enough, could a historian like John Boswell justifiably use it for a history of early Christianity in his landmark study *Christianity, Social Tolerance, and Homosexuality?*[7] Was it historically valid to assume real continuities between 'gay communities' in ancient Rome and modern New York, San Francisco, London, Berlin or Amsterdam, as Boswell and others seemed to suggest? What was the relationship between the homosexual past and the gay and lesbian (and bisexual, trans and increasingly diverse and queer) present, with its clear identities or refusals of identity? Was it possible, indeed, to hope for a comprehensive history of homosexuality at all?

Recovering the Lesbian and Gay Past and Historic Present

The fundamental commitment of pioneering lesbian and gay historians in the 1970s and 1980s was to a more comprehensive, more inclusive history, both in terms of areas covered, and in people listened to. This was essentially at first a work of recovery, of discovering and listening to the voices of those who had been 'hidden from history'.[8] It is not surprising that the new histories were closely associated with the development of a 'history from below', offering a genuine grassroots history. The path-breaking documentary collections *Gay American History* and *Gay/Lesbian Almanac*, which inspired many subsequent research projects, were authored by an independent scholar, Jonathan Ned Katz, rooted in the gay liberation movement.[9] For too long, Katz argued, lesbians and gays had been invisible in history, an 'unknown people'. Through involvement in the new movement, 'we experienced the present as history, ourselves as history makers. ... We experienced homosexuality as historical.'[10] This pointed to a practice of history against the grain, a democratic collective activity that was both scholarly and political. For those involved in the lesbian and gay communities in the USA in the 1970s and 1980s, the recounting of an alternative history was about their identities, their stories, an essential narrative that linked their contemporary struggles with a history of resistance and survival. The late Allan Bérubé, influenced by a reading of Katz, saw gay community history as a form of activism. He pioneered a dynamic presentation of grassroots history using slide shows, which he toured across the USA. A number of grassroots projects sprang up in various US cities in the 1970s collecting documentary evidence and oral histories of lesbian and gay life, including memories of working-class women and 'butch–femme' relationships, which contemporary radical feminists strongly disapproved of, and which otherwise might have escaped the historical gaze (see chapter 7). Similar community-based activities occurred in Britain, Canada, Australia and elsewhere.[11]

The study of emancipatory movements, including contemporary ones, became a crucial way into gay and lesbian history, especially as they explicitly emphasized the significance of grassroots action and strong elements of self-making. Studies by James Steakley, Toby Marotta, John D'Emilio and myself saw forms of activism and the emergence of distinctive homosexual identities as intricately intertwined. My own work outlined a process of definition and self-definition, exploring the legal, medical, psychological, political and cultural processes at play, and individual and collective identity affirmation and creation in Britain. D'Emilio traced the emergence of a new grassroots minority consciousness before Stonewall that shaped the conditions for a new movement and identity in the USA. Such work established a lineage, a progressive history of oppression and struggle, whilst emphasizing the elements that went into identity formation.[12]

This approach was both encapsulated and immediately problematized in a collection edited by Ken Plummer, *The Making of the Modern Homosexual*, in 1981 which became a controversial touchstone for emerging themes.[13] The affirmation of identity was a central feature of these early histories, but as the various contributions to Plummer's book made clear, the meanings of same-sex activities at different times varied enormously. It also became obvious, as gay men, lesbian, bisexual and transgender people chaotically sought common aims in a new social movement, that identity was not only enabling but potentially divisive.

As a history of same-sex relations between women developed in the 1970s and 1980s it was increasingly apparent that lesbian and gay male history might be linked by common taboos, prejudices and discrimination, but there were distinctive stories to be told, not least in the significance of identity. For historians such as Carroll Smith-Rosenberg and Lillian Faderman, the overwhelming preoccupation at first was with friendship and support networks amongst women for which a modern sexual categorization seemed barely relevant. Smith-Rosenberg delicately portrayed romantic friendships amongst women in the nineteenth century where erotic connection was at best ambiguous. Faderman, more explicitly, argued that a lesbian sexual identity was an imposition by sexologists on a 'continuum' that extended across all women, and which was expressed in close, mutually supportive friendships. Whilst for gay men at this stage gay was explicitly a *sexual* identity, for many 'women-identified-women' lesbian was as much a political/cultural category as a sexual one. There was a vigorous counter-argument to this: historians like Martha Vicinus, whilst documenting close friendships amongst women, were also able to demonstrate the highly sexualized nature of many female relationships. The emergence of the diary for the 1820s and 1830s of the English landholder Anne Lister of Shibden Hall, near Halifax in Yorkshire, illustrated the passionate erotic and romantic (and also property-related) preoccupations that entwined relations amongst women, but that in a sense dramatized the issue. The core issue for lesbian historians was how to interpret the meanings and subjectivities that such emotional and sexual entanglements gave rise to.[14] This was a problem that had wider resonance in exploring the historical manifestations of same-sex sexuality.

Deconstructing and Reconstructing the Homosexual

It was here that Mary McIntosh's essay 'The Homosexual Role', though directly addressing sociological issues, offered a starting point for a new approach to lesbian and gay/queer history. Her suggestion that homosexuality was a historically variable and culturally specific social category, giving rise to a range of social roles and identities, was politically charged, though immediately appealing to gay theorists aware of rapidly changing identifications and subjectivities.[15] Though exclusively about male homosexuality, her article had obvious implications for a history of lesbianism as well. McIntosh's intervention pre-dated by a decade the more famous work of Michel Foucault. As his biographer Didier Eribon has made clear, the first volume of Foucault's *History* was a product of many elements: a scepticism about the so-called Lacanian recovery of Freud, a rejection of the liberatory rhetoric of the Freudo-Marxists, and a deep scepticism about the emancipatory rhetoric of the new gay liberation movement. Establishing a social constructionist approach was certainly not Foucault's aim, and it was in many ways deeply ironic that he was to become an iconic figure for radical liberationists.[16] But there can be no doubt about his impact. In particular, his suggestion that 'the homosexual' had only emerged as a specific type of personage in the late nineteenth century, in a new discursive regime where people were being increasingly defined in terms of their sexuality, proved enormously influential. For much of the Christian era same-sex activity had been categorized under the amorphous category of sodomy. Now homosexuality had a specific meaning, increasingly defined by medicine, psychiatry, the penal system, and through new forms of identity: 'The sodomite had been a temporary aberration; the homosexual was now a species.'[17]

This, inevitably, opened up more questions than it answered. How significant was persecution of the sodomite? When did recognizable notions of homosexuality and 'the homosexual' emerge? How did this relate to women? Historians differed. Were the early modern cities of the Italian Renaissance a crucible? Or perhaps Dutch cities and London during the seventeenth and eighteenth centuries? Was the late nineteenth century more critical? Or was it the 1940s or 1950s before modern concepts fully developed? For some, such intellectual convolutions seemed critical for understanding the making of identities; for others, they seemed a dangerous irrelevance, because they ignored the continuities of gay life and identities.[18]

The resulting constructionist/essentialist controversy produced antinomies and polarities which now seem extreme. No one had argued against the idea that homosexual practices, and forms of social organization, have existed in many societies across different time spans: the evidence for this was transparent and increasingly well documented. Nor should it necessarily involve having to take a fundamentalist position on whether a 'homosexual orientation' (a concept that only fully emerged in the 1970s and 1980s) is *caused* by biology, psychology or social factors. Most historians are not well qualified to take an absolutist position on this, and anything else is simply belief. After all, most sex 'experts' had failed, and still do fail, to agree. From a historical perspective what matters is not what causes homosexuality in individual subjects, but how attitudes, concepts and subjectivities are shaped in particular historical circumstances, regardless of aetiology.[19]

In retrospect, some of the harsh oppositions that framed the debate seem overdone, especially as we come to understand the different intellectual and political agendas at play. John Boswell is a case in point. He was perhaps the most articulate defender of essentialist positions, though he politely disclaimed the honour. In understanding Boswell, it is important to grasp the complexity of his own intellectual commitments. *Christianity, Social Tolerance, and Homosexuality* was as much a dialogue with the Roman Catholicism of which Boswell was a critical adherent as with homosexual history. This book, like its successors, was part of a sustained effort to recover a less anti-sexual and anti-gay strand within the Christian tradition. For Boswell, Christianity was crucially about community across time, and in the same way the concept of 'gay' represented for him a continuity without which community was impossible – even if that community was remarkably like the burgeoning male gay communities he was familiar with in New York and San Francisco.[20] It was also a contribution to a much wider historical debate on classical and early Christian attitudes to sexuality that Foucault himself was to engage with in the two posthumous volumes of *The History*, and historians such as Peter Brown and Bernadette Brooten were to make important contributions to.[21]

It was this wider debate that underlined some of the limitations of Boswell's approach. Brooten drew attention to Boswell's indifference to lesbianism in her study of classical and early Christian attitudes towards female homoeroticism. Like Boswell, she was critical of Foucauldian views on identity, and recognized continuities in lesbian life, but she argued that it was gender inversion rather than sexual practices that was seen as a problem in pre- and early Christian attitudes.

What all these debates highlighted was the complexities of understanding the relationship between social categorization and individual sensibilities, subjectivities, identifications, social worlds and ways of life, which an increasingly theoretically sophisticated empirical research was highlighting. Much of it focused on the city. Alan Bray, in a classic study of attitudes to homosexuality in Renaissance England, had started his research by seeking to disprove constructionist approaches but had concluded by noting the absence of a distinctive homosexual identity or role, whilst documenting at the same time the evidence for same-sex activities in seventeenth-century London. Randolph Trumbach explored in great detail what he saw as a major shift in the organization of gender practices in eighteenth-century London, which reshaped the ways in which same-sex activity was conceived as an aspect of an emerging modernity.

Studies of the city as a crucible of burgeoning sexual cultures showed dramatically the differing temporalities and identifications around same-sex activity that co-resided in the anonymity of urban spaces. The city was a site of 'a constant titillation of the senses', of fleeting sexual encounters, and of sexual modernity, a laboratory of sexual possibilities.[22] George Chauncey's *Gay New York* provides a classic study of this from the epicentre of twentieth-century modernity. The emphasis on self-making paid homage to the constructionist arguments whilst carefully recognizing the co-existence of diversity in the urban spaces, and avoiding any sense of teleology which suggested the present was an automatic product of the past: 'The "gay world" actually consisted of multiple social worlds, many of them overlapping but some quite distinct and segregated from others, along lines of race, ethnicity, class, cultural style and/or sexual practices.'[23] The book shows how sexual identities are always provisional, in process, subject to the changing pushes and pulls, possibilities and limitations in a society where who and what you are, what your sexuality is, increasingly matters, but matters in different ways at different places and times.

New York experience from the late nineteenth century was paralleled by studies of other great international cities, such as Berlin, Paris and London. Matt Cook's *London and the Culture of Homosexuality, 1885–1914*, an early example of what has been called the New British Queer History, draws on literary scholarship as well as lesbian, gay or queer theory. It deploys urban geography as easily as the new social history. Cook is interested not so much in the *longue durée* of homosexual history as in the complex ways in which homosexuality was woven into the fabric of urban cultures at particular moments.[24]

Cook's London is a world of danger and of possibility, of new meanings and old patterns, a world where male homosexuality can be encountered in trains, tube stations, theatres, streets, music halls, public houses, squares, Turkish baths, urinals, parks, cafés, gentlemen's clubs, settlement houses, churches, hotels, shops and barracks, and yet be totally illegal. This was a world of friendships and of casual sexual encounters, of high-minded philosophizing about the nature of love, and of low-life encounters. This was the City of the Plain, the new Babylon, vividly described by Morris B. Kaplan in his *Sodom on the Thames*, where vice and virtue lived side by side, the home both of transgressive radicalism and of Hellenic romanticism, of the brilliant theatrics and tragedy of an Oscar Wilde, and of a covertly developing 'Cause' of homosexual emancipation. For Kaplan and Cook the neat categories of the sexologists, who in the late nineteenth century were just honing their craft, and of the gay historian who from the 1970s sought to establish the lineaments of a common history, crumble when you look at the urban melange.[25]

A sense of the sheer difference of the past is at the heart of Matt Houlbrook's *Queer London*. This work is in many ways a parallel to Chauncey's, covering much the same period. This again is a world of diverse life patterns rather than settled identities, where 'queans' and 'queers', 'homosexuals' and 'trade' live and engage side by side, often unknowingly. There is a strong note of nostalgia as the author looks back at a lost world, where discrimination existed, but life was also lived fully in the interstices of urban life. The enemy are those who sought to squeeze themselves into the traps of conformity in the later period, with the emergence of the middle-class queers who set out to reinvent themselves as the respectable homosexual of the 1950s and 1960s.[26] Both Chauncey and Houlbrook are suggesting that the 'modern homosexual' only really began to emerge in the post-war world, not from the logic of history but as a result of contingent events and practices of resistance and subjectification, and this personage remained one amongst many in a world of sexual complexity.

The emphasis on the city has been productive, but can also have a distorting effect on historical accounts of the emergence of contemporary homosexualities. Recent studies of same-sex relations amongst northern English non-metropolitan men at the turn of the nineteenth and into the mid-twentieth centuries, some heavily influenced by Walt Whitman and

Edward Carpenter, show both the fluidity of sexual practices amongst men, and the rigidity of gender relations between men and women. Similar research on rural America, especially the 'Deep South', have vividly brought to life cultures of gender and sexual nonconformity, focusing on widespread male same-sex practices and male-to-female transgender within a deeply conservative dominant sexual order, and in the virtual absence of the minoritizing identities emerging elsewhere.[27]

Such examples remind us that there were multiple makings of homosexual experience over the past century, leading not to sanctified gay or lesbian identities but to a proliferation of identifications, subjectivities and ways of being. There were harsh penalties, sustained prejudice, medical interventions, haphazard but often painful legal penalties but also vibrant cultures and self-making in this complex queer world.

The Queer Challenge

Such a simple little word, David Halperin observed about 'queer'. 'Who ever could have guessed that we would come to saddle it with so much pretentious baggage – so many grandiose theories, political agendas, philosophical projects, apocalyptic meanings?'[28] This is deliberately polemical, but it points to the conflicting meanings which criss-cross queer. Queer as a concept is as fluid and ambiguous as the worlds it sought to address. Its roots lie in the old denigratory term for homosexuals, which had been largely superseded by the adoption of 'gay' in the 1970s and pushed back into a bitter memory. It was revived in the new militancy of the late 1980s, especially in the USA, around AIDS and the anti-gay backlash. It represented a new assertion of resistance and defiance. The subsequent highly theoretical interventions – the subject of Halperin's wit – went further, questioned the fixity and arbitrariness of lesbian and gay identities, and endorsed a politics of subversion, dissidence and transgression. 'Queer is by definition whatever is at odds with the normal, the legitimate, the dominant', as Halperin put it in his 'gay hagiography', *Saint Foucault*, which sought to reclaim the philosopher from high theory and for a radical sexual politics.[29] This gives the concept a clear critical stance, but also a certain elusiveness, especially over its own conditions of existence. The often unacknowledged lineage of queer theory lies deep in the social constructionism and Foucauldian analyses of discourse and power that it critiqued, as well as in wider poststructuralist theory, the deconstructionist writings of Jacques Derrida, and excursions into Deleuzian desiring machines.

A move beyond social constructionism, however, was what many queer theorists explicitly endorsed. Eve Sedgwick critiqued both Foucault and David Halperin, whose *One Hundred Years of Homosexuality* had enthusiastically endorsed constructionist approaches, partly on the grounds that sexual identities were more unstable than constructionism seemed to imply – though in fact many gay and lesbian historians had no difficulty in agreeing with this. Powerful and influential as Sedgwick's challenge actually was, in retrospect it seems rooted less in theoretical scepticism than in political pragmatics. Her key book, *Epistemology of the Closet*, is not only a dialogue with the literary canon, but also a passionate engagement with the state of US sexual politics in the age of AIDS. She seeks to displace the essentialist–constructionist deadlock with a different if less sharp binary, of minoritizing and universalizing paradigms. The first assumes that homosexuality is a characteristic of a small, distinct and more or less fixed minority; the second sees homosexuality as an issue that shapes the lives of people across the spectrum of sexualities. She herself clearly aligns with the universalizing approach, arguing that many of the major modes of thought and literary products of the late nineteenth and early twentieth centuries are structured and fractured by an endemic crisis of homo–hetero definition. The ultimate reason for her rejection of the term, however, as becomes clear in her critique of anti-gay politics in America during the 1980s, is that constructionism gives an unnecessary hostage to fortune, allowing socially conservative and fundamentalist propagandists to argue that if homosexuality is socially constructed, so it can be socially reconstructed or reversed. She adopts in effect a form of 'strategic essentialism' as defined by the postcolonial theorist Gayatri Spivak. This makes a valid point: many sexual activists have found themselves in the position of defending a position that they did not theoretically accept. The trouble with Sedgwick's argument is that it conflates rather than clarifies the two different meanings of 'socially constructed'. The first does indeed explore how personal meanings and identities are socially shaped at the level of individuality. But it is not necessarily linked to constructionist arguments as used by historians or social scientists, who are more interested in how categories, structures of power and discourses produce historically specific meanings, and ultimately suspend questions concerning the causation of specific orientations.

There were other differences of emphases. Whereas pioneers of lesbian and gay history in the 1970s and 1980s had been largely concerned with the evolution of the category of the homosexual, queer approaches were more interested in exploring the power of the binary divide that gave rise to the category in the first place, and with the embeddedness of heteronormative values and structures. The concept of heteronormativity was in part a reformulation of the idea of compulsory heterosexuality, which had taken various subsequent forms – the heterosexual panorama, the heterosexual imperative, the heterosexual matrix, the heterosexual assumption, and so on. But it was derived also from the emphasis that Foucault had put on the settling of norms rather than sovereign power as the framework in which sexual meanings and discourses were lived within modernity. This was a productive if challenging emphasis, but had the odd effect of reasserting rather than deconstructing the power of the binary divide, and in some cases of universalizing the idea of heteronormativity, now seen as a principal dynamic of social organization, regardless of historical context.[30]

Beyond the Binary

The emphasis on 'performativity', on the *doing* of sexual and gender identities, following Sedgwick and Butler, was to be a key influence on the development of sexual history. In particular, interest in what came to be known from the 1990s as transgender was to prove a major preoccupation of queer historians. It destabilized not only sexual categories but especially the hitherto fundamental divide between men and women, male and female, masculinity and femininity. Feminist theorists had made a crucial distinction, derived from the work of American sexologists John Money and Robert Stoller, between 'sex', based on basic biological markers, and 'gender', which was seen as a social category that was historically variable. Queer theorists went further. For Judith Butler sex is an idea produced within relations of gender, which are social practices we act and re-enact incessantly to 'create the effect of the natural, the original, and the inevitable'.[31] From this perspective transgender offered a basic subversion of the sex-gender order, and a potent source of radical dissidence. For Marjorie Garber, author of *Vested Interests*, cross-dressing '*is a space of possibility structuring and confounding culture*' (italics in original), reflecting not just a crisis in the categories of male and female, but 'the crisis of category itself'.[32]

Transvestites and transsexuals had been heavily involved in the first burst of gay liberation at the Stonewall riots in June 1969, but their relationship with mainstream gay politics as it developed had been uneasy and ambiguous. The ambivalence was reflected in the first historical accounts of the new movement, and in the community history. Allan Berubé's famous slide show 'Lesbian Masquerade' was ostensibly about lesbians who passed for men, but could as readily have been presented as a history of trans people. As transgender activism found a new voice in the 1990s, so a new history emerged building on what previously had been seen as a history of homosexuality.[33]

Foucault made his own contribution to a growing interest in gender nonconformity with this famous dossier on Herculine Barbin, a mid-nineteenth-century hermaphrodite living in provincial France, who lived in 'the happy limbo of a non-identity' until forced to live unhappily as a man – and ultimately commit suicide. An obscure local tragedy became for Foucault and his collaborators a metaphor for a culture where saying who you are by telling of your sex is coming to matter.[34] An increasingly important literature has explored hermaphroditism, intersex, transvestism, transsexuality and 'female masculinity', revealing the ambivalence, confusions and adaptations that dwell within the apparent order and regularity of gender normality.[35]

In the same way, challenges to the logic of identity helped liberate the perverse and the perversions for historical investigation. There was a double imperative here. On the one hand there was a stress on the perverse as the worm in the bud at the heart of Western imagination, setting the parameters for the normal, the fracture that in a sense delimited all sexualities. But on the other hand, in Gayle Rubin's well-known phrase, characters straight from the pages of Krafft-Ebing were marching onto the stage of history, and of historical study: bisexuality, sadomasochism, necrophilia, paedophilia, all became the basis of new identities, and the subject of serious scholarship.[36]

This developing literature pointed in one direction to an explosion of new histories of identity – of the trans person, the bisexual, the BDSMer, and so on. In another direction they could be deployed to challenge the fixity of subject positions and identity, offering fundamental challenges to the prison house of sexual normality. What sexology defined as perversions, which liberal theorists labelled as sexual aberrations, and the writers of the various editions of the American Psychiatric Association's *Diagnostic and Statistical Manual* saw as sexual disorders, could be seen by queer writers as opening the possibility of new forms of sexual relating outside the heteronormative order, with utopian undertones. For Muñoz, 'Queerness is essentially about the rejection of a here and now and an insistence on potentiality or concrete possibility for another world'. For Love, 'utopian desires are at the heart of the collective project of queer studies and integral to the history of gay and lesbian identities'.[37]

As Biddy Martin has warned, there is an 'enormous fear of ordinariness' in all this which elevates radical detachment, anti-societalization and transgression to the level of 'a reactive sublime', leaving no space for ordinary lives. Discipline and normalization are not the only ways power operates in modern societies, and a flat anti-normativity is not necessarily the most efficacious political or conceptual challenge to the forms of constraint and abjection people face. For queer radicals, like Muñoz, however, 'being ordinary and being married are both antiutopian wishes'.[38]

   This utopianism was the counterbalance to a dark dystopianism that characterized some theoretical approaches to
queer history by the turn of the millennium, and for which
Sedgwick's search for an understanding of shame is a useful
marker. Two of the leading queer historians, David Halperin
and Valerie Traub, convened a conference on gay shame in
Michigan in 2004 and subsequently produced a substantial
volume of papers from it. One of the declared aims of the
event was to resist the professionalization of queer studies
and to return it to community practice. The result, the volume
itself appears to confirm, was to sharpen divisions between
the two as activists and theorists spoke dramatically different
languages.[39] The impulse to pursue the darker side of queer
history was a deliberate counter to the progressive story that
many writers were happy to tell. The history of non-normative
sexualities is littered with the detritus of violence, fear, hatred,
persecution, trauma, stigma and guilt as well as shame, which
it is important to bring to memory.
   But it is one thing to default towards a Whig interpretation
of history and a teleological optimism. It is surely another to
mark the history of homosexuality as eternally sculpted by
shame. George Chauncey, who spoke at the Gay Shame conference, remarked that shame is no more natural than race,
sexuality or anything else. He recognized the existence of
shaming/shameful rituals of humiliation, but rejected the idea
that pre-gay liberation history is dominated by shame.[40]
   The debate on shame brings emotion and affect to the
heart of queer history. But in its darker form it can be seen
as an aspect of the 'anti-social turn' in queer theory, associated with the theorists Leo Bersani and Lee Edeleman, and
their rejection of 'queer futurity'.[41] Many found this body of
work compelling because it compounded a deeper sense
of loss and melancholia amongst a particular generation of
theorists. But as the social anthropologist Henrietta Moore
pointedly remarks, theories which assume the existence of
pain, humiliation, exclusion, abjection, suffering and subjection as the given condition fail to explain why these things
exist, and reduce masses of people to victimhood. They are,
she suggests, products of a left melancholia, and ignore the
ways in which people creatively imagine their modernities
and futures.[42]

Making Connections

In her book *Disturbing Practices* Laura Doan critiques what she calls 'ancestral history', marked by a quest for stable and identifiable sexual subjects, and conventional social history with its commitment to the empirical, and suggests these are profoundly at odds with a queer theory that 'blasted to smithereens' the possibility of fixed identities. Taking this argument to its logical conclusion, she also auto-critiques her own subtle and influential genealogy of a lesbian identity in twentieth-century Britain in *Fashioning Sapphism* (itself richly empirically based) as marred by an assumption that she knew more about female sexuality than the individuals she was researching. Now she suggests that the purpose of queer critical inquiry is not to provide a usable past but to explain aspects of the sexual past that resist explanation in terms of identity history. The real efficacy of queer history is methodological rather than ontological, with 'queer' a verb more than an adjective, performative rather than substantive: queering as well as querying same-sex history.[43]

Such an approach takes the logic of problematization and denaturalization to a point where all modern categorizations are challenged. There is a scepticism about patterns and explanatory schemas, in favour of an emphasis on what Brian Lewis, in his discussion of the New British Queer History, describes as 'fragmented experiences, self-understandings, desires and behaviours',[44] offering no longer a grand narrative but a kaleidoscopic picture.

Scepticism about meaning and direction, however, need not mean no links and relationships can be made. In *How to Do the History of Homosexuality*, Halperin explores the radical otherness of the sexual past, especially of the ancient world. He now rejects the epistemological distinction between homosexual acts and homosexual identities, supposedly derived from Foucault, that he made use of in his early work, and stresses the potential continuities that can endure in queer subjectivities, as products not of biology but of cultural traditions and experience.[45] Valerie Traub explores similar themes in *The Renaissance of Lesbianism in Early Modern England*. She is concerned with the 'impossibilities' of disinterring and interpreting representations of female-to-female erotic desire in the past.[46] We lack the key to the code that would unlock the organizing conceptual categories of the periods she is exploring, but the trajectory of the book traces nevertheless how a discursive regime of the impossibility of lesbianism is gradually displaced by a governing logic of suspicion and possibility. These shifts provide the conditions for a range of social types to emerge whose subjectivities came to be fixed in identities – masculine females, female husbands, tommies, sapphists, inverts, on to female homosexuals and lesbians. In her history there is no developmental logic, no inevitability, no simple supersession of one category by another. The concern is with how female desire is made intelligible in different ways at different times, and in how different categories co-exist in parallel temporalities. But the point is that categories do emerge with effects on individual lives and social perceptions. In retrospect we do see movement, patterns, narratives, structures and identities emerge through the mists of the past.

In her book *Getting Medieval*, Carolyn Dinshaw also seeks a queer history that is a contingent rather than determined history, but nevertheless finds ways of connecting past and present. She links traditional institutions for parish priests, accusations of sodomy amongst heretics and orthodox Christians, the deposition of a male transvestite prostitute, the ostensibly heterosexual fellowship of Chaucer's pilgrims and the verbal sparring of the mystic Margery Kemp in the fourteenth and fifteenth centuries with the culture wars of the 1980s in the USA and sodomy in the film *Pulp Fiction*. The queer historical impulse, she suggests, is towards making connections across time between lives, texts and other cultural phenomena left out of sexual categories then, and out of sexual categories now.[47] In essence, what this queer history is suggesting is that instead of a fruitless search for precursors of modern identities in a fragmented history, we can validly seek identification with people who are both radically different and emotionally close to us – discovering the joy 'of finding counterparts in the past, problematic though it may be'.[48]

From this perspective queer history can be seen as part of the same impulse that gave rise to the new lesbian and gay history of the 1970s and 1980s in the first place. The challenge then as now was not just to celebrate but to question, not to seek the truth of sexuality but to denaturalize it, not to confirm a settled history but to problematize, not to systematize the past or order the present, but to unsettle it. By historicizing 'the homosexual', queer historians have opened the way to challenging all fixed categories, not least heterosexuality, and to revealing, in all its richness, the complexity of the sexual past, and of the present.

4
Gender, Sexuality and Power

Dangers and Pleasures

The rather dry and academic-sounding 'The Scholar and the Feminist IX' conference, held at Barnard College, New York City, on 24 April 1982, turned out to be anything but scholastic or dull. It was destined to become a critical moment in the evolution of second-wave feminism. The Barnard conference crystallized and fed into what became known as the 'sex wars' in the USA, with resonances in Europe and elsewhere, that embroiled feminist activists, theorists and historians for much of the 1980s and beyond.

The sex wars were fought over a range of issues including pornography, gay male sexuality, sadomasochistic and butch–femme relations between women, reproductive freedom, the sexual abuse of children, and sex education.[1] The wider context was the apparently irresistible rise of a morally conservative New Right in the USA from the 1970s, coinciding with an apparently out-of-control health epidemic – AIDS – that largely affected gay and bisexual men, and other unpopular minorities, and fuelled a backlash against them. What made the feminist controversies so fevered was that in this wider context, some radical/revolutionary/cultural feminists (the self-descriptions varied) appeared to be allying on issues of sexuality with the most reactionary forces in America. This was symbolized by the efforts of two major figures in American radical feminism, the legal scholar Catharine MacKinnon and the charismatic and apocalyptic anti-porn polemicist Andrea Dworkin, working with conservative (male) state legislators, to pass ordinances outlawing 'the graphic sexually explicit subordination of women whether in pictures or in words' in Minneapolis and Indianapolis in 1984, followed by similar efforts elsewhere.[2] All proved ultimately unsuccessful, but what especially incensed sexual dissenters and radicals was the invocation of conservative state power to limit freedom of speech – including that of other feminists. As British feminist historian Joanna Bourke later remarked, 'such approaches jettison emancipatory agendas of plurality and solidarity by involving the State as the arbiter of sexual legitimacy'.[3]

For the feminist thinkers involved in the Barnard imbroglio, defence of free speech and contestation of state regulation and repression were two key elements in any feminist agenda. But behind this was a profound political and theoretical divide, focused on the historic meanings of gender, sexuality and power. Two key essay collections published within a year of each other, the volume of conference papers, *Pleasure and Danger*, and *The Powers of Desire*, encapsulated in their titles and contents the issues at stake.[4] As Ellen DuBois and Linda Gordon put it, contemporary feminists inherited two conflicting traditions from nineteenth-century feminist thought. The strongest, virtually unchallenged in the first wave of feminism, emphasized the dangers of sexuality for women. The emphasis on sexual violence and on the exploitative nature of prostitution vividly illustrated this, and continues to be a central motif in international feminism to the present. The second strand sought to affirm female sexuality in all its diversity, to explore desire and pleasure, but it remained a largely subterranean strand, often linked with wider leftist or utopian politics.[5] What was needed was a more nuanced history of female sexuality which balanced pleasure and danger, passion and power, and contributed to a broader understanding of the historical making of sexuality.

Sexual Violence and Sexual History

Sexual violence was a key issue around which such controversies were played out. In the 1970s the issue of sexual violence, and rape, had rapidly become the symbolic focus of debates about male power and the motivating force of sexual history. The enormously influential book *Against our Will*, by the journalist Susan Brownmiller (1978), had crystallized a certain view that was powerful because it was so clear and apparently aligned with common sense.[6] Rape is 'nothing more or less than a conscious process of intimidation by which all men keep all women in a state of fear', the single most important causative factor in the original subjugation of women by men, the key to female dependence, and the roots of patriarchy.

Other radical feminists echoed these themes. For Robin Morgan, pornography was the theory, rape was the practice, while 'the Man's competitiveness and greed' were responsible for 'sexism, racism, war and ecological disaster'. Kathleen Barry in *Female Sexual Slavery* drew attention to the similarities between feminist campaigns against the Contagious Diseases Acts in Britain in the 1880s and feminist attacks on pornography in the 1970s. Mary Daly, in her book *Gyn/Ecology*, lamented the emptiness of male sexuality, while stressing the nurturing, loving, open and egalitarian nature of women. A particular reading of sexual and gender history was created in the service of current political preoccupations. As Alice Echols remarked, as feminism became synonymous with the establishment of the 'female principle' it had come to reflect and reproduce dominant cultural, and early sexological, assumptions about women – and men.[7]

Andrea Dworkin's notorious assertion that pornography *was* violence against women was clearly part of the same framing analysis, though there were significant differences amongst this school of feminists. MacKinnon, Dworkin's partner in the anti-porn crusade, was heavily critical of Brownmiller for arguing that rape was about power rather than sexuality, but at the same time she distanced herself theoretically from traditional biologistic arguments. For MacKinnon sexuality was the social process which creates, organizes, expresses and directs desire, shaping women and men. The erotic sexualizes power. But simultaneously she polemicized against what she conceived of as the driving force of the sex radicals. 'The history these historians of sexuality write is the history of desire: of the impelled, compelled, wanting, grasping, taking, mounting, penetrating, thrusting, consummating. It is the history of ecstasy and its prohibitions and permissions.' For MacKinnon, *Pleasure and Danger* and *Powers of Desire* are exemplars of 'sexology-inspired retrofit versions of gay and lesbian history and the history of prostitution'. Writers on these subjects were developing a type of history, she argued, based on the assumptions that sex was good, and more sex was better; sex is pleasure. Against this, she argued, the feminist task was to insist on male culpability for violence.[8]

MacKinnon was the key figure in the elaboration of a concept of gender, sexuality and power that claimed to be anti-essentialist whilst decrying feminist, gay and Foucauldian efforts at historicizing sexuality, and was to become highly influential amongst a select group of feminist historians. In *The Spinster and Her Enemies*, the British (later Australia-based) Sheila Jeffreys outlined a history in which the anti-violence agenda of late nineteenth-century feminists was thwarted by a male backlash, in which sexologists like Havelock Ellis played a central part in legitimizing male aggression. In subsequent works she critiqued the sexual revolution, the anti-feminism of queer politics, transgenderism, the global sex trade, the rise of religion and its impact on women's rights, and the beauty trade, covering the range of issues that became central to radical feminist analyses and activism into the 2000s. The message was consistent. Women and children are intimidated and inferiorized through male sexuality and male violence. Perversions are the extreme form of what is inherent in ordinary male sexuality. Gay men are complicit in male privilege. The forms of domination may be socially scripted but always in the context of male power.[9] Men are the problem. Despite its claims to be historically grounded and non-essentialistic, it is difficult not to see in this a discourse with its own essentializing drive and moral absolutism.

My aim here is not to refight old controversies but to show how a particular set of assumptions about men and violence shapes historical perspectives. Contemporary historians of rape give due credit to Brownmiller's work for drawing attention so powerfully to the crucial importance of sexual violence, but they seek to put rape into a wider historic, social and economic context. Joanna Bourke argues that 'Rape is a form of social performance. It is highly ritualized. It varies between countries, it changes over time. There is nothing timeless or random about it.' Janie Leatherman similarly challenges essentialist views in her study of rape in war, and argues that sexual violence does not develop in isolation from a society's pre-existing socio-economic and culturally shaped gender relations. Estelle Freedman concurs that the meaning of rape is fluid rather than transhistorical, continually reshaped by specific social relations and political contexts. In particular, Freedman draws attention to the racialized meanings of rape in the American context, and critiques Brownmiller for fanning the fires of racism. Rather than a monistic, uni-causal account these historians are seeking both to address the specificities of male (and other) violence and to problematize: 'Sexual abuses have a history. By demystifying the category of rapist we can make him less frightening and more amenable to change.'[10]

Historicizing Female Sexuality

'Reliance on an iconography of female victimization', Judith Walkowitz commented, 'can undercut the political impact of feminists' own public initiatives.'[11] What marks the alternative feminist history is an approach that seeks to go beyond a singular analytical explanation (men, male power, patriarchy) that reduces women to the status of perpetual victim, and seeks instead to root gender and sexuality within a complex, multifocal nexus of power relations, in which women constantly struggle against their subordination, and become active agents. The women involved in shaping this pluralistic feminist sexual history had their roots in the women's liberation movement, but were often shaped also by a socialist-feminist tradition that was sensitive to class and anti-racist arguments, seeking to tease out the intersections between the different dynamics of power.[12] They were strongly engaged in the arguments around social constructionism and social and later cultural history, especially in the emphasis on language, discourse, representation and narrative, and (for some at least) psychoanalysis. Above all, they both contributed to and drew on a fundamental re-evaluation of the relations between gender, sexual systems and power that was to become enormously influential. 'Against a unified picture of male social power and misogynist cultural production,' Walkowitz wrote, 'feminist critics of the anti-pornography campaign increasingly invoked a world changed less by unities and binary divisions than by gaps, fragmentations, and contradictions, a world peopled by historically constructed shifting selves with no fixed gender-identity of subject or object.'[13] As with contemporaneous studies of homosexuality, thinking about female sexuality in history inevitably problematized its meanings and implications.

Linda Gordon's *Woman's Body, Woman's Right* is a key work in this development of a sophisticated feminist sexual history. It was a book deeply rooted in the feminist struggles of the time around women's reproductive rights, but at the same time it was a pioneering study of the birth control movement within the context of sexual history. Previous studies had offered technical and medical histories of contraception, or profiles of prominent activists, such as Margaret Sanger. Neither of these approaches had stressed the importance of birth control as a social movement. In exploring the social movement itself Gordon came to realize that this could not be understood as a simple narrative of progress. The different phases of its history were shaped by the specific circumstances of the time, especially as they impacted on or were interpreted by women. Major institutions of sex and reproduction, she argued, such as the family and codes of morality, were established as much by women's struggles to protect themselves as by men's struggle to protect their property.[14]

Gordon's book and subsequent works such as Rosalind Petchesky's *Abortion and Woman's Choice*, paralleled by near-contemporary studies by Angus McLaren and others on the UK, showed abortion and birth control to be part of a wider battle for sexual rights and reproductive freedoms, with women central to them.[15] Gordon's book was attacked at the time, for its rejection of a progressivist narrative, and for its downplaying of heroic leadership. But Gordon does strongly emphasize that conflicts about reproductive rights are *political* conflicts, and that involves an understanding of the gender and sexuality systems, class and race structures and language.

Judith Walkowitz's studies of prostitution, feminism and social purity in the late nineteenth century in Britain show similar nuances. In *Prostitution and Victorian Society* she argued that the Contagious Diseases Acts, which sought to control the spread of venereal disease in certain English garrison towns by enforcing compulsory inspection and detention of suspected women, offered a critical focus for the study of class and gender relations, and the possibilities of female resistance. The acts generated enormous popular mobilization, from working-class men and women as much as from middle-class feminists, and provided powerful insights into the rise of the institutional state, the development of the women's movement, and changing social and sexual mores. The role of working women was central to the analysis. Those labelled as prostitutes in towns like Portsmouth and Southampton 'emerge as important historical actors, as women who made their own history, albeit under very restrictive conditions'. They were not rootless social outcasts but poor working women trying to survive in towns that offered them few employment opportunities and that were hostile to young women living alone.[16] But through the turmoil of the controversy, and the legislative changes that took place in the 1880s, together with the interventions of social purity reformers, the delicate balance of many working-class communities was deeply unsettled, and increasingly the divide between the respectable women and the prostituted hardened, creating a sharply demarcated outcast group.

In her early essays in the 1970s Walkowitz had shown the influence of the same labelling and deviance theory that was reshaping the history of homosexuality, but her 1980 book is clearly influenced by an early reading of Foucault. The Contagious Diseases Acts are now understood in Foucauldian terms as technologies of power to oversee and manipulate the lives of the unrespectable poor. In place of a single Victorian sexual ideology Walkowitz shows a complexity of often conflicting beliefs and practices, and an ongoing struggle to develop a hegemonic set of values, never fully achieved.

The influence of the social purity movement, involving key feminists, was to become a central focus of feminist controversy and divide. For writers such as Jeffreys, social purity feminism had courageously challenged male sexual violence and had pioneered the 'true' feminism which presaged the sort of revolutionary feminism that she advocated. In her essay 'Male Vice and Female Virtue' Walkowitz explicitly challenged this narrative, and sought to demonstrate the contradictory impact of social purity, especially on vulnerable women. In a subsequent reflection she acknowledged a 'family resemblance' rather than a complete identity between the preoccupations and interpretive strategies on sexuality and social order in the late nineteenth century and in the present, and proposed a feminist vision which 'posits a world of complex cultural meanings where perhaps the most strenuous task facing feminists would be to shape representations'.[17] As the language suggests, Walkowitz is here marking a significant theoretical shift that goes beyond social history and signals an engagement with a new cultural history.

Sexuality and the Theory Wars

The questions that were becoming central to the debates about sexual history – about gender, power, the historical shaping of sexual identities and subjectivities – were a long way from the initial concerns of traditional social history with class and popular resistance (and the preoccupations of radical and revolutionary feminists about male violence and power were even further distant). The work of historians such as Linda Gordon and Judith Walkowitz were, however, pushing the boundaries of what constituted social history and beginning to engage with more culturalist themes, taking on board the influence of Michel Foucault, developments in cultural anthropology, and theoretical shifts in cultural theory towards poststructuralism. This had been presaged as early as the first issue of the feminist journal *Signs* in 1975, which had introduced the 'new French theory' of Julia Kristeva, Hélène Cixous and Luce Irigaray to US feminists, combining a fierce philosophical/psychoanalytic/linguistic critique of twentieth-century master thinkers with a lyrical 'writing of the body' that challenged the male 'phallocratic' order in the name of a radical difference.[18]

These intellectual shifts paralleled wider debates in the historical profession, especially in the USA, which became known as the 'theory wars'. The 'new historicism', a term coined by Stephen Greenblatt in 1982, was declaredly influenced by an eclectic range of thinkers from Karl Marx and Louis Althusser to the cultural critic Raymond Williams, and the anthropologists Victor Turner and Clifford Geertz. This stimulated an important body of work, especially among literary scholars, that was centrally interested in interdiscursivity, synchronic coincidence rather than causality, concern with the workings of power, and a growing focus on sexuality, though the debt to feminist and gay history was initially obscured. The key moment in the impact of these new developments on sexual history came with the publication of Gallagher and Laqueur's *The Making of the Modern Body*. Now the body itself became an object of historical investigation, and this was confirmed by Laqueur's subsequent work, *Making Sex*.[19]

These shifts towards a more culturalist history are reflected in Walkowitz's book *City of Dreadful Delight*, published in 1992. She locates the Jack the Ripper narrative in late nineteenth-century London as part of a formative moment in the production of feminist sexual politics and of popular narratives of sexual danger. Her study examines the competing cultural elements that are incorporated into the Ripper narratives, as well as those elements that are excluded and resisted, especially those in which women were not silenced or terrorized victims. Walkowitz is here exploring much more than the identity of the Ripper, which has engaged so many writers for over a hundred years. She is seeking to illuminate a new sexual landscape in London, and in England as a whole.

This work remains rooted in a commitment to history as a discipline, and to the importance of the category of experience (which gender theorists like Joan Scott were problematizing) in a material world. But she is now adding a poststructuralist concern with the ways in which people organize meaning in social contexts, and experience is mediated through language. Walkowitz acknowledges the problems posed to traditional history by cultural history: the absence of narrative closure (who the Ripper was is of little concern to her), the absence of fixed gender or class polarities (meanings cannot be derived from these categories, which are fluid and changing), and the existence of multiple voices (many of which are contradictory, shifting over time and in different social situations). This sort of history is less concerned with change over time than with the shifting patterns through which sexual and gender meanings are produced, the emotions they invoke, and the constant interactions of a complex present and a living past.

The emphasis on subjectivity and emotion was fuelled by a growing interest in psychoanalysis, which early second-wave feminist theorists had once vigorously rejected. Juliet Mitchell's *Psychoanalysis and Feminism* had pointed in new directions, arguing for the need to complement an analysis of capitalist structures with an understanding of the unconscious structuring of patriarchal relations and female subordination through the subject's entry into language and gendered identity. This rather abstract formulation was a challenge to more detailed historical excavation. Historians such as Sally Alexander, Barbara Taylor and Michael Roper posed important questions about how psychoanalytical insights into gender, with their tendency towards universalism, could be deployed in historically specific analyses, teasing out the subjectivities and emotions which sustained and destabilized gender stability.[20]

Rethinking Power

Culturalist approaches stressed the importance of issues of subjectivity and affect in similar ways to the queer challenge within lesbian and gay history. Within both, however, was a problem that radical feminists had put so vigorously on the agenda: the relationship between gender and sexuality, identity and feeling, and the overarching question of the nature of power, and how it was to be understood in historical analyses. In her essay 'Gender: A Useful Category of Historical Analysis', Joan Scott suggested that gender was both a constitutive element of social relations based on perceived difference, and a primary way of signifying power, with shifting historical meanings and significance.[21] Every society, the social anthropologist Gayle Rubin famously argued, 'has a sex/gender system – a set of arrangements by which the biological raw material of human sex and procreation is shaped by human, social intervention and satisfied in a conventional matter, no matter how bizarre some of the conventions may be'.[22] Gender, far from being the stable and eternal basis for the organization of social life, was the historically and culturally variable and potentially unstable means by which different societies organized sexual differences. The constellation of institutions, beliefs and ideologies and social practices that organizes the relations between men and women in any particular society is not fixed for all time. It constitutes a specific 'gender order' that is a product of history, indeed of many histories, and is in constant evolution as new gender projects develop, are consolidated or contested, lived or denied.[23] In *Making Sex*, Thomas Laqueur influentially suggested that the eighteenth century was a key moment in this evolution in Europe. In medical discourse, he argued, there was a move away from the ancient tradition of seeing women and men as constituting but one sex, with women's bodies an inverted and inferior version of men's, towards recognizably modern versions of two polarized, and potentially antagonistic, categories.[24]

The relationship of the historically shifting gender order to the complexities of the making of sexuality was, however, contested amongst sexual historians. Gayle Rubin, whose early essay on the sex/gender system had been very influential, offered a more refined analysis a decade later. A radical theory of sexuality, she argued, 'must identify, describe, explain and denounce erotic injustice and sexual oppression ... it must build rich descriptions of sexuality as it exists in society and history'.[25] This necessitated an analytical and political distinction between sexuality and gender in order to understand the historical nature of the hierarchies and power relations that shaped sexual systems and enshrined and enforced heterosexuality. Sexuality and gender, she argued, form the basis of two distinct arenas of social practice. They are different 'vectors of oppression', with gay and lesbian struggles appropriate to one, and feminist struggles to the other. Drawing on Rubin, Eve Sedgwick had proposed in *Epistemology of the Closet* (Axiom 2) that the study of sexuality was not co-extensive with the study of gender, and therefore anti-homophobic inquiry was not co-extensive with feminist inquiry. 'Sexual systems', the structured ways in which sexual behaviour and practices were shaped and given meaning through institutions, should be the main focus of sexual history.

We can see in this argument a commitment to write, in the context of the sex wars, a history that is multi-causal, rejecting macro-theoretical explanations (Capitalism, Patriarchy, even Gender) in favour of grounded studies of particular configurations of power around sexuality. It is clearly indebted to Michel Foucault's rejection of a grand theory of power, in favour of what he called an analytics of power. Power was a process, not a thing that could be seized or held or imposed. It was immanent in all social relations, but took particular institutional forms within specific historical conditions, operating as much through discourses of power-knowledge as through physical force.

In perspective, however, this distinction between sexuality and gender looks somewhat artificial. There are complex, mobile relations between the two. Ultimately the complexities of gender and sexuality are ethnographic and historical questions rather than theoretical, because these categorizations and distinctions only have meaning in specific historical and cultural contexts.[26]

Intersections

The complex interactions of the forces that shaped sexual history were increasingly recognized by feminist historians from the 1970s, with the key term 'intersections' already being widely used by Vance in her introductory essay to *Pleasure and Danger*.[27] It was a significant theme in the first comprehensive history of sexuality in the USA, D'Emilio and Freedman's *Intimate Matters*.[28] The interlocking, mutually reinforcing impact of various forms of power and domination around race, class, gender and sexuality had been first articulated by black feminists as it became clear that the universalizing tendencies of white feminist analyses did not speak to the experience of all women. The black lesbian

Combahee River Collective had written of the difficulty of separating race from class from sex oppression, because in their lives they were experienced 'simultaneously'.[29] Affirmations of sisterhood, female culture and feminist community, black critics argued, had ignored questions of race and class; while feminist critiques of the family as a vehicle for patriarchal oppression and the constriction of female sexuality ignored the importance of the black family as a focus both of opposition to racism and of survival.[30] Intersectional analyses sought to show how different experiences of oppression, discrimination and exclusion worked together to reinforce one another in the uniqueness of subject position: they were lived not as separate forms of oppression but as inextricably interlocking and densely lived experiences, producing their own forms of resistance.

From this perspective, race and class were not add-ons to a history of sexuality: they were central to the organization and power dynamics of the sexual order. In the USA racial divides have come to be seen as formative and constitutive, above all because of the centrality of slavery to American history. A recent collection of essays on the global experience of slavery argues for the 'mutual entanglement' of slavery and sexuality, with sexuality 'actually at the heart' of how slavery worked in many societies.[31] Historians in the USA have shown how the institution of slavery, and since its formal abolition in the 1860s its long legacy in Jim Crow laws and institutionalized racism, were structured by a racialized sexuality, where the deployment of sexuality intersects with the deployment of race, and where sexuality is a determining component of racial – and class – formation. Racialized sexuality exists at the point where the virtual powerlessness of certain sexual subjects intersects with the prohibitive power of various state and civil apparatuses, underwritten by the threat or actual use of coercive violence.[32]

Fear and sexualized violence have been at their most obvious in the lynchings of black men for sexual relations with white women, but subtler forms of violence and coercion have been no less powerful on the shaping of black female sexuality. Evelynn M. Hammonds's article 'Towards a Genealogy of Black Female Sexuality' powerfully argued that from the nineteenth century black female sexuality was defined in precise antithesis to white women's, as hypersexual. Black women campaigners from the latter part of the century sought to counter that by stressing their own Victorian rectitude and morality, but without being able to dismantle the pre-existing stereotypes. Despite many forms of resistance, black women have been unable to express their own sexuality fully, with effects that persisted into the AIDS crisis, which is Hammonds's specific concern.[33]

White racialized sexuality is the silent, unmarked norm in all this, and a considerable scholarship has recently explored this. In her 'southern gothic tale of violence and despair', *Sapphic Slashers*, Lisa Duggan has documented the ways in which the narratives of 'lesbian love murder' in 1890s Tennessee overlap with the racist narratives about the lynchings of alleged black rapists, to shape a toxic racial discourse that proved highly influential. The murder of Freda Ward by her 'girl lover' Alice Mitchell in Memphis in 1892 coincided with the driving out of the anti-lynching crusader Ida B. Wells from the same place. Both contributed, Duggan argues, to defining the white home as the central symbolic site for nation through processes of exclusion of both wild, unruly, sexually dangerous women and violent, overpowering black male sexuality. In *The Heart of Whiteness*, Julian B. Carter demonstrates how normality and heterosexual eroticism co-evolved in the interwar years, and so embedded were they in the relations of power that the racial implications of the new sexual discourses became hard to see – what he calls the 'power-evasiveness of normality'. Racially charged ideas of what constituted civilized ways of life were wrapped into new discourses of familial and romantic love that became dominant after World War II, especially in the celebration of heterosexual marriage.[34]

This is one explanation of why radical critics of the sexual order have been so hostile to marriage, especially most recently in the debates about the legalization of same-sex marriage. Historians have shown the centrality of marriage law in the USA in enforcing race segregation by first of all not allowing marriage amongst slaves, and then by outlawing interracial unions and miscegenation, so that marriage continued to be seen as a white institution into the twenty-first century.[35] Similarly, reproductive choice was structured by race, and class, with discouragement, including enforced sterilization, for non-white women, especially outside marriage.[36] The prominent discourse of eugenics was heavily racialized in the early twentieth century, and this served to undercut the feminist and socialist direction of the early birth control movement in the USA through its efforts to regulate the reproductive capacities of poor and black women. There is strong evidence, nonetheless, of black support for birth control as a way of advancing racial progress and economic independence. Racialized discourses were all-pervasive, but also produced resistance and resilience, and as Rennie Simson put it, 'it was on this basic foundation of self-reliance that the sexual sex of the black female was constructed'.[37]

Race, gender and class intermingled powerfully in the discourses of imperialism that became hegemonic in Europe in the late nineteenth century. Ann Stoler's work has shown the centrality of normative gender and sexuality to the maintenance of a racially stratified colonial order (in the Dutch Indies in her case) through domesticated detail as much as colonial regulation.[38] Sexual intermingling of colonizers and colonized, and various patterns of interracial prostitution, dramatized racial fears, in Europe as well as America. Although initially reluctant to intervene in direct regulation of colonial sexual life, British colonial administrators became increasingly concerned about interracial sexual encounters which undermined the status of the colonizers. Regulation of prostitution became a critical prop of imperial rule. Prostitution, or casual sexual encounters by colonial subjects, which to the Victorian mind were much the same thing, offered proof positive of their lack of civilization and their immorality, though they were seen as necessary for the white male colonizers themselves. The Contagious Diseases Acts which had so crystallized feminist and social purity opinion in the 1880s were to prove the model for colonial legislation.[39]

In the same way, anti-homosexual legislation in England proved a helpful template for the colonies (see chapter 6). The age of empire is also the period that saw the birth of homosexuality as a distinctive category, and historians have observed the strong fascination of empire (or at least the bodies of male colonial subjects) for homosexual writers, from Edward Carpenter and Oscar Wilde to André Gide, as well as for sexologists. Havelock Ellis, for example, like many of his colleagues, showed a fascination with race and eugenics in exploring sexual types.[40]

The racialized body is simultaneously heavily classed, and this has provided the focus for important work on sexuality in nineteenth- and twentieth-century Britain in particular. Leonore Davidoff's influential article 'Class and Gender in Victorian England' remains a powerful exploration of the eroticization of the class divide. Her exquisite analysis of the relationship between the writer and minor poet A. J. Munby and his servant, companion and eventual wife, Hannah Cullwick, not only vividly portrays the sexualization of class differences but shows how these are embodied and racialized. Munby's diary obsessively records the hands of working-class girls, their colour, shape and texture. Hannah's hands, in their roughness and griminess also came to represent a racialized difference. In the rituals of domination and submission that Munby and Hannah enacted she regularly addressed him as 'massa', in the assumed language of the American slave.[41]

On Manliness, Masculinity and Men

Gender theory, particularly under the influence of poststructuralism, stressed the relational nature of masculinity and femininity – each existed and only acquired meaning because of the other. But there was an initial resistance to engaging with men in history, both from feminists who felt that it would be at the expense of women's history, and from amongst the panjandrums of the historical profession, who couldn't quite see its relevance. John Tosh, a British historian of masculinity, recalled that in the early 1990s, when his own first studies began to appear, 'it was far from clear what the history of masculinity comprised, and to the majority of historians the very idea was eccentric and provocative'. Men, Michael Kimmel echoed, were believed to 'have no history'.[42]

For a gender theorist like the sociologist Raewyn Connell, masculinity, to the extent it could be readily defined at all, is at the same time a place in gender relations (that is defined by its relation to femininity), the practices through which concrete men and women place themselves in relation to the

gender order, and the effects of these practices in bodily
experiences, personality and culture, and particularly in the
subjectivity of men, in shifting historical configurations. This
gives rise at any particular time to a host of masculinities
co-existing and interacting, hegemonic, subordinate, marginalized and oppositional, all of which are shaped in specific
historical circumstances.[43]

One of the effects of this theoretical approach was to
encourage historians to move away from the use of a broad,
overarching concept like patriarchy in favour of the idea of
hegemonic forms of masculinity, stressing the importance of
norms, rules, beliefs and principles through which male
power and privilege were constructed and exercised in specific moments of history. Connell herself has suggested that
the first key moment in modern European history was propelled by the Spanish conquistadors in South America in the
sixteenth century, who defined themselves in terms of prowess
and sexuality against the Other provided by the conquered
peoples of the New World, and the history of masculinity
was to be shaped and reshaped continuously by the imperial
and colonial encounters. There was an inextricable link
between ideologies of respectability, sexual repression, nation
and empire in shaping dominant ideals of manliness in
nineteenth-century Europe, based on bonds between men
and a sublimation of homosexual attraction.[44] The imperial
moment at the end of the nineteenth century shaped new
anxieties. Tosh saw the new enthusiasm for empire amongst
middle-class and lower middle-class men in the 1890s as a
response to growing status anxieties and insecurities fostered
by agitation for women's rights and new sexual uncertain-
ties.[45] Imperial enthusiasm was in part a 'male flight' from
domesticity, a notion that has been highly influential though
controversial.

Tosh argued that in the middle years of the Victorian
period there was an unprecedented commitment by middle-
class men to domesticity, though it was beset by contradictions, especially around sexuality. Male homosociality was
often in conflict with commitment to home and family. The
rigid division of labour and separate spheres cut across the
ideals, and the domestic ideology was belied by the existence
of widespread prostitution and the prevalence of the double

standard of morality. By the late nineteenth century the strains were apparent, giving rise to an acute sense of crisis.[46]

Many historians have pinpointed a 'crisis of masculinity' at various points over the past two hundred years or so – the late eighteenth century, the middle Victorian years, the late nineteenth century, the 1920s, and so on up to the present. Perhaps the point is not so much that they are wrong, as that in the ongoing shaping of masculinities and femininities there is a perpetual sense of crisis, or at least instability. The costs of a gender order which so privileged masculinity but made inordinate demands upon it were felt most acutely by women. But there were costs too for men, both for those who strove more or less successfully to embody hegemonic values and ideals, and for those who couldn't. Lesley Hall's study of *Hidden Anxieties: Male Sexuality, 1900–1950*, based on thousands of letters sent to the birth control pioneer Marie Stopes from men in all parts of society seeking advice about sexual matters, shows vividly the price men had to pay for male domination. A study of couples in Britain in the inter-war years, based on oral history interviews, similarly demonstrates that the emerging ideals of companionate marriage and mutuality dwelt uneasily with male assumptions and sometimes crippling fears.[47]

Such studies have fundamentally undermined 'mythopoetic' and transhistorical ideas of masculinity that offer to explain the dynamics of sexual history, and point instead to the contingencies that shape the everyday realities of gendered sexuality. Ultimately, the purpose of such work is not to produce men's history as an end in itself but to enrich our understanding of history as a whole.[48]

5
Mainstreaming Sexual History

Into the Mainstream

From the 1970s critical sexual history has had a dual aim: first, to speak of crucial aspects of personal and social life that had hitherto been silenced or obscured – identities, subjectivities, bodies, emotions, risks, pleasures and dangers; second, to question and problematize the taken-for-granted, 'the natural', and to understand sexuality as a pre-eminently social phenomenon, at the heart of power relations and historical experience. These approaches transformed feminist and lesbian and gay history, though they have had mixed success in reshaping mainstream history. The traditional citadels of historical scholarship opened the door to feminist scholarship in general terms, but proved more resistant to the implications of critical or queer history. At best we see the emergence of an additive history (social history, plus gender, plus sexuality) rather than a transformative history, in which a critical awareness of sexuality changes the lenses through which the past and the present are viewed. David Halperin, perhaps wearily, suggested that a critical sexual history was more likely to enter the mainstream through the queering of literary and cultural studies than directly through more traditional social history, and this is echoed in Laura Doan's plea for a queer critical history as a way of changing the mainstream.[1]

Mainstreaming involves recognizing the centrality of sexuality to the operation of power in a wide range of historical processes in the modern world. This been a major theme within sexual history since the 1970s. My own initial attempt in 1981 at a survey of British sexual history from 1800, *Sex, Politics and Society*, was as much a history of changing patterns of family life, gender, domesticity, intimacy and shifting forms of regulation and patterns of agency as one of erotic activity, within the wider context of industrialization, urbanization, imperialism, scientific endeavour, politics, the rise of the welfare state, social movements, and changing religious, moral, legal and medical practices.[2] In their pioneering overview of sexual history in the USA, *Intimate Matters*, D'Emilio and Freedman took a similar stance, stressing that for them the history is a tangle of power relations that constantly reconstructs sexual norms. They offered a narrative that was inclusive about gender, class, race, ethnicity, region and orientation, even though, as they admitted, they were inhibited at this early stage by the limitations of sources, especially in relation to African-American experiences.[3]

Both these studies critique a linear model of historical progress from repression towards sexual liberation, but each from a perspective of the present suggests a trajectory that foregrounds the growth of individual and collective agency, though always in the context of new potentialities of power, regulation and resistance. Lesley Hall, in her study of gender and sexual change in Britain since 1880, quite rightly emphasizes the often painfully slow rate of change, and the deep continuities – the *longue durée* – that shape sexual life.[4] But it is important also to mark the points of transition, and ruptures, that propel change, and offer the glimpse of new possibilities. Despite the continuities, the sexual regimes of Western societies have changed fundamentally over the past two hundred years, though in a fitful rather than predetermined fashion. D'Emilio and Freedman argue that in the USA the sexual system has moved from a family-centred reproductive one in the colonial period, to a romantic, intimate yet conflicted sexuality in nineteenth-century marriage, to a commercialized sexuality in the modern period, when sexual relations provide a personal identity and individual happiness – as well as reproduction. But the transitions have not been straightforward. These overall patterns were constrained and limited by different chronologies in different social groups and different regions, and shaped by deeply entrenched social hierarchies, especially of gender, class and race, which sexuality helped both to sustain, and sometimes to undermine.

The point is that sexuality is not marginal to wider historical developments, it is integral to them. Sexuality is a prism through which we can understand more fully the scale, intensity and effectivity of social change. In the examples that follow I examine key moments in the development of sexual modernity in the West, and seek to show that as sexuality goes, so goes society, and as society goes, so goes sexuality.

The Birth of Modern Sexuality?

I begin with the debate about the origins of modern sexuality. Foucault's conceptual framework in the introductory volume of *The History of Sexuality* (modified in subsequent volumes) is based on a division between the classical or *ancien régime* of erotic practices and the modern regime of sexuality. He rather vaguely links this to the rise of capitalism, though it plays no operative role in his history. His main interest is in what makes certain things possible and others not in the emergence of sexual discourses and the intricate apparatus of sexuality. For him it is the development of the very idea of sexuality itself that is the key discursive revolution from the eighteenth century, with the nineteenth-century development of new sexual categories as the crystallizing moment. His influence can be seen in a host of book titles that speak of 'before' sexuality, the 'making', the 'invention' or the 'origins' of sexuality, and even 'after' sex.

The danger of such an approach is that it apparently downplays or denies the vast range of sexual experiences and histories that existed 'before sexuality', in the face of a vast literature now which documents it. I have chosen in this short book for practical reasons of space and coherence to concentrate on the debate on sexual modernity, but I have referred to some of the debate in relation to same-sex practices in history, and in chapter 6 I explore in more detail non-Western patterns and the different meanings of modernity. I am acutely conscious of the point made by Phillips and Reay in their book *Sex before Sexuality* that 'Premodern people lived without our familiar sexual categories and should not be forced to occupy them retrospectively.'[5]

Broadly, I would argue that the modern West has been preoccupied with *whom* people had sex with (male or female, same-sex or other-sex, same-age or younger or older) while other periods have been preoccupied with questions of excess or overindulgence, activity or passivity, sin or salvation.[6] The challenge is to demonstrate that a periodization such as Foucault's has meaning for such crucial shifts, and this has proved controversial for historians, some emphasizing earlier shifts – as for example in the Protestant Reformation, which opened the way to rethinking the significant of sex in marriage and the sexuality of women – or suggesting indeed that no significant change happened at all.[7] But the eighteenth century has proved especially enticing for historians.

A recent intervention in this debate by a British scholar, Faramerz Dabhoiwala, in his *The Origins of Sexuality*, boldly focuses on the great changes that swept through Western society (including the European diaspora in North America) in the late seventeenth and eighteenth centuries, which he calls 'the first sexual revolution'.[8] Central to these, he argues, is the dawn of the Enlightenment, the 'age of reason', and with it the breakdown of religious authority, combined with a host of associated changes, including the emergence of female voices in public life and a transformation in the modes of communication in society. The core motivation was a 'momentous ideological upheaval' which gave rise to new forms of sexual liberty. The earlier sexual regime had been based on the assumption that immoral actions and beliefs were dangerous because they corrupted individuals and undermined society, and needed to be rigorously controlled by the church and society. The Enlightenment brought a new spirit of sexual toleration, which grew out of the exhaustion of religious conflict, so that by 1750, Dabhoiwala argues, most forms of consensual sex had drifted beyond the reach of the law, and by the end of the century every previous assumption about sexuality had been seriously challenged. He concedes that this sweeping transformation was limited by class and gender and, he could have stressed, by new forms of discipline around sexual nonconformity, especially homosexuality, in the nineteenth century, but he leaves no doubt that for him this first sexual revolution was a necessary precursor to the sexual revolutions of the twentieth century, and a decisive moment in the emergence of modern society.

This affirmation of a revised and essentially mono-causal teleology of sexual change has proved controversial. It foregrounds changes in ideas rather than any material grounding. It offers a refurbishment of the thesis that sexual freedom is a result of secularization, which gradually confined religion to the private sphere, but that ignores the continuing role of religion in shaping sexual moralities well into the contemporary period. The disentanglement of legal and moral codes from religious sanctions has been tortuous and prolonged in the West, and is not complete even today. Religious modes of thought, moreover, shaped early feminist thinking and the ideologies of many radicals throughout the nineteenth and twentieth centuries who were in the vanguard of sexual reform. And the exceptions that Dabhoiwala acknowledged to his overall thesis, relating to class and women, are hardly marginal but central to any idea of a social and/or sexual revolution.

Echoing Foucault, historians are generally agreed now that far from there being a regime of silence or discretion governing sexuality, contemporaries talk about sex and sexuality endlessly. Sexuality is central to Malthus's jeremiad on excessive population at the end of the eighteenth century, and suffuses the preoccupations of commentators on everything from the French Revolution to the conditions of women in factories and mines, from the housing conditions of the poor to the meanings of childhood and childhood sexuality. Sexuality became a source of continuing uncertainty and anxiety, giving rise to recurrent panics, a battleground for different perceptions of what society was and should be.[9]

It is difficult, however, to interpret this ever-growing cultural preoccupation with sexuality as evidence of a regime of greater freedom. It suggests on the contrary a growing concern with the control of sexuality through the regulation of bodies and behaviours. A key element of this, a number of historians have argued, was a fundamental transformation in ideas of gender and of heterosexuality and homosexuality, and of associated practices. A complex, interconnected set of social, economic, political as well as cultural developments between the late seventeenth and early nineteenth centuries, Thomas Laqueur suggests, lowered the barriers to marital – and extramarital – fertility, as revealed by demographic history. In the course of industrialization there was 'a demonstrable increase in access to heterosexual intercourse, a sort of sexual democratization which made it easier to couple'.[10]

Although he does not offer any causative link, these arguments complement Laqueur's famous thesis that a new model of gender emerged in the eighteenth century based on the existence of two complementary sexes, with their own distinctive bodies, necessarily linked, but potentially antagonistic. The anxiety over masturbation, increasing from the middle of the eighteenth century, reflected in part, Laqueur argues, growing fears of the weakening of sociability amongst men. Anxieties over sex with the self were an indicator of new fears about the uncontrollability of male sexuality in a society where the weakening of communal controls often freed men from the responsibility for pregnancy and parenthood.[11] An even bolder assertion of the significance of the eighteenth century, particularly in establishing the tramlines for new concepts of heterosexuality and homosexuality, comes from Randolph Trumbach. He argues that the sexual system dominant from around 1500 in North-West Europe was decisively supplanted by 1750 by a quite different one dominated by new notions of masculinity and femininity, and by the emergence of a distinctive role for same-sex activity with the elaboration of the notions of a third (male same-sex) and fourth (lesbian) gender.[12]

In both versions, a hierarchical (and complementary) model of gender and sexual relations was being displaced by a difference (and potentially antagonistic) model that was to dominate the next two centuries. Neither Trumbach nor Laqueur attempts a full exploration of the wider social processes that had shaped these shifts, and many have critiqued their models as essentially ideal types that mask the complexity and contradictory impact of what was actually happening in different cultures at different timescales.[13] But a challenging narrative of change does nevertheless emerge. Increasingly, sexual norms that had made little distinction between male sex with men or women, as long as the sex with men was with those who were inferior by reason of class or age, became more firmly heterosexualized. There may have been greater sexual freedom for men (Laqueur's 'sexual democratization') in the last decades of the eighteenth century, but it was frequently at the cost of increased violence against women, and the heightened regulation and control of the female body that were to be identified later as a key element of the Victorian sexual regime.[14]

Historians have rightly critiqued the myth of Victorian sexual repression, but it would be difficult to see the nineteenth century anywhere in Europe or America as the unproblematic home of sexual toleration or Enlightenment. Sexologists and sex reformers, after all, had self-consciously positioned themselves against Victorian morality, even if they exaggerated its dominance and universality, and sought their own scientific Enlightenment. Anna Clark reminds us that Western civilization has been imagined 'as the triumph of rational values over barbarism and ignorance' but contemporary historians have tended to find the picture much more unsettling, and less hopeful.[15]

The Normalization of Heterosexuality

Historians until quite recently have largely ignored the history of heterosexuality. It has been the unmarked term, the unspoken norm. Given the dominance of reproduction in thinking about sexuality throughout the Western tradition this is not surprising, but as sexuality in general has been historicized so has heterosexuality. It needs, as Tin suggested, to be taken out of the order of nature and placed within the order of time.[16]

Language as ever is critical to our understanding. The inventor of the term 'homosexuality', Kertbeny also created the term 'heterosexuality', but it was not at first clearly part of a binary divide. Originally referring to 'psychical hermaphrodism', or what later came to be known as bisexuality, it had an erratic history. Jonathan Ned Katz notes its first use in the *New York Times* as late as the early 1920s, and it came into popular use only in the 1930s.[17] It was the 1940s and

1950s before exclusive and sexually fulfilling heterosexual relationships were to be serenaded universally as the basis for a stable society. Heterosexuality's rise and rise marked a critical shift from the procreative imperative to pleasure in the sexual culture of the twentieth century, but it also evolved into the key disciplining discourse of its notional opposite, homosexuality.[18]

There is of course a complex relationship between the emerging concept and its referent. Family historians write confidently about heterosexuality from early medieval times. The Protestant Reformation has been seen as a key time for its development, especially with the emergence of a strong belief in the importance of sex within marriage.[19] We have seen writers on the first sexual revolution suggesting that its origins were in the eighteenth century; while the 'biological imperative' only became central to sexological discussions a century later. The growth of distinctive subcultures of prostitution, pornography and homosexuality in the nineteenth century indicates a sharpening separation of the normative and the improper, but it was only in the latter half of the nineteenth century that recognizably modern models of marriage based on love and public declaration became hegemonic in Britain and (white) America, and new ideals of marital relationships began to soften the ideology of separate spheres.[20] Alongside these developments historians have documented in ever more refined details the burgeoning diversity of the (hetero)sexualized city: cultures of prostitution, pornography, pub culture, music hall, gossip, 'slumming', classified advertisements, and so on as part of the sexualization of everyday life.[21]

The safest conclusion we can draw from these developments is not that heterosexuality as a set of reproductive and pleasurable practices did not exist before a defined (and variable) time in the past, but that its elaboration as a normative system and power-laden discourse has a distinctive but erratic history. It was only in the twentieth century that its history crystallized. It has been shaped and defined both by shifting attitudes to its Other, homosexuality, and by a range of social discourses and practices whose histories are clearly traceable. These include the formalization of marriage from the mid-eighteenth century onwards, evolving ideals of mutual pleasure between men and women, the availability of birth control, new patterns of consumerism and, above all, the changing position of women. The increasing sexual openness of the 1920s saw a partial renegotiation of male–female relations that stressed mutual pleasure in marriage as a key to marital stability. This had precursors in earlier periods, but became more explicit and generalized in the burst of 'informalization' following the end of World War I.[22] For Laura Doan a key moment was the publication in 1920 of Marie Stopes's paean to *Married Love*, which crystallized an ideal of heterosexual marital bliss, for which effective birth control became an essential element.[23] Other historians have pointed to the radical experimentation in bohemian circles in the 1920s in Greenwich Village, New York, and elsewhere, or the gender and sexual openness of Weimar Germany. Ideas that at the end of the nineteenth century had been confined to feminist or socialist circles, on companionship and mutuality in relationships, birth control, female sexual pleasure, even 'free love', began to enter wider circles, giving rise to a new popular literature on love, sex and intimacy.[24]

We must not exaggerate the transformative impact of these changes. Patterns were uneven and variable across countries. Historians tend to agree there was a muted modernity in Britain during the interwar years, which Szreter has attributed in part to the persistent influence of the social purity strand of feminism, and a strong emphasis on abstinence in its sexual cultures. His book with Fisher, based on oral history testimonies, is in part a hymn to the quiet decencies of a sexually restrained life.[25] Sexual knowledge continued to carry a taint into the 1920s and beyond, and sexual misery affected the life of women above all. The focus on female transgressions was a prism through which to identify concerns about modern femininity – 'modern women', 'the flapper', and more generally social mobility and modernity itself.[26]

On the wider European scene, Dagmar Herzog sees the dominant theme of the interwar years as the 'unprecedented efforts on the part of national and local governments to intervene in their citizens' private lives'.[27] This was true of democratic as much as authoritarian countries, as sexuality increasingly became a matter of central political importance. But it is in the fascist countries and the Soviet Union that sexuality became most explicitly a focus for the new technologies of power. Herzog rebuts the conventional view that the Nazi regime could be defined simply as the imposition of the values of *kinder, küche, kirche*, and shows how fascism embraced heterosexual sexual pleasure in its distorted version of sexual modernity to bind people ever more closely to their destiny. Following Foucault, she agrees that pleasure can never in and of itself put itself in opposition to power; it can be a tool in its very operation. The opposite side of this, however, was manifest in the camps, where, as Herzog puts it, 'Killing was not enough; the death of the soul was aimed at – and in the assault on their sexuality, the victims were targeted in their innermost selfhood.'[28] The shifts in policy in the Soviet Union in the 1930s, as the liberal reforms on homosexuality and abortion of the early revolution were abandoned, spoke to the same violent rejection of the humanistic tradition. This was the dark heart of European sexualities, which refutes any easy progressivism.

New attempts at regulation were not confined to Europe, however. Even in the USA, a 'Straight State' was being entwined in a growing Federal bureaucracy from the 1930s, during its most famous progressive period, the 'New Deal'. The reforming, welfare-minded post-war governments in Western Europe and the USA after World War II were deeply socially and sexually conservative. In the USA, from the mid-1940s, especially, to the late 1960s the state was crafting tools to target homosexuality, in relation to immigration, the military and welfare, in the context of an engulfing Cold War. This was part of a wider 'American obsession' through which the heterosexual–homosexual binary was being inscribed into science, medicine and everyday life, simultaneously targeting homosexuality and elevating heterosexual relations.[29]

The Great Transition

The 1950s were a crucial period in the regulation of Western sexuality. On the one hand they carried the legacy of the 1930s and the disruptive impact of war, tightening in many ways a social illiberalism that went hand in hand with the promotion of heterosexuality. On the other, the seeds of dramatic change were in retrospect clearly visible.[30] From the 1950s, most historians agree, there has been a historic shift in sexual beliefs and intimate behaviour, with its epicentre in the old West, but with powerful resonances on a global scale. This is what I have called elsewhere the 'Great Transition'.[31] Historians, however, tend to disagree on causes, meanings, temporalities, implications and effects. Gert Hekma, Alain Giami and their collaborators in their book *Sexual Revolutions* suggest there were no regular patterns across regions and countries, and no common agenda for its main actors, chiefly members of the post-war baby-boom generation in the West, and the postcolonial baby-boom generations in the global South. The process has been messy, contradictory and haphazard, with different rhythms across different countries and cultures. But whatever it was, it undoubtedly drew in and involved millions of people, reimagining and remaking their lives in a multitude of different ways. Whether this involved a new 'sexual freedom' or 'sexual liberation' is another matter.[32]

Conservative thinkers have generally critiqued the 'cultural revolution' of the 1960s for fundamentally sapping the traditional values which had underpinned Western civilization, leading, in the words of the conservative American historian Gertrude Himmelfarb, to the 'de-moralization' of society. For the influential American sociologist Daniel Bell, this was the decade when the Puritan ethic was fatally undermined by an ideological transformation which put hedonism, ultra-individualism and consumerism to the fore. The turmoils of the 1960s were, for the conservative American political scientist Francis Fukuyama, at the heart of the 'great disruption' which broke the foundations of trust and social capital that sustained Western democracies, and accounts for the moral confusions and cultural divides that characterize the succeeding decades.[33]

Although on the opposite side of the political spectrum altogether, leftist philosophers have been equally pessimistic, and have seen the endless proliferation of speech about sexuality in the 1960s as masking the illusory nature of the freedoms on offer. Herbert Marcuse, who briefly became a radical icon of the decade, foresaw the danger of technological rationality working through the erotic to bind the individual to the status quo. Pleasure generated submission. The partial or 'repressive desublimation' offered by advanced consumer societies is a guarantor of the survival of oppression and exploitation. Such views, reliant, like conservative views, on a notion of sexuality as a volcanic force that could be repressed, liberated, or channelled through sublimation into sustaining the status quo, have tended to disappear following the constructionist revolution, but elements have continued in radical critiques of mindless consumerism, or suggestions that liberalization is merely a shift in the modes of power, regulation and control. Dagmar Herzog has recently wondered whether the concept of repressive desublimation might not still have a role in understanding the contradictions of contemporary sexual freedoms.[34]

There was undoubtedly in the 1960s a real transformation in leading Western countries in material conditions, lifestyles, family relationships and personal freedoms for the majority of ordinary people.[35] Those shifts were, however, deeply ambiguous. One of the stimuli to second-wave feminism in the 1970s was precisely a feeling that the sexual revolution had been for men – including leftist men – rather than for women. It was very much also a heterosexual revolution more concerned with regulation and control of deviance than positive endorsement of different ways of life. The lesbian and gay movements of the 1970s emerged *against* the main directions of the 'sexual revolution' of the 1960s. What did become central, however, was a new sense of agency in sexual matters.

Gertrude Himmelfarb has made a revealing comparison between the alleged 'sexual anarchy' of the nineteenth century *fin de siècle* and the 'sexual revolution' of the late twentieth century. 'A century ago', she suggests, 'the "advanced souls" were just that, well in advance of the culture, whereas now they pervade the entire culture. This is the significance of our "sexual revolution": it is a revolution democratized and legitimized.'[36] Although Himmelfarb comes to condemn rather than praise this singular achievement, most historians would agree with her central argument. This was, Escoffier has recently reflected, a cultural revolution in which the social framework within which sex took place was radically transformed – the everyday sexual scripts, the great cultural narratives of sex, gender, age and race, and the scientific understanding of sexuality all dramatically changed. Gradually from the 1940s, but with a strong spurt forward in the 1960s, Cas Wouters has argued, social conduct became increasingly less authoritarian, more differentiated and varied for a wider public, with an increasing variety of behavioural and emotional patterns of behaviour becoming socially acceptable.[37]

This was for Wouters largely a shift in the psychology of the emotions. Giddens emphasizes other elements, particularly 'detraditionalization', the undermining of traditional value systems and structures such as religion and the family, and 'individualization', the social process that emphasized the centrality of individual autonomy and choice. Together, he argues, they have underpinned new patterns of intimacy, and a rebalancing in social relations in a new phase of social development, 'late modernity'.[38]

As these approaches suggest, it is more useful to see the 1960s as in many ways but a staging post in a continuing process, part of a long and still unfinished revolution. The pace of change varied across the global North and global South, different national traditions, regions, classes and ethnic populations. There were new efforts at social regulation as well as greater freedoms. Many of the breakthroughs towards greater liberalism in the 1960s and 1970s faced reaction in the following decades, especially in response to the AIDS epidemic from the early 1980s. There were victims as well as gainers of the changes. But under the surface of events, at a deep level of popular agency, profound changes were indeed taking place, especially in the affluent parts of the globe: a shift of power between the generations, as young people began to define the cultural zeitgeist; a shift in power between men and women, as women made new claims for rights and equality; a rebalancing of the relationship between sexual normality and abnormality, as LGBTQ people claimed recognition and rights; an undermining of the fixity of gender, giving trans people more voice and legal recognition; the separation of sex and reproduction, as more effective birth control made parenting increasingly a choice; the separation of sex and marriage, which was no longer seen as the only acceptable gateway to sexual expression; the separation of marriage and parenting, as women on a massive scale gave birth outside marriage, and the number of single parents grew hugely; the separation of heterosexuality and parenting, as same-sex parenting, always present, became a key aspect of lesbian and gay domesticity; and the separation of hetero-sexuality and marriage, as same-sex marriage and civil part-nerships were recognized in various parts of the world. Haphazardly, unevenly, with different rhythms in different parts of the West, a new sexual world was emerging.

AIDS and the Burdens of History

What made the AIDS epidemic so traumatic and historically significant was that it emerged in the 1980s in the midst of these wider changes. It was a massive human tragedy, of historic proportions, with millions of deaths on a global scale. But 'AIDS' rapidly became also, as the cultural theorist Paula Treichler graphically described it, an 'epidemic of sig-nification', a nexus of meaning, representation, moral con-testation and historical controversy. AIDS was framed and burdened from the start by many different and often difficult histories, of past epidemics, would-be scientific theories, medical interventions, social policies, prejudice, discrimina-tion, racism and homophobia.[39]

AIDS appeared when sexual mores were in unprecedented flux, old social disciplines were declining, and literally millions of young people were in movement and willing and eager to experiment with their sexual behaviour. Above all, what coloured the response to the epidemic from the start was that it first manifested itself amongst gay men, an increasingly assertive, but politically unpopular commu-nity that was already experiencing an element of backlash against the gains of the 1970s. The moral panic around AIDS that broke in the media in the early 1980s focused on homo-sexuality, and had a profound impact on the delayed and hesitant responses to the epidemic by governments in the USA, Britain and elsewhere until the epidemic was almost out of control.[40]

Ironically, the historical work on identity that lesbian and gay historians had produced was to prove central to the understanding of the crisis, especially in relation to identity. An essentialist view of homosexual identity implied a focus on individual aetiology, carrying the danger of reifying and bio-medicalizing sexual identities, of fixing them as if they were true and permanent.[41] The argument that sexual identities are not given but contingent, fluid rather than fixed, was to prove an important insight into the nature of the epidemic that eventually fuelled more sensitive medical and social interventions. HIV illnesses might tell the truth about a person's sexual activities, but could not tell any truth about identity. This insight was to become central to culturally specific explorations of the epidemiology and cultural conditions of the epidemic in non-Western societies, where Western categories, though increasingly circulated, had little cultural purchase or historical meaning.

The historical work on the medicalization of sexuality also proved critical to the understanding of the crisis.[42] The definition of HIV as sexually transmitted immediately called up powerful resonances of sexual diseases from the past, especially syphilis, with its identification with the prostitute as someone saturated with sex and danger, and in the USA particularly with racialized difference as well. The homosexual was now the pollutant. As Allan M. Brandt observed, sexually transmitted infections have been deployed as a symbol of a society marked by sexual corruption and contamination, a sign of deep-seated sexual and social disorder. For Frank Mort, 'AIDS is the contemporary moment in a much longer history, the extraordinarily complex interweaving of medicine and morality with the surveillance and regulation – even the very definition – of sex.'[43] The social meanings of AIDS were heavily overdetermined by a powerful medico-moral politics and history, which had become particularly toxic in the 1980s.

But there was another history here, of community self-affirmation and collective agency that had its roots in the social movements of the 1970s. One of the unique features of the whole early story of HIV/AIDS was the degree to which those most affected by it were involved in both defining the problem and intervening against it. Until the late

1980s the only coherent non-medical response came from largely gay community-based organizations.[44] The alliance between the gay community, people with HIV and AIDS, and public health officials that developed widely proved to be a harbinger of a profound shift in the relationship between medicine and society.[45] The work of AIDS activists had been preceded by feminist health movements, and was succeeded by a host of other campaigns, but the essence of all of them was the mobilization of people who themselves were at risk to take some control of their treatment and care. The community-based response to AIDS, as Altman documented, was a critical factor in defining the epidemic, and what had started in America and elsewhere as a desperate response to public neglect became a crucial aspect of the global response. New knowledges could come from below as well as from the traditional biomedical elite – precisely the argument in the 1970s rejection of sexological definitions, and sexology-inflected history. The AIDS crisis, Epstein argued, 'is a case in which the normal flow of trust and credibility between experts and laypersons has been disrupted. The autonomy of science has therefore been challenged; outsiders have rushed into the breach.'[46] In this new turn of the battle for credibility, who could speak, who could be listened to, AIDS activists had made themselves experts about prevention strategies, antibody testing, anti-discrimination legislation, health care delivery systems, treatment – and the meanings of sexuality itself.

From the mid-1990s there was a normalization or routinization of HIV/AIDS in most Western countries following the introduction of new antiviral drug therapies. This was not the end of the epidemic. Its incidence continued to increase even in the affluent West, and elsewhere in the world it became pandemic. But where resources were available (a major qualification), it was well on its way to becoming what early campaigners had seen as the best to be hoped for, a chronic manageable disease. Yet its vicissitudes continue to haunt the global historical imagination. It was obvious at the time, but becomes even more so in historical context, that the HIV/AIDS crisis was a flashpoint that illuminated the sexual landscape in an unprecedented way.

Same-Sex Marriage and New Patterns of Intimacy

An unexpected consequence of the AIDS crisis was the emergence of same-sex marriage as a key issue. While some lesbian and gay activists in the USA had attempted to claim marriage rights in the 1970s, as George Chauncey has shown, same-sex marriage had little prominence in the early years of gay liberation.[47] On the contrary, many lesbians and gay men alike shared the widespread feminist hostility to marriage, and were inclined to see it as an institution hostile to lesbian and gay people. Attitudes to same-sex marriage were, however, to change dramatically between the late 1980s and the 2010s. Over little more than a decade a broad policy consensus emerged that pushed towards recognition of same-sex registered partnerships and eventually equal marriage rights.

This shift was heavily overdetermined by different national traditions and histories. In the USA, campaigners began by focusing on judicial action and popular mobilization for full and equal same-sex marriage, while Denmark, followed by the rest of Scandinavia, started with limited recognition, using tried and trusted lobbying and parliamentary processes.[48] In France, the legislation that established PACS (*pacte civil de solidarité*) in 1999 followed classic republican traditions and protocols by not recognizing the separate cultural identities of lesbians and gays, and allowed civil unions for heterosexual and homosexual couples alike. In the Netherlands, radical changes fitted in readily with the tradition of 'pillarization' that assumed the co-existence of different rights claims in a complex plural society. In the United Kingdom, the Civil Partnership Act gave same-sex couples who contracted partnerships virtually the same rights as heterosexuals who married, but called it something else to dodge over-hostile reaction – a classic example of 'liberalism by stealth'. In the USA, on the other hand, same-sex marriage became a key battlefront in the 'culture wars' that had been raging since the 1970s.[49]

The AIDS epidemic had dramatized the absence of any formal recognition of the strong bonds of friendship and commitment that had sustained gay men through the epidemic. Lesbian parents were similarly confronted in the 1970s and 1980s by intense institutional and media hostility because of the perceived threat they posed to the traditional familial order, hostility which the AIDS epidemic had accentuated. The rise of a growing movement for reproductive rights by lesbian and gay male parenting groups, accompanied by the so-called lesbian and gay 'baby boom' from the late 1980s, constituted, in the words of its historian Daniel Rivers, a 'critical but unrecognized' part of the sexual revolution.[50] Both AIDS and parenting, as Chauncey documented, dramatized the key role played by marriage in the USA in not only organizing institutional recognition of heterosexual coupledom but also opening the way to social entitlements and health care. Marriage was not simply a desired citizenship right; it was a key to essential social safeguards, and in many cases to survival.

Such arguments were bolstered by a historiography that sought to show the long historical existence of alternative patterns of intimacy. Early lesbian histories had emphasized the marriage-like nature of many romantic friendships between women in the nineteenth century, and lesbian history had uncovered many examples of actual (though illegitimate) marriages between women where one of the partners was able to pass as a man. Mock marriages between men had also been uncovered in the Mollies Clubs in early eighteenth-century London, and had been mentioned by Mary McIntosh in 'The Homosexual Role'. Most famously, John Boswell in *Same-Sex Unions* lists a range of cultures where same-sex unions were accepted, from ancient China to some Native American tribes, the Middle East to South America – pretty much in every continent as well as in early Christian Europe.[51]

Boswell's work was in large part a continuation of his debate with the Catholic tradition about the ways in which the church had suppressed its own history of toleration of homosexuality and of same-sex marriage-like arrangements. Unsurprisingly, the book aroused intense controversy – over definitions, the meaning of sources, and the historical and contemporary implications. Alan Bray, with a similar Catholic and gay background to Bowell's, adopts a rather more austere but perhaps more radical thesis in his final book *The*

Friend, published posthumously in 2003. The religious rites and oaths of same-sex friendship that he traces were not, he argued, simply parallels to heterosexual marriage, which in any case was not formalized till the eighteenth and nineteenth centuries, but were one aspect of the rich complexity of social arrangements in and around the extended family and social networks. He is extremely cautious, even equivocal, about the sexual nature of such unions, but in one example he cites there can be no doubt. He sees in the commitment arrangements of Anne Lister a suppressed echo of these medieval arrangements, where the sexual elements are, on the evidence of her four-million-word diary and thousand surviving letters, unequivocal. In these, Bray argues, 'there stands out in unmistakeable detail the degree to which a settled friendship could still be comprehended by family and friends in the 1830s as creating bonds that overlapped with and shaded into those created by a marriage'.[52] By the end of the nineteenth century, however, they had all but disappeared from historic memory as heterosexual marriage became the norm.

Bray's work is one of the most far-reaching efforts to shift the grounds on which the history of homosexuality (and heterosexuality) has been written, dethroning erotic practices as an organizing principle while offering affective intimacy in its place.[53] The most apparently orthodox family arrangements in the past have, as Deborah Cohen vividly shows, co-existed with various subtle ways of accommodating embarrassing social deviance, including homosexual relatives, single motherhood, adultery and bigamy. And the deliberately unorthodox sought their own pathways, making things up as they went along. Matt Cook's evocation of various queer domesticities in twentieth-century London suggests there was no binding or singular model of intimate life, despite the common experience of homosexual subjects of a hostile legal climate and deep-seated prejudice. So much depended on social situation, class experiences, personal opportunities and cultural, and ultimately political or social movement, commitment. And the lines between 'normal' and 'queer' lives were often 'rather blurred'.[54]

Histories such as these weave a tapestry of intimate lives in their density, intricate patterns and connectedness. They attempt to 'trouble' existing histories of home and family which neglect queer or generally unorthodox lives. They also offer insights into the interiority of private lives, and the 'deeply affective unconscious interpersonal dynamics of intimacies', which point to the hazards and perils of intimacy as well as the hopes and harmonies.[55]

As the rise of interest in same-sex marriage shows, the very multiplicity of intimacies increasingly challenges societies to say how they should be socially and culturally recognized. The notion of sexual or intimate citizenship, particularly as defined by Plummer, has come to stand for the achievement of full inclusion in society both through the achievement of rights and through a transformation of the nature of inclusivity, not as a limited toleration of difference within a pre-existing order but as a full acceptance of difference as constitutive of a democratic, dialogic, egalitarian society.[56]

This has opened up new historical explorations of the development of the relationship between sexuality, gender, race and citizenship, and in the process generated heated new controversies. Some queer or radical critics of the sexual order in America have seen claims to marriage and intimate citizenship as examples of 'homonormativity', complicit with neoliberal restructuring of contemporary culture. Some have gone further and detected the emergence of a new discursive unity between homosexuality and conservative nationalism in the wake of the 'war against terrorism' – what has become known as 'homonationalism'. Jasbir Puar opines that gay marriage is not simply a demand for equality with heterosexual norms, but more importantly a demand for reinstatement of white privileges and rights, rights of property and inheritance in particular.[57]

Although this is clearly articulated in terms of American experience, similar critiques echo in queer debates in Europe over same-sex marriage. Gert Hekma has seen in the acceptance of liberal sexual reforms a gay world that has opted for a sexual order based on a drab notion of equality, of sameness rather than difference, at the expense of more radical and challenging sexual patterns.[58] A world of proliferating stories about sexuality and intimacy, ranging from multiple relations and polyamory to the ever-burgeoning ease of sexualized interactions online, is not one that is likely to see such controversies readily abate.

On the other hand, there is plentiful evidence that once same-sex marriage is legalized it rapidly becomes an everyday experience, not as a new norm for everyone, but as one choice amongst many. The study by Heaphy et al. of civil partnerships amongst young gay and lesbian people in Britain after their introduction in 2005 shows how they had very rapidly become completely taken for granted, an ordinary possibility for ordinary people.[59] Certainly there was no evidence here of a desire to disrupt the sexual order, or the meanings of marriage. On the other hand, there was equally no evidence of the acceptance of a traditional moral system of sanction and disapproval of different ways of life. It was simply that homosexuality was ceasing to be the defining difference between young people. If this is the case then it suggests at the very least a profound undermining of the heterosexual/homosexual binary that has been so decisive an influence in the past two centuries – and a challenge to a sexual history which relies on that binary for its defining terms.

6

The Globalization of Sexual History

Globalizing Sexual History

'Borders *do* exist and have meanings', Marc Epprecht, a historian of African sexualities, has remarked, even though those meanings are not stable or consistent.[1] For state builders and activists alike in postcolonial nations, history in general, and national sexual history in particular, have become vital battlegrounds for reassessing their past and defining the contours of the present.

Yet it is also obvious that a meaningful historical enterprise cannot easily be confined within the borders of a national imaginary, however deeply rooted and insular its cultural heritage may seem. Cross-national currents have shaped local sexual cultures in the past and are transparently doing so in the present on a global scale. From the sixteenth century onwards, in what can now be seen as the first wave of globalization, European soldiers, travellers, traders, colonial administrators, moralists and missionaries, followed later by archaeologists, anthropologists, pioneering sexologists and sex reformers, simultaneously revealed the diversity and multiplicity of sexual and gender worlds, and massively disrupted the delicate sexual ecologies of the lands they 'discovered'. The brutal colonial encounters between European countries and much of the rest of the world, from early modern times through the heyday of European empires from the late nineteenth century to World War I and beyond, in a second wave of globalization, were even more formative. They not only reorganized the lives of the colonized Other but also reshaped sexual meanings in the metropole itself. It was surely no coincidence that the new sexual science and the earliest efforts at constructing a sexual history emerged simultaneously at the height of empire. But it is the more recent waves of globalization that have precipitated a 'transnational turn' in sexual history, since the 1990s, reflecting a wider interest in what Dennis Altman graphically labelled as 'global sex'.[2]

The current wave of globalization refers broadly to the process of global integration of economic, social, cultural and communication activities which has gathered pace since the 1980s, and is transforming social relations at all levels on a world-wide scale. Superficially, it is a neutral term to describe such transformations in global interactions. But since the 1990s it has also been seen as a transnational political and cultural project, closely linked with Americanization and neoliberalism, which in turn has generated transnational anti-capitalist and anti-globalization movements. I am using it here, as neutrally as possible, to describe interlinked processes which together are transforming the context and meanings of human interactions at all levels: a *stretching* of social, political, cultural and economic relations across frontiers; an *intensification* and growing strength of global interconnectedness, interactions and flows; and a *speeding up* of global interactions, especially through the development of more rapid and accessible transportation, media and information technologies, circulation of goods, capital and peoples.[3]

Sexuality is inevitably subject to these forces of globalization, which are bringing into contestation and confrontation different beliefs, behaviours and assumptions. Global flows are reshaping the context and meanings of intimacy and the erotic, and opening up in new ways the historical imagination: flows of goods and services and sexual consumerism; flows of people seeking love, sex and friendship, fleeing poverty, war or persecution, being trafficked, seeking new opportunities; flows of sexually transmitted infections, especially of HIV/AIDS; flows of pornography and sexually explicit material; flows of sexually arousing or suppressing drugs; flows of reproductive technologies and women seeking reproductive freedoms; flows of children, escaping social breakdown, seeking refuge or being trafficked; flows of sex tourists seeking pleasure (and sometimes partners); flows of religion, of science, of new media and forms of communication; flows of digital sexualities, websites, blogs, social networks, sexual dating; flows of ideas, ideologies and belief systems; flows of identities, male, female, trans, gay, bisexual, queer; flows of campaigns, international organizations, and social movements; flows of conferences, workshops, seminars, academics and moral entrepreneurs; and flows of claims for rights, for sexual justice and human rights.[4]

While these globalizing flows affect all parts of the world, their impact is uneven on individuals, groups, states and regions because they are enmeshed in huge disparities of power and gross inequalities, and this is manifest in continuing sexual injustices, especially against women, children and lesbian, gay, bisexual or trans-identified people.[5] Ken Plummer suggests that such 'real world' differences are simultaneously the source of the greatest joys and of the deepest miseries of human life: joys because exploring the multiplicities of sexual possibilities can bring great pleasures and opportunities to millions; miseries because we have to live with the potential for perpetual conflicts and violence over differences.[6] At the same time, global perspectives produce new opportunities for transcending the limits and restrictions of tradition, and give rise to oppositional social movements, and claims for human sexual rights and social justice.

Historians and Transnational Sexual History

Historians have become increasingly preoccupied with analysing these global sexual flows, drawing on a rich and ever-growing sociological, anthropological, political, economic, medical and queer literature that documents their positive and negative impact in both denying and embracing sexual and gender difference – though much of this literature is still from a Northern perspective. Accounts by scholars from other parts of the world are 'still rare', note Saskia Wieringa and Horacio Sívori in their collection on *The Sexual History of the Global South*.[7] Even in a civilization as rich and well documented as China's, Susan Mann has suggested, the history of sexuality and gender has until recently been badly neglected, despite masses of historical evidence from philosophers, religious leaders, writers, artists, parents, doctors and ordinary people, and despite intense state interest in both imperial, republican and Communist periods.[8] The same can be said about other major sexual systems. But a vigorous local as well as international scholarship is now taking up the challenge. Wieringa and Sívori's book deliberately draws widely on significant Southern scholarship, which was encouraged by an internationally funded exchange programme to support research on the history of development. Works such as Nyeck and Epprecht's volume on *Sexual Diversity in Africa*, Hoad's on *African Intimacies* and Tamale's collection on *African Sexualities* showcase a growing and diverse scholarship, demonstrating there is no such thing as a single 'African sexuality', as colonial myths propounded. Tamale's work, documenting the sexual diversity of the continent through poetry and oral testimony as much as more formal records, dramatizes the fact that the sexual archive in the global South does not lie ready waiting to be discovered. It is being created in the very process of constructing a sexual history.[9] A similar point is made by Anjali Arondekar in relation to another major culture where sexuality and gender have been a central aspect of the struggle between colonizer and colonized: India. Constructing multiple alternative archives is a way of remedying the erasures of a conflicted and disputed past, and underlining complex, intertwined histories.[10]

As in the development of Western sexual history, a key aspect of the modern development of a critical sexual history on a global scale has been concerned with same-sex sexuality – from China and India to Latin America, Africa and the overlapping but not identical Islamic and Arab worlds. One reason for this is that as in Western countries historical work has been strongly associated with the emergent struggles of activists, and more specifically with the impact of HIV/AIDS, which provided the stimulus (and the international funding) for local sexual histories. Queer historians have been pioneers in exploring the globalization of dissident sexualities and genders, drawing on postcolonial scholarship and perspectives as well as well-established critical historical approaches.[11] A key aspect of their arguments is that in pursuing the dissident or nonconformist they are illuminating the wider sexual regime, drawing the contours of and querying heteronormative assumptions. Research on the ways in which same-sex practices are lived and represented can reveal hidden power dynamics in many spheres of social, intellectual and political life. These practices are integral to the social organization even when (or perhaps especially when) they are excoriated and despised. But this underlies a key dilemma in doing transnational sexual history: the extent to which we can deploy the categories that have been so resonant in Western scholarship (even when they have been problematized) in non-Western sexual and gender cultures.

Scholars in the early twentieth century had no compunction in deploying the new language of sexology, of homosexuals and heterosexuals, in referring to other cultures, even though at the time they had little resonance in the West, let alone the rest of the world (see chapter 2). The new wave of critical sexual history from the 1970s historicized such terms, but it has not stopped a proliferation of efforts at exploring 'gay life' across the globe, which has produced in return fierce polemics against the 'gay international' and 'homonationalism'. But even more general queer criticism of ethnocentric assumptions and essentialism in transnational sexual history is not always especially helpful. Queer theorizing, Marc Epprecht suggests in relation to the African historical context, carries too much of its North American origins, embodies too many Western theoretical assumptions and too much Western empirical evidence, smacks of cultural imperialism itself, and is often 'strikingly old-fashioned'.[12] The challenge for the sexual historian is always how to enter with empathy and understanding into the meanings, rituals, forms of knowledge, subjectivities and feelings of another culture without imposing alien meanings.

Central to critical sexual history is the assumption that sexuality as a continent of knowledge and practice has a very specific history in Western epistemology. How relevant can it be to other cultures? Susan Mann comments on the strangeness of deploying a cultural category that did not exist in China for most of the period of her study. She suggests, nevertheless, that there are justified reasons for doing so. If the categories we use do not fit, we get to see differences, variation and change over time. People are introduced to ways of being unlike their own, and begin to recognize a broad range of human possibilities.[13] One powerful effect of this is not to see approximations of Western concepts in all other histories of sexuality, but to recognize through other histories the cultural specificity, even strangeness of Western concepts. A transnational sexual history, Epprecht has argued, is more than a world history, or a study of global effects. It is about circulation, transcendence, inequality, hybridity, dynamic encounters and exchanges both across and within borders.[14] A transnational approach to sexual and gender history is not about separation but about interconnections, and should illuminate the history of the USA or Britain or Germany as much as the histories of Brazil, China, Indonesia or myriad African countries.

Patterns of Sexual History

Michel Foucault's famous distinction between the *scientia sexualis*, the scientific concepts of sexuality which shaped Western notions, and *ars erotica*, the practices of pleasure and ritual which ostensibly shaped much of the rest of the global erotic economy, has been amongst the most savagely critiqued of his concepts, especially by historians of the global South.[15] The distinction is widely seen as misleading in its interpretation of Western sexuality, and patronizing, neocolonialist and utopian in relation to non-Western sexual cultures, strangely echoing the romantic vision of the pleasures and dangers of the primitive that many early sexologists and later sex tourists displayed, and critical sexual historians of today are supposed to have got over. As Mitchell Dean has persuasively suggested, Foucault's arguments are fundamentally at odds with the methodological principles of his own critique of cultural totalities and his embrace of effective/ genealogical history.[16] But whatever the inadequacies of his own schema, and of those who follow him too religiously,

Foucault's adventures into transnational classifications have been highly influential, and can be seen as part of a long effort to see patterns in sexual history on a global scale.

One of the most (in)famous and influential efforts at a global division and classification is the theory of a 'Sotadic Zone', offered by the British mid-nineteenth-century traveller and adventurer Sir Richard Burton in the 'Terminal Essay' of his translation of *The Arabian Nights*. He postulates the existence of a geographical zone, shaped by climate as much as by race, culture or biology, where intergenerational sexual activity between men and boys is tolerated or fully integrated into sexual mores. The zone embraces the Mediterranean litoral, the Middle East and Iran through to large parts of India and Indochina, into China, and the South Sea Islands through to South America. This mythical framework is of more than antiquarian interest. As historians such as Epprecht, with regard to Africa, which was largely excluded from the zone, and Massad, in relation to Arab civilizations, which were very much included, have argued, exclusion or inclusion within the Sotadic Zone has had a continuing impact on Western perceptions of and policies on these regions, and in shaping their contemporary historical understandings.[17]

'African sexuality' was portrayed as resolutely heterosexual and homosexuality as an imported vice, arguments still deployed by nationalist leaders and religious conservatives in attacking Western-backed campaigns for sexual rights, and international responses to the HIV/AIDS crisis. The former South African president Thabo Mbeki's disastrous denial of HIV as a cause of AIDS was shaped, it has been powerfully argued, by his suspicion of Western attitudes towards 'African sexuality'.[18] By contrast, Arab sexuality was portrayed by colonizers as effeminate and corrupt, and especially exploitative of women, which has fed into Arab nationalist and religious fundamentalist opposition to Western moralism, which in turn has fired Western Islamophobia. The mapping of a 'geography of perversion'[19] has had profound effects. Categorizations, as we have seen throughout this book, are more than neat divisions. They embody relations of power, and have consequences.

Sexual cultures always overflow our efforts to classify: they are always more plural and diffuse than taxonomists like to imagine. At the same time, it is unlikely that the patterns they make are entirely arbitrary. The critical point is to recognize (not impose) patterns where they can be detected, and to deploy them as heuristic devices to clarify rather than grids to determine. The Swedish sociologist Göran Therborn, in his book *Between Sex and Power*, detects five basic types of global family forms, within broad religious frameworks, which provide the shaping contexts for sexualities and gender formations. These are sub-Saharan African families (shaped by Animist beliefs); European and North American (Christian); South Asian (Hindu); East Asian (Confucian and Buddhist); and West Asian/North African (Islamic). Therborn also mentions various sub-forms, such as South-East Asian and Creole American. As Plummer points out in his discussion of this work, these categorizations are not hard and fast, and they have been, and are, subject to dramatic changes.[20] But their legacies continue to shape contemporary values, especially in underlining that sexual regimes are not independent variables but fundamentally linked to structures of gender, family and wider social organization.

Plummer himself suggests the existence of 'global tectonic plates' moving slowly and organizing forms of life all around them. He names these as world religions, which far from being in decline seem to be burgeoning on a global scale; civilizational regions, along the lines suggested by Therborn; migratory human groupings – diasporas, colonizations and hybrid sexualities; and social divisions, such as those of gender, racial and ethnic, generational and economic, with extremes of poverty and wealth increasingly the determinant of life chances.

These are highly suggestive for historical work, especially in underlining that global divisions and differences cannot be confined within straightforward national, continental or 'civilizational' boundaries. The era of globalization has produced intensified regionalism as much as global homogenization, and the development of specific cultural interventions – and inventions.[21] The celebration of 'Asian values' by South-East and East Asian politicians, with the traditional family and Confucianism seen as the essential cradle of economic take-off, has influenced studies of China and its diaspora. The same is evident in the historical construction of 'European values', up to and including the presentation of the European Union as the embodiment of a new liberalism in relation to sexuality and intimate life.

A further vital aspect of globalizing energy can be seen in the vast growth of international networks and social movements – of women, of LGBTQ people, in relation to HIV/AIDS and reproductive rights, for human sexual rights, against sexual and childhood trafficking, as well as the conservative or fundamentalist religious movements and their affiliates – which have been massively boosted by globalization. International networks are not new. Josephine Butler's campaign against sexual exploitation of (Western) women in the so-called 'white slave trade' gave rise to international congresses as early as the 1880s, and can be seen as an important precursor of contemporary international campaigns against the trafficking of women and children largely from the global South. Early sexual science was especially productive in generating global links and mutual influence. Magnus Hirschfeld's World League for Sexual Reform in the 1920s and early 1930s brought together sex researchers and reformers from around the world, with a significant contribution from people in what we would now see as the global South, which influenced key sexologists such as Havelock Ellis.

As the existence of such movements and international networks suggests, the reality of international divisions is messier than the tidy-minded categorizer would often care to admit. Boundaries are fluid, cultures inevitably change over time, and influences go both ways.

The Colonial Legacy and the Postcolonial Critique

Western colonialism, Tom Boellstorff has observed, is 'the most significant antecedent to contemporary globalization'.[22] The management of sexuality and reproduction was a key aspect of colonial governance, which grew in significance in the heyday of empire from the late nineteenth century. It was central to the 'civilizing mission', which sought to bring

sexual order and discipline to the colonized, and was manifest in a range of practices, from new laws and institutions
to labour regimes, that entered directly into the organization
of everyday life.[23] These were technologies of power designed
to redraw the boundaries between men and women in accor-
dance with imperial notions of what was appropriate or
desirable. In British-controlled India, as Sinha has documented, the effeminization of Bengali men was a specific
technique of domination, an intervention justified by the
colonial regime as a response to the oppressive treatment of
women in the local culture. It was only the less clearly colonized nature of China that protected its men from a similar
redrawing of masculinity, Mann has argued.[24]

One of the most tangible and long-lasting legacies of empire
which, as we have seen (chapter 4), historians are now exploring is the regulation of homosexuality. Over half of the eighty
or so states that still criminalize homosexuality are members
of the Commonwealth, former dependencies of the British
Empire. They carry the burden still of British legislation now
(if only fairly recently) confined to the dustbin of history in
the old 'mother country'. The British imposition of the anti-
homosexual article 377 of the Indian Penal Code, which
echoed England's penalization of sodomy and gross indecency, still remains the basis for Indian regulation. Its terms
were eventually extended to all British colonies in Africa,
South-East Asia and the Caribbean as well as the white settler
colonies in the late nineteenth and early twentieth centuries,
and as late as the 1920s was imposed on Iraq, which had come
under British imperial hegemony after World War I.[25] It is a
supreme historical irony that contemporary Britain, with a
newly burnished sexual liberalism, alongside the USA and
other Western states, has recently positioned itself as a global
defender of homosexual rights against its former colonies and
dependencies, especially in Africa and the Arab and broader
Islamic world. As Joseph Massad, one of the most trenchant
critics of this history, has caustically observed, whilst the
imperial West attacked Islam's alleged sexual licentiousness,
the modern liberal West now attacks the alleged repression of
sexual freedoms in the present Islamic world.[26]

In *Desiring Arabs*, Massad is concerned with two issues
he sees as fundamental to the continuing power nexus

between the old imperial West and the Arab world: the distorting impact of Western interventions on the perceptions of Arab sexuality and Islam, both globally and within the Islamic world itself; and the disastrous role of gay human rights activists in the contemporary politics of sexuality in that world. His work is heavily influenced by Edward Said's critique of 'orientalism', and is to a large extent an application of that critique to Arab sexuality. So the book is not so much a history of Arab sexuality as a dissection of the representations of the sexual desires of Arabs, and how they came to be linked to 'civilizational worth', and a desiring target for Western sexual adventurers and gay romanticism for centuries – a view, Massad suggests, that has been given a new life by recent gay historians and anthropologists.

Whilst Massad is critical of anti-homosexual attitudes in the contemporary Arab world, which he suggests are an emulation of Western Christian fundamentalist attitudes, his most passionate critique is of the 'Gay International', who reproduce the discourse of Western sexual identities as universal. This universalization, he polemicizes, inflicts 'epistemic, ethical, and political violence' on the rest of the world by human rights campaigners who thereby assault the human rights of their postulated subjects and destroy the existing subjectivities organized around other sets of binaries.

This polemic is if anything sharpened in other studies. Puar condemns 'the racism of the global gay left and the wholesale acceptance of the Islamophobic rhetoric that fuels the war on terror'. This, she argues, is part of the rise of 'homonationalism', in the wake of the 9/11 attacks on the USA, whereby new forms of national, racial or other belongings, especially of 'sexual liberalism' in Europe, the USA and Israel (a particular target), can be affirmed against a collective vilification of Muslims.[27] Such arguments have made a significant impact, but they also exemplify the dangers of attempting a mono-causal explanation of a complex history. Whatever the vagaries of gay rights advocates and the essentialism of some of the arguments (and histories) offered to the world, they can hardly be blamed for attitudes and practices that are deeply rooted in various cultures, whether Muslim or Christian. To suggest otherwise would be to imply that what is oppressive, misogynistic, homophobic or transphobic in Arab societies is merely a reflection of Western intervention.

Other historians have offered a more nuanced picture. There appears to be general agreement that 'before homosexuality' there was a complex and diverse sexual ecology in the Islamic world, including a widespread acceptance of men falling in love with boys, expressed in poetry as well as physical gestures of affection, but pre-modern Islam did not tolerate homosexuality per se, and there were severe Islamic injunctions against anal intercourse (as there were in the Christian world).[28] The most famous Arab historian of sexuality, Abdelwahab Bouhdiba, portrays Islam as a sexually enlightened religion, but firmly emphasizes the ideal of monogamous, heterosexual relationships ordained by the Koran, which was subsequently corrupted by patriarchalism and homoeroticism.[29] The evidence suggests a hardening line against homoeroticism from the late eighteenth century, in part through interactions with the Christian and modernizing West. The toleration of sexual heterodoxy in the dominant Islamic power, the Ottoman Empire, began to be challenged, with increased zeal by modernizing reformers from the end of the nineteenth century, and by the new nationalism developing in Turkey and the successor states of the Ottoman Empire from the 1920s.[30] An 'entire cultural silencing mechanism', Ze'evi suggests, was deployed to cleanse the sexual discourse. These nations did not need the intervention of human rights advocates to stimulate official hostility towards homosexuality. Contrariwise, Western intervention has not caused the rise of more diverse sexual cultures in the Arab world. Recent studies suggest the liveliness of popular sexual culture, with an increased emphasis on sexual autonomy in countries as different as Egypt and Iran – an incipient 'sexual revolution' shaped by local cultures amongst young people, not by international norms and values.[31]

Sexual Regimes, Sexual Lives

Just as the organization of sexuality and gender was central to the colonizing endeavour, so modernization and nation-building in the postcolonial world have characteristically involved strong intervention in the regulation of gender and sexuality by state bureaucracies, and the elaboration of explicit ideologies regarding the role of the family, usually at the cost of the exclusion of homosexuality.

Active intervention in reshaping everyday life has been explicitly the case in the context of self-consciously revolutionary transformations, when the world was 'turned upside down', and opportunities for the creation of the 'new man' and 'new woman' seemed an imminent possibility. The results have been at best ambiguous. The Russian Revolution provides the classic example, of revolutionary hopes and the harsher reality of revolution betrayed. The transformative impact of the early sexual reforms in the Soviet Union, on marriage, divorce, abortion and homosexuality, may have been exaggerated by contemporary enthusiasts and early historians, but they were soon in any case negated by the Stalinist counter-revolution of the 1930s, and the USSR became a byword for sexual conservatism until its demise.[32]

In the case of China, deep-seated ideas have been recirculated, reinvented and given new meanings over a long period, with the state always playing an 'overwhelmingly important part', in Mann's words, in defining the criteria for performing gendered identities. These interventions became more pervasive and coercive in the twentieth century, and a family-based polity and citizenship have been as central to the Chinese Communist regime as to its imperial predecessors. There have been significant changes in the sexual culture since the 1980s, but the Communist government continues to take steps to ensure a normative model of heterosexual marriage and a carefully regulated reproduction policy, most notoriously through the one-child family.[33]

Cuba was widely seen as the lodestar of a new type of popular revolution in the 1960s. The leadership showed no lack of transforming ambition, and there remains in Cuba a deep nostalgia for the revolutionary hopes. One of the founding myths of the revolution, Carrie Hamilton has suggested, was that of male heterosexual potency linked to political invincibility.[34] Perhaps not surprisingly, many of the changes the leadership set in train were deeply conservative. Despite the reforms designed to improve the position of women, the revolutionary regime in the early days sought to enforce traditional, even Catholic, values deeply rooted in the colonial culture, on marriage and the nuclear family – values which were often at odds with local, working-class and rural practices, where consensual unions and extended families were common. Early historians of the revolution very quickly began to express acute disillusion, especially because of the strong anti-homosexual currents that went with the machismo that characterized the revolutionary leadership.[35] Despite significant recent changes, especially towards homosexuality and transgender, promoted by Mariela Castro, niece of Fidel and daughter of President Raul Castro, as head of the regime's sex education organization, oral history accounts show a deep sense of loss and reluctance to speak, with continuing inhibitions amongst women in discussing sexuality, especially outside marriage and the family.

A central aspect of these revolutionary efforts has been the drive to restore a sense of national pride and destiny, and this has been a recurrent theme in the sexual histories of many other states in the global South, as in the West. Japan's sexual history was dramatically reshaped by deliberate state policy from the late nineteenth century in an effort to adjust to standards of global respectability. The regulation of geisha houses was stiffened, a Confucian emphasis on the family and on the maternal role of women was reaffirmed, and homosexuality was declared illegal (though this was quickly rescinded).[36] In the interwar years the Thai state deliberately set out to transform the gender patterns which had been portrayed in Western representations as ambiguously androgynous. Key to this has been Thai notions of 'phet', which incorporates sexual difference (male versus female), gender difference (masculinity versus femininity) and sexuality (heterosexual versus homosexuality). The new gay categories that have emerged in recent decades are not so much new sexualities as new genders in line with Thai traditions.[37]

In Brazil, Larvie has argued, 'The sexual peculiarities ascribed to the Brazilian population have been a source of consternation for governing elites since the early colonial period.'[38] This has led to recurrent interventions, whether to reinforce the heterosexual order through eugenic and social hygiene policies in the first half of the twentieth century, or recognizing (or inventing) sexual categories in the 1990s in the wake of the AIDS crisis, so that international and national campaigns against the epidemic had subject groups to address.

As these histories demonstrate, 'modernization' did not mean simply adopting Western norms. On the contrary, in most cases there was a play of tradition and modernity, but the unifying element was an active state involvement with the aim of making the state fit for a postcolonial world, and the deployment of a historical narrative to legitimize its practices. This was most strikingly apparent in those countries where the battle to define sexuality and gender was most clearly inscribed in the struggles against colonialism. Anti-colonial theorists like Frantz Fanon had been deeply concerned with the European myths about African sexuality, and the ways in which colonial interventions had emasculated African masculinity. This fed into a homophobia which has been a central motif in many postcolonial sexual regimes.

In their collection *Global Homophobia*, Weiss and Bosia argue that 'political homophobia' has become a 'core instrument of governance' in the contemporary world, though with a differential impact on male–male and female–female relations.[39] As deployed by postcolonial states from Central and East Africa to Indonesia, and post-Communist states including parts of Eastern Europe and above all post-Soviet Russia, it has a range of practical merits: deflecting attention from wider economic and social restructuring, reacting to or even pre-empting gay rights mobilization, reaffirming heterosexual values, especially through raising the spectre of same-sex marriage, and above all asserting 'traditional values' as the bedrock of national unity against the sexual Other. In Iran, capital punishment for same-gender sexual expression can be seen in the context of the assertion of 'sexual sovereignty' by the Islamist regime, and a strong affirmation of the naturalness and centrality of traditional male and female roles. It has led to the strange position that Iran is a world leader in gender reassignment surgery. 'Sex change' is apparently preferable to homosexuality. Elsewhere, homophobic and transphobic discourses have been strengthened by the evangelical interventions of Western conservatives.[40] In countries such as Uganda, Malawi and Liberia it is American fundamentalist Christians who have actively stimulated violent homophobia through propaganda against liberals, who are accused of imposing sexual deviance on African countries. The LGBTQ activists in those countries, as Kaoma notes, are in danger of suffering 'collateral damage' from the American culture wars.[41]

In historical perspective, the tragedy is that a focus by postcolonial state builders on the impact of Western colonization, and attacks on the zeal of human rights campaigners and the 'global gay', have led to the suppression of a rich indigenous history, pre-dating colonial interventions, of same-sex and gender nonconforming ways of life even in the most oppressive or homosexuality-denying countries. Cultures as diverse and varied as India, the Philippines, Brazil, pre-Columbian America and many others have deep-rooted cultures of gender nonconformity that have too readily been assimilated into Western notions of sexual inversion or homosexuality. Even the recent adoption of variations of the terms 'gay' or 'lesbian' across equally diverse cultures can be seen as very specific adaptations to local cultures, which have not substituted for but added to pre-existing patterns. In Indonesia, as Boellstorff has shown, the emergence of the categories of 'lesbi' and 'gay' since the 1980s is part of the creation of a translocal 'gay archipelago' across the state's myriad of islands scattered over thousands of miles, providing an 'imagined community'.[42] In South Africa, black Africans were intensely involved in articulating same-sex identities through activism and publications long before the fall of Apartheid, without simply aping Western categories, even if words like 'gay' or 'lesbian' are deployed. More widely in Africa, despite deep-seated opposition there have been notable advances in campaigns for sexual justice in recent years, including on gay rights.[43] In these and many other examples, what is at stake is an intense process of internal negotiation through which new meanings and new interpretations of belonging and local citizenship are emerging.[44] The various forms of activism may not share a common genesis, or any necessary identity with Western models, but they demonstrate a common dynamic of resistance to dominant gender/sexual ideologies in their cultures. The claim for human sexual rights has become a prime transnational vehicle for this activism since the 1990s.

History and Human Sexual Rights

The idea of 'human rights' had its origin in the American and French Revolutions of the late eighteenth century, and has had a complex and tortured history ever since. For them to be *human* rights as opposed to natural or particularist rights, Hunt has argued, all humans across the world must possess them equally, and only because of their status as human beings.[45] But the construction of the idea of a common humanity, and what a full humanity might embrace, has had to be struggled for in the past two tumultuous centuries and remains highly contested. Prior to the early 1990s, sexuality was strikingly absent from international human rights discourse. The Universal Declaration of Human Rights, adopted by the United Nations General Assembly in 1948, had famously declared the 'inherent dignity' and 'equal and inalienable rights' of all members of human society, but its definition of the right to family life and privacy proved limited in practice in supporting any claim to sexual rights. Over time the universal subject of human rights has been broadened to encompass different racial or ethnic origins, different faiths or none, varying health needs, and different forms of gender, but the UN (or rather its diverse members) proved reluctant to acknowledge issues of sexual diversity or transgender. The international argument for a wider agenda embracing sexuality in its broadest sense only began to emerge fully into international debate with the Vienna Conference on Human Rights in 1993, the UN Declaration on the Elimination of Violence against Women later that year, the world population conference in Cairo in 1994, and the women's conference in Beijing in 1995.[46]

Sexuality came onto the international human rights agenda mainly, at first, through debates over privacy and reproduction. There are obviously strong links between reproductive rights and wider questions of sexuality, especially in relation to core themes like bodily integrity, personhood, equality and diversity, and to the social and cultural contexts which encourage injustice and violence. While a strong international discourse on reproductive rights has emerged powerfully, its history underlines the difficulties in negotiating common meanings across different societies, dependent on different traditions, circumstances and relations of power between men and women.[47]

The main push, however, has come from within the international LGBTQ movement, which gave rise to organizations such as ILGA (International Lesbian and Gay Association, founded 1978), the International Gay and Lesbian Human Rights Commission, which so upset Joseph Massad, and various transgender organizations.[48] Two documents have particularly focused debate and campaigning in the early twenty-first century. The Yogyakarta Principles, published in 2007, in effect argued that LGBTQ rights were already inherent in existing international human rights law, and assumed the fixedness of sexual identity categories. The later Declaration of Montreal, presented at the International Conference on LGBT Human Rights in 2006, sought to soften the essentialism of this position in deference to critics, and attempted to go beyond Western definitions of sexuality.[49]

As Peteschky noted, while the claim to rights can be enabling, it can as easily lead to an intensification of conflict over which rights and whose rights have priority.[50] If sexual cultures vary enormously and have specific historical formations, how do we distinguish those claims to rights that have a universal resonance, and those which are highly culturally specific – and possibly antipathetic to large numbers of citizens around the globe? A recognition of the human rights of women, for example, does not mean that as yet it is possible to develop a common assumption about what those rights mean in practice, as controversies over the legitimacy of women wearing the veil, enforced or arranged marriages, access to birth control and the like underline. There is an obvious danger in a multiculturalism or cultural relativism that protects cultures which discriminate against women or homosexuals. Many, however, see equal dangers in imposing Western 'Enlightenment values' on the global South. Lennox and Waites, in responding to Puar's critique of homonationalism, underline that affirmation of human rights in relation to sexual orientation must be careful to address a wide range of human rights issues, including racism and global power relations, especially those linked to colonialism and imperialism.[51]

Such debates within the discourse of human rights, however, illustrate the core problem: human rights do not exist in nature. They are not there to be discovered written on tablets of stone. They have to be invented – and invented in situations where what it is to be human is itself deeply challenged, not only across global divides but within Western epistemology and historical understanding. As Bourke puts it, 'the concepts of "man" or "human" are merely metaphysical generalities: they do not exist without the substance conferred by specific societies, legal systems and their concrete protections'. It is not so much that humans have rights, but that rights make humans.[52]

A strong strand of conscious 'anti-humanism' pervaded the poststructuralism that fed into critical sexual history: famously, Foucault looked forward to the figure of 'man' disappearing as the sea clears the sand. By 'humanism' Foucault seems to mean that tradition which finds a human essence in the autonomous subject of Enlightenment rationalism, the constitutive individual of liberal thought.[53] A special vitriol is reserved by theorists of 'posthumanism' for the 'moral humanism' of an advanced liberal thinker such as Martha Nussbaum, critiqued for her 'humanistic cosmopolitanism' rooted in 'American liberal individualism', despite her strong support for LGBTQ and wider sexual rights.[54] In its place Braidotti offers an 'ecophilosophy of multiple belongings', based on an 'ethics of becoming', 'expanding the notion of Life towards the non-human or zoe', offering a 'neo-materialist discursive ethics based on non-unitary subjectivity'. This self-conscious, intellectualized anti-rationalism owes a great deal to the vitalist philosophy of Gilles Deleuze and Félix Guattari, and seeks to embrace the post-digital as well as the non-human animal in the posthuman world.[55] The difficulty with it, however, is that it offers little in everyday practices for combating the inequities, discriminations, violence and abuses of the material world, especially where they impact on sexual and gender lives. In rejecting the narrowness of one particular interpretation of humanism, there is an acute danger of evacuating altogether the idea of a common humanity.

In *Cosmopolitan Sexualities*, Ken Plummer provides a vigorous defence of what he calls 'critical humanism', which recognizes a rich diversity of human goals but within a framework of agreed and negotiated common values, a 'differential universalism' that seeks not to impose a single notion of humanity but to offer the possibility for working through differences and divisions.[56] As Tom Boellstorff observes in his history of a pioneering virtual world, 'Second Life', its reconfiguration of selfhood and sociality is only possible because people rework the virtuality that already characterizes human beings in the actual world. This is another way of saying that humans live in cultures that are human constructs. They might appear incommensurable at times, but they can never be hermetically sealed from one another. Because of this connectedness, dialogue must always be possible, and in the possibility of dialogue across the chasm of difference lies the potentiality for new understandings of what it is to be human.[57]

A discourse of human sexual rights has, since the 1990s, become the main focus for discussion of the relationship between our common humanity and diverse sexual needs and gender variability. It has, as we have seen, been highly contested, but in its existence it carries with it the hope and promise of a continuing conversation. In the words of Carol Gilligan, 'underneath the terror, the war, the bullying, there is a human face. And voice, however suppressed.'[58] At its best, a sexual history rooted in global perspectives can help make that voice heard.

7
Memory, Community, Voice

Unofficial Knowledges and Counter-History

In this final chapter of the book I return to one of the strands that gave rise to a new, critical sexual history: to the grass-roots, community-based histories that burst out of the feminist and lesbian and gay movements of the 1970s, and have had a continuing energy and influence since. I do this not to privilege those histories over the professionalized, usually university-based history that has become the norm in most Western countries (though less so in the global South) but to suggest the intensely symbiotic nature of the relationship that continues between the two, and the power differences they nevertheless embody.

In a recent history of what was once the largest British lesbian and gay organization, the Campaign for Homosexual Equality, the author Peter Scott-Presland begins with an apologia: 'I write with the insecurity of not being a "proper" historian, queer theorist, or indeed any kind of academic ... and inevitably wonder if this is enough.' He needn't have worried. The book, published in 2015, the first volume of a planned three with the overall title of *Amiable Warriors*, is immensely detailed, engaged, passionate, scholarly, chatty, rumbustious and highly readable, embracing the reader with the excitement of new beginnings, ambitious goals and collective endeavours, and the vicissitudes, pleasures and pains of many individual lives. But the author, a long-term activist, not only excuses himself for not being a professional historian, he sharply distinguishes his work from the efforts of academic LGBT or queer scholars. He comes to the 'reluctant conclusion' that queer studies encourages 'an arid, self-regarding exchange between academics which gets further and further away from primary sources and what actually happened'. Against this he seeks to write a history that appeals to a general, and especially young LGBTQ, readership, 'who are now discovering a reawakened interest in their own history and roots'.[1]

The relationship between a popular, grassroots-oriented history and history as practised in the university was examined with similar sentiment and even greater passion by Raphael Samuel, a teaching and researching historian by trade and lifelong intellectual troublemaker, gadfly and subversive by inclination, in his late masterwork, *Theatres of Memory*, first published in 1994.[2] Samuel was the founder and presiding genius of the History Workshop movement, an ardent espouser of 'history from below' and of new forms of history. He was acutely alert to new directions in historical practice, and a major influence on many pioneers of the new sexual history, and in turn he warmly embraced and supported their work. He had a deep commitment to the democratization of the historical imagination, and to questioning authority in all forms, but particularly the authority of the discipline of history as he had experienced it, hierarchical and hermetically sealed in a way that stifled creativity and new ways of seeing the past. Like Scott-Presland, he believed that history left to the professional historian was apt to present itself as an 'esoteric form of knowledge', fetishizing archive-based research, encouraging intellectual inbreeding, introspection and sectarianism. For Samuel, history was not the prerogative of the professional historian, and should not be left to them. It was rather a social form of knowledge, the work of many different hands, embracing an 'ensemble of activities' in which 'ideas of history are embedded in a dialectic of past–present relations'. This was the domain of unofficial knowledges, whose sources were 'promiscuous', going way beyond the official documentary record and drawing not only on real-life experiences but also on memory, myth and desire.

No doubt in many ways this was polemically unfair, as Bill Schwarz details in his foreword to a new edition of Samuel's book in 2012.[3] But its arguments resonate with the experiences of many pioneering sexual historians. Much of the early feminist and lesbian and gay history in the 1970s and 1980s was, as we have seen, developed outside the academy, and often against the academy, shaping alternative knowledges about the past, and creating a counter-history to challenge the silences and occlusions of the keepers of the official flame. A historian of gender history recalls the crucial role played in its growth by adult education, neighbourhood women's centres and informal history groups widespread in the USA and Britain. And when feminist historians began to move into the universities in the 1980s, it was as often in departments of sociology, social policy, cultural studies or education as in history.[4] If anything, developments in gay and lesbian history were even more marginalized, with few university opportunities for younger historians until the early 2000s. The Australian gay historian Graham Willett stresses that the subject has continued to a large extent to be 'community-focused', partly at least out of necessity. He underlines, however, the degree to which this has been a source of great strength as well, combining the commitment and insights deriving from community connections with the high standards of academic skill that good history required.[5]

Allan Bérubé was an exemplary model of this dual commitment. *Coming Out Under Fire*, Bérubé's major book, combined high standards of conventional scholarship with deep community roots.[6] The research for what became the book began through the regular slide shows on lesbian and gay history he gave at hundreds of venues in the USA in the late 1970s and early 1980s. As Joan Nestle, the co-founder and guiding spirit of the Lesbian Herstory Archive set up in New York City in 1973, observed about her own contemporaneous work, travelling slide shows became 'our major organizing tool', 'our most powerful way to work against the feelings of cultural deprivation and personal isolation'.[7] The material Bérubé amassed, including a cache of letters from US service personnel passing through, and later settling in,

San Francisco during World War II, came to him often from people who had heard or heard of his talks. Further evidence came from memories captured in interviews and discussions. And crucially, he was supported in his research and writing not by any official sources of funding, but through part-time work, his community activities, a legacy from his late lover, and many individual supporters.

In their introduction to the collection of Bérubé's essays published after his death, D'Emilio and Freedman emphasize that he believed passionately in the power of history to change the way individuals and even whole groups of people understood themselves and their place in the world. History was an aid to activism and a world-changing tool. The same passion animated Joan Nestle, who sought to capture and preserve the memories of a pre-Stonewall lesbian culture that was fast fading and in danger of being forgotten. Her aim, she declared, was to analyse and evaluate the lesbian experience, and to encourage lesbians to record their experiences to form a 'living herstory'. The colonized, she observes, are doomed to lose their history. Through the archives, she and her colleagues sought liberation with memory: 'one of our battles was to change secrecy into disclosure, shame into memory'. Remembering was an 'alchemy' that transformed mockery, hatred and fear into community.[8]

Memory and Community

The fundamental argument of Samuel's *Theatres of Memory* is that memory, far from being a mere passive receptacle or storage system, is an active, dynamic shaping force that is dialectically related to historical thought rather than being some kind of negative Other to it. At stake in the historical endeavour is who controls memory, with all its ambivalences and ambiguity. Historically the task had fallen to the professional guardians through their institutional power and dominating presence in the schools, the academy, the archives, the journals and other publications that shape what can be said or thought, and police the absences in the collective consciousness. As the oral historian Paul Thompson remarked, 'The very power-structure worked as a great recording machine shaping the past in its own image.'[9] There was a disdain of unofficial records, including what was to become a powerful tool of the new history, oral testimony. The result, as we have seen, was a long silencing of the history of sexuality and gender in general, and of non-normative sexuality and gender nonconformity in particular. The alternative knowledges constructed by the new sexual historians gave voice to a counter-memory: stories of sexual violence, gender inequality, normalizing practices, guilt and shame, suffering and endurance, humiliation and resilience, passion and pleasure, resistance and identity. A counter-memory is associated with trauma and suffering, but also with triumph over the odds. It may embrace elements of nostalgia, a bitter-sweet memory of times that have passed – but then so does official history. It may be selective and myth-making in its own ways. Memory is always partial, and historians must always beware of seeking final Truth in recollections of the past. But if there cannot be a single Truth in the highways and byways of disparate memories, there are surely to be found pathways to multiple truths. Alternative histories do more than excavate a buried past, though that is a crucial if hazardous task. They also create and reshape memories that give greater meaning to the present, and do so through constructing alternative archives of emotion and by providing voice to feelings and experiences that may have been long stifled or forgotten.

The Sexual Archive

The archive is the conserver and producer of memory. It also has the power to discipline and constrain memory by its omissions and commissions. For Foucault, the archive embodies power relations, and like confession is a tool of subjugation, an aspect of the urge to classify and define that gave rise to the deployment of sexuality. The archive is a theoretical twin to his notion of a discursive formation, which does not so much reproduce knowledge as produce it.[10] If this is the case, then we can see how creating alternative archives, both in the conventional sense of material collections of records and memories, and in the more Foucauldian sense of identifying all the traces of a particular historical period and cultural manifestation and using them to understand genealogies, has been so crucial to the making of a critical sexual history. New archives embody new ways of constructing the past – and have the potential to be as formidable, to a different end, as the traditional sort.

By 1990 the Lesbian Herstory Archive could already boast of 10,000 volumes, 12,000 photographs, 200 special collections, 1,400 periodical files, 1,000 organizational and subject files, thousands of feet of film and video, art and artefacts, posters and T-shirts, buttons and personal memorabilia. Once housed in the apartment of the co-founders Joan Nestle and Deborah Edel in New York City, from 1993 it had a home of its own in a three-storey building in Brooklyn, paid for by hundreds of gifts and subscriptions.[11]

This was very much a material archive, but it also extended beyond a traditional remit through actively involving its users through slide shows, talks, presentations, and by providing a safe space for women-loving women. Its presence was itself a vital aspect of producing meanings and memory – often going way beyond conventional definitions of the archive. This was a model that later scholar activists could build on, in increasingly unconventional ways. Judith (Jack) Halberstam offers an account of her website for a class in critical gender studies at the University of California, San Diego. Through digital links to independent record labels and queer bands she hoped to create 'an archive of subcultural material' that will enable students to find out about, write about and connect with queer bands and queer zines and ephemera, thus making a "new future" for queer history by making a place for materials that otherwise would be lost in the ebb and flow of a paper history'.[12] One day, she suggests, memories of comic books and performers and dyke bands might be 'as important to queer studies as Freud or Lacan'. For the queer archive has to extend beyond a place to hold or collect material. It has to become a 'floating signifier' for the kinds of lives implied by the crumbling paper remnants of shows, clubs, events and meetings.

The 'stock in trade' of the LGBTQ archive, Ann Cvetkovich observes, is ephemera of various types,[13] not only flyers for marches or dances (the traditional 'grey material' of libraries), but matchbook covers, used to exchange phone numbers in gay bars, condoms packaged to support safer sex at special events, and vibrators – all held by San Francisco's GLBT Historical Society of North California, but replicated in many similar archives from Berlin to Melbourne, Toronto to Johannesburg. Collections like these propose that emotions and feelings, associated with nostalgia, personal memory, fantasy and trauma, make a document or artefact significant and worthy of conserving. The 'queer archive', the editors of a special issue of *Radical History Review* suggest, is 'evasive and dynamic. ... A space where one collects or cobbles together historical understandings of sexuality through an appraisal of presences and absences.'[14]

These are elements of what Cvetkovich has called an archive of feeling. Sexual history demands a radical archive of emotion in order to document intimate life, sexuality, love and activism, illness and loss, all areas which are difficult to chronicle through the materials of a traditional archive. The HIV/AIDS crisis was especially central to a growing sense of the fragility of life, and the urgent need to preserve the records of lives lived, and lost. But the same impulse to preserve and memorialize is true of the archiving of women's memories of violence, trauma, reproduction, parenting and caring as well as sexual exploration. The archive provides a resource, a collection of stories, a set of representations, a memorial, a time capsule, creating a field of inquiry and construction, embodying and solidifying a new structure of feeling.

There has been an extraordinary efflorescence of specialist archives since the 1970s, many with deep social movement roots. Their disparate histories, however, are revealing of the tensions inherent in building a creative archive. In Britain, the largest collection of feminist material is the Women's Library, whose roots are in the archival records of early twentieth-century suffrage organizations, and some social purity organizations. These remained in the hands of the feminist organizations themselves until they fell under the responsibility of what was to become London Metropolitan University in the 1970s, and were eventually housed in a prize-winning dedicated building open to the wider public. Financial difficulties, however, led that university to pass responsibility for the collection to another, the London School of Economics, in 2013. Here it joined a major social science and political archive collection, including the largest British LGBTQ collection, the Hall-Carpenter Archives. What from one perspective seemed an ideal solution to the problem of preserving a major historical legacy and situating it in a broader history nevertheless occasioned passionate opposition from a number of feminist and sexual historians, who felt that the hard, independent, community-based work of creating feminist archives open to all – as they had achieved it in local women's history groups, or community-based women's history centres – was in danger of being lost.[15] A similar dilemma had faced the Hall-Carpenter Archives some years earlier. The archives had been started by enthusiastic community activists, and were for a time supported as an independent organization by the Greater London Council. On the GLC's dissolution (partly because it had funded non-traditional organizations), the precious archive had been housed in private homes and store rooms until the LSE provided a home. Built around the records of the Homosexual Law Reform Society and its charity arm the Albany Trust, the Gay Liberation Front, the Campaign for Homosexual Equality and a number of AIDS support organizations, plus various private papers, the collection has become an indispensable location for LGBTQ historical research by grassroots and professional historians alike. But the cost was the archive's institutionalization.

The same tension is apparent in sexual archival collections across the world. The Australian Lesbian and Gay Archives in Melbourne remain resolutely independent, sustained by community support. On the other hand, the Australian Women's Liberation and Lesbian Feminist Archives are now housed in the University of Melbourne.[16] The GLBT Historical Society in San Francisco is a major archive, and also houses a GLBT History Museum, the first stand-alone museum of its kind in the USA, based in Castro Street, the historic heart of the lesbian and gay community in that city. However, the archive of the One Institute, the early homophile organization founded in the early 1950s, and now the focus of what claims to be the largest LGBTQ archives collection in the world, has been housed at the University of Southern California since 2010. In Johannesburg, GALA,

Gay and Lesbian Memory in Action, the only dedicated LGBTQ archive in Africa, founded in 1997, remains an independent organization but works closely with neighbouring universities on various projects supporting sexual justice.

The growing reality is that as sexual history becomes more and more mainstream, and society generally liberalizes, the hard divide between grassroots and official memorializing and archiving is softening. Public libraries and even national archives are rapidly becoming focuses for sexual and LGBTQ research, from university libraries to the New York Public Library, from local libraries to the British Library in London (which is home to a major collection of LGBTQ oral histories). The British National Archives, like the Danish, now advertise their LGBTQ-relevant material.[17]

Sexuality research in general and LGBTQ history in particular are no longer marginal activities: they have become a major aspect of the historical endeavour. Central to that achievement is the recognition that there are many stories that were not recorded, many diverse ways of living sexuality and gender that history forgot, or where memory was partial and distorted. That remains the case in many parts of the world, of course, but in the more privileged spaces, not simply in the global North, sexual diversities, and therefore diverse histories, have shaped the sexual archive. I mention here, almost at random, a tiny sample to suggest the plurality: Rainbow Jews in London and the Rukus! Black LGBT Archive, both housed at the London Metropolitan Archives; the Leather Archives in Chicago, housed in their own building paid for through a mortgage funded by community events in the USA, Canada and Europe; the Transgender Archives at the University of Victoria, British Columbia, built around a community activist's personal collection; Outspoken: Oral History from LGBTQ Pioneers, an online video and audio collection of gay liberation activists' memories; Pride History Group, Sydney, with its recordings of 100 Voices; the LGBTQ Oral History Digital Collaboratory, a five-year project starting in 2014, connecting archives in the USA and Canada to explore new digital technologies and methodologies. From the major feminist and LGBTQ archives to more specialist collections, from university libraries to community bases, sexual history is gaining legitimacy and voice.

Voice

It is gaining voice literally through effective use of oral history. Oral history, as Paul Thompson reminds us, is as old as history itself. 'It was the *first* kind of history. And it is only quite recently that skill in handling oral history has ceased to be one of the marks of the great historian.'[18] There is a profound reason for this. Human beings, Plummer has argued, are above all narrators and story tellers, and society can be interpreted as an endless series of stories that help make society work.[19] Sexual stories are integral to that: as old as society, they were long embodied in folk memories and oral tales, and became central to the more scientific efforts from the late nineteenth century: the narratives of the founding sexologists are frequently constructed around the voices of the sexual subjects they classify and categorize. So it is not surprising that oral testimony came to play an increasingly important role in a nascent sexual history from the 1970s.

A major characteristic of modern sexuality as theorized by Michel Foucault has been the urge to confess, and essentially to confess about who you are by telling of your sexuality. Through practices such as confession individuals render themselves governable, subjecting and subjectifying themselves in and through a web of power relations. Yet all such practices hold the possibility of subverting the very authority they embody. Speaking out about your experiences and feelings was a characteristic feature of the early women's movement and the gay movements in the 1970s, through consciousness-raising and stories of survival and coming out, and these were reflected in the earliest writings of those movements. The confessional mode, instead of being a mode of subjection, became one of self-assertion. In her book on confession, nostalgia and memory, Susannah Radstone hypothesizes that in the West the urge to confess may now be giving way to an era of memory.[20] Nostalgia and memory have been key ideas in recent debates about modernity and postmodernity, with Marxist critics especially seeing nostalgia as a characteristic postmodern mood. It can also be related to, though it is not identical with, a melancholia which cultural critics have seen as pervasive in the contemporary (Western) world, signalling a sense of loss, and which I earlier marked as a crucial element in queer theory and history. But it could also be a force for agency and change. For Cvetkovich, oral history captures some of the lived experience of participating in a counter-public, offering a testimony to the fact that it existed – and made certain things possible.[21]

Oral history is not of course inherently radical in its approach and methods: it can be as easily deployed to record the memories of the rich and powerful as the poor and down-trodden, the conformist as much as the dissident. But there were elements within it that were closely allied to the spirit of the new activism, and activist history: it was implicitly collaborative and cooperative, dependent on the trust and mutual understanding inherent in the oral interview, creating links across generations and types of people; it potentially carried a strong emotional charge and urgency, often touching on issues that may have been repressed or too painful to bring easily to voice, which is why a number of theorists have linked oral history to psychoanalysis;[22] it reached people's memories in a way that few other techniques could do, creating new knowledges and hence perceptions of the world.

As early as 1977 in the USA, *Frontiers: A Journal of Women's Studies* published a special issue on 'Women's Oral History' (summer 1977). Oral history journals more widely increasingly carried articles on women's and sexual history. As the sociologist Mike Savage has observed, the narrative method could be used by feminists as a means of reasserting the power of women talking to other women. Oral history offered a 'feminist encounter' in the practice of doing history.[23] A plethora of studies have followed, exploring issues of intimate experience that might otherwise never have seen the light: changing patterns of family, including the rise of same-sex families, the upbringing of girls and boys, the emotional and material conflicts and dependencies of adolescence, the struggles of youth for independence, courtship, sexual behaviour within and outside marriage, the memories of single mothers in Catholic Magdalene houses or Mother and Baby homes forced to give up their children, survivors' tales of sexual violence, experiences of contraception and abortion, the lives of sex workers, stories of homosexuality and gender nonconformity in oppressive times, the impact of war and social change, the transformative effect of social movements and sexual communities, and so on.[24] Now we can hear these voices in books, periodicals and pamphlets but also on radio and television, through documentary and feature film, and increasingly online.

A key feature of oral history has been the often intense involvement of the researchers with the community and narrators that are being researched. People are drawn to the use of oral history methods often because of an emotional identification or political commitment – which does not in any way abnegate scholarly standards. Two classic texts of 1993 on lesbian and gay themes vividly illustrate this, both making creative use of oral history methods, whilst being open about their authors' own involvement in the communities they describe, and their personal investment in the memories they produce: Esther Newton's *Cherry Grove, Fire Island*, and Elizabeth L. Kennedy and Madeline D. Davis's *Boots of Leather, Slippers of Gold*. The first is an ethnography of 'America's first gay and lesbian town', the second a vivid recreation of a lesbian community in Buffalo, New York, from the 1930s to the 1960s.[25] Both deal with the complexities and specificities of lesbian and gay identities as they changed from the 1930s, and the class and racial tensions that shaped the communities, though their perspective is inevitably shaped by the differences between the relatively affluent and largely white and male culture of a holiday resort and the working-class, butch–femme lesbian culture of Buffalo. These two books stand out both for their scholarship and for their rootedness in the worlds they describe, marked by a sense of reciprocity and gratitude between authors and the narrators they worked with.

That is a key aspect of eliciting testimony that might otherwise not be articulated. But the power relations of the interview situation remain hazardous. In the edited collection on the practices of queer oral history *Bodies of Evidence*, there are vivid examples of the inhibitions, evasions and multiplicities of meaning in any given interview situation, especially when the power differentiations are sharply delineated. In her essay in the book, Carrie Hamilton recounts the difficulties of exploring the history of female sexuality in post-Soviet Cuba via an account of three interviews she conducted with Laura, a black woman who was a declared and active supporter of the revolution. It was only on the third interview that Laura began revealing her own lesbianism, which had earlier been obscured by her use of the male pronoun for her lover. A major factor in this tentativeness was the fact that earlier interviews had been co-conducted with an interviewer appointed by the Cuban authorities, whose heteronormative and pro-regime sentiments were transparent in the questioning. The wider context is detailed in Hamilton's book *Sexual Revolution in Cuba*, which tells of the fraught circumstances surrounding the oral history project of which Laura's interview was part.[26] Despite official backing from Mariela Castro and being signed off by her father, the president, the project experienced bureaucratic difficulties, and an insistence that the interviewees were identified through official channels, such as committees for the defence of the revolution, local branches of the Ministry of Culture, or via recommendations from Communist Party militants. Eventually the project was closed down, largely because it became clear to the authorities that people were willing to talk about the failures of the revolution as well as its achievements. The project was unofficially revived a few months later, and further interviews conducted – including Laura's third.

Not surprisingly, the early interviews had been marked by nervousness and trepidation on the part of narrators when speaking of intimate sexual feelings and experiences, especially those that ran against the dominant narrative of the revolution, whether on sexual norms or racial and class divisions. The promise of anonymity did not help: on a 'small island' like Cuba everyone knew everyone else. The later interviews, however, with less official surveillance, were more relaxed and informal – and as Hamilton shows in relation to Laura, more revealing – and cathartic.

Most oral history does not have to contend, like participants in Cuba, with anything as obviously dramatic as a world-historic revolutionary experience. But the transformations of everyday life that are remaking sexual and gender experiences across the globe can pose similar challenges to individuals' sense of self and belonging. Like all archival material, oral history records do not speak in one direction only. It should remind us again that there are multiple sexual histories and multiple voices who can speak of such complexities. Oral history can help us hear the respectable as well as the disrespected, the ordinary as well as the exotic, the conservative as well as the radical. The challenge is to grasp the power of multiple voices in history – and to do them justice.

Living Sexual History

Community-based history, like sexual history more widely, is based on a reflexive relationship between past and present. Inevitably, present preoccupations shape not only the questions we ask of the past, but also the form that ideas of the past take. A sense of the past is filtered through memory, commitment, ideology, prejudice, hope, fear and politics. What we see as the past is shaped by the present, which is why it is so contested. But if the past remains a battleground it is also in part because the past is not dead: it lives on in the present, through institutional embodiments (law, religion, education, belief systems, norms, traditions, and so on) and personal and collective identifications and memories. I chose to end this book with a discussion of community-based history because it is here that the living nature of history is most sharply felt. But the entire history of the history of sexuality has underlined that personal and collective belongings are inextricably entangled with the ways in which the past lives in the present. That subjective quality poses inevitable dangers, which is why scholars of sexual history have often gone out of their way to justify extravagantly the academic attributes of their work. The (partial and incomplete) mainstreaming of sexual history is a testimony to the high quality of the work achieved, but also to the dangers of treading on sensitivities and anxieties that still surround the subject. Yet sexual history remains vivid and relevant to many people because sexuality and gender issues are not resolved, either in those parts of the world where sexual liberalization appears to be most securely grounded, or in many parts of the global South where struggles over sexuality and gender are struggles about the very nature of the society people desire. Sexual history may no longer be as explicitly political as it was at second birth in the 1970s, but by the very nature of its subject matter, it can never be neutral.

Sexual history at its best has rewritten the way we see the past. But perhaps its most dramatic achievement has been to make us see the historic present in a new way: as a world of diversity, plural values and constant change. That may have always been the case. Now we can speak of it.

Suggestions for Further Reading

These suggestions should be used in conjunction with the notes to each chapter. I use the latter to provide precise references when I refer to important arguments or quotations. To avoid unnecessary duplication, in this section I largely focus on additional reading. I have referred to some of the classic texts where appropriate, but the main emphasis is on recent scholarship which illuminates both the debates about sexual history and the history of sexuality itself.

1 Framing Sexual History

A good overview of the development and implications of sexual history is provided by H. G. Cocks and Matt Houlbrook (eds.), *The Modern History of Sexuality*, Basingstoke: Palgrave Macmillan, 2006. See also H. G. Cocks, 'Approaches to the History of Sexuality since 1780', and Katherine Crawford, 'The Good, the Bad, and the Textual: Approaches to the Study of the Body and Sexuality, 1500–1750', in Sarah Toulalan and Kate Fisher (eds.), *Sex and the Body: 1500 to the Present*, London: Routledge, 2013, pp. 38–54, 23–37. See also what is in effect a companion volume, Kate Fisher and Sarah Toulalan (eds.), *Bodies, Sex and Desire from the Renaissance to the Present*, Basingstoke: Palgrave Macmillan, 2011, which also discusses historiographical issues. Julie Peakman has edited *The Cultural History of Sexuality*, in six volumes, London: Berg, 2011 (hardback) and London: Bloomsbury, 2014 (paperback). Several of the individual volumes are cited elsewhere in what follows. Stephen Garton, *Histories of Sexuality: Antiquity to Sexual Revolution*, London and New York: Routledge, 2002, is a well-informed and intelligent guide to key issues and themes in the emerging sexual history. Robert A. Nye (ed.), *Sexuality*, Oxford and New York, 1999, provides a comprehensive collection of articles by key authors, classical and modern, with an insightful 'Introduction: Historicizing Sexuality', pp. 3–15. Another important edited collection is Kim M. Phillips and Barry Reay (eds.), *Sexualities in History: A Reader*, New York: Routledge, 2002. On the historicization of sexual concepts see Arnold I. Davidson, *The Emergence of Sexuality: Historical Epistemology and the Formation of Concepts*, Cambridge, MA: Harvard University Press, 2001. On generations and temporalities see Elizabeth Freeman, *Time Binds: Queer Temporalities, Queer Histories*, Durham, NC: Duke University Press, 2010. For my own perspectives see *Making Sexual History*, Cambridge: Polity, 2000, and *The Languages of Sexuality*, Abingdon, London and New York: Routledge, 2011.

2 The Invention of Sexual History

There is now a flourishing scholarship that unravels the role of sexology and sexologists. For an account of the emergence of sexual ideas in the nineteenth and early twentieth centuries see Robert Deam Tobin, *Peripheral Desires: The German Discovery of Sex,* Philadelphia: University of Pennsylvania Press, 2015. Histories of sexology, which to an extent accept sexology on its own evaluation as an enlightened science, include Paul Robinson's *The Modernization of Sex: Havelock Ellis, Alfred Kinsey, William Masters, Virginia Johnson*, London: Paul Elek, 1976; and Vern L. Bullough, *Science in the Bedroom: A History of Sex Research*, New York: Basic Books, 1994. Bullough was one of the earliest in the 1970s to lament the absence of sexual history. His own contributions include Vern L. Bullough, *Sex, Society and*

History, New York: Watson Publishing International; and Vern L. Bullough and Bonnie Bullough, *Sin, Sickness and Sanity: A History of Sexual Attitudes*, New York: New American Library, 1977. For the antecedents of sexology see Roy Porter and Mikuláš Teich (eds.), *Sexual Knowledge, Sexual Science: A History of Attitudes to Sexuality*, Cambridge: Cambridge University Press, 1994; and Roy Porter and Leslie Hall, *The Facts of Life: The Creation of Sexual Knowledge in Britain, 1650–1950*, London: Yale University Press, 1995. On the links between the construction of sexual knowledge and historical interpretation see Kate Fisher and Rebecca Langlands (eds.), *Sex, Knowledge, and Receptions of the Past*, Oxford: Oxford University Press, 2015. On the USA see Helen Lefkowitz Horowitz, *Rereading Sex: Battles over Sexual Knowledge in Nineteenth-Century America*, New York: Knopf, 2002. Other works which disentangle the scientific aspirations and more complex reality of sex research, especially in the USA, are Anne Fausto Sterling, *Sexing the Body: Gender Politics and the Construction of Sexuality*, New York: Basic Books, 2000; Roger N. Lancaster, *The Trouble with Nature: Sex in Science and Popular Culture*, Berkeley: University of California Press, 2003; Janice M. Irvine, *Disorders of Desire: Sexuality and Gender in Modern American Sexology*, 1st edition 1990, revised edition Philadelphia: Temple University Press, 2005; Lisa Downing, Iain Morland and Nikki Sullivan, *Fuckology: Critical Essays on John Money's Diagnostic Concepts*, Chicago: University of Chicago Press, 2015.

For overviews of constructionist (and post-constructionist) arguments see Joseph Bristow, *Sexuality*, 2nd edition, Kindle version, New York and London: Routledge, 2010; Steven Seidman, *The Social Construction of Sexuality*, 2nd edition, New York: W. W. Norton; Jeffrey Weeks, *Sexuality*, 3rd edition, Abingdon and New York: Routledge, 2009; Stevi Jackson and Sue Scott, *Theorizing Sexuality*, Maidenhead: Open University Press, 2010. For two recent examples of the continuing invention and medicalization of 'sexual problems' see Barry Reay, Nina Attwood and Claire Gooder, *Sex Addiction: A Critical History*, Cambridge: Polity, 2015; Thea Cacchioni, *Big Pharma, Women, and the Labour of Love*, Toronto: University of Toronto Press, 2015.

3   Querying and Queering Same-Sex History

For overarching histories of homosexuality see Louis Cromp-ton, *Homosexuality and Civilization*, Cambridge, MA: Harvard University Press, 2003; Robert Aldrich (ed.), *Gay Life and Culture*, London: Thames and Hudson, 2006; Leila J. Rupp, *Sapphistries: A Global History of Love between Women*, New York: New York University Press, 2009. For key edited collections see Martin Bauml Duberman, Martha Vicinus and George Chauncey (eds.), *Hidden from History: Reclaiming the Lesbian and Gay Past*, New York: New American Library, 1989; and Henry Abelove, Michèle Aina Barale and David M. Halperin (eds.), *The Lesbian and Gay Studies Reader*, New York: Routledge, 1993. For a recent overview with pedagogy in mind see Leila J. Rupp and Susan K. Freeman (eds.), *Understanding and Teaching US Lesbian, Gay, Bisexual and Transgender History*, Madison: University of Wisconsin Press, 2014.

For studies of major theorists of homosexuality see Elena Mancini, *Magnus Hirschfeld and the Quest for Sexual Freedom: A History of the First International Sexual Freedom Movement*, New York: Palgrave Macmillan, 2010; Ivan Crozier (ed.), *Sexual Inversion: A Critical Edition (1897)*, by John Addington Symonds and Havelock Ellis, London: Pal-grave Macmillan, 2008; Hubert Kennedy, *Ulrichs: The Life and Works of Karl Heinrich Ulrichs, Pioneer of the Modern Gay Movement*, Boston: Alyson, 1988. For debate on homo-sexuality in the classical world see John Winkler, *The Con-straints of Desire: The Anthropology of Sex and Gender in Ancient Greece*, London: Routledge, 1990; James Davidson, *The Greeks and Greek Love: A Radical Reappraisal of Homosexuality in Ancient Greece*, London: Phoenix, 2008; Craig A. Williams, *Roman Homosexuality*, 2nd edition, Oxford: Oxford University Press, 2010; and David H. J. Larmour, Paul Allen Miller and Charles Platter (eds.), *Rethinking Sexuality: Foucault and Classical Antiquity*, Princeton, NJ: Princeton University Press, 1997. On medieval concepts see Robert Mills, *Seeing Sodomy in the Middle Ages*, Chicago: Chicago University Press, 2015.

For national and movement histories see (on the USA) Michael Bronski, *A Queer History of the United States*,

Boston: Beacon Press, 2011; Lillian Faderman, *The Gay Revolution: The Story of the Struggle*, New York: Simon and Schuster, 2015; (on Scandinavia) Jan Löfström (ed.), *Scandinavian Homosexualities: Essays on Gay and Lesbian Studies*, New York: Harrington Park Press, 1998; (on France) Jeffrey Merrick and Michael Sibalis (eds.), *Homosexuality in French History and Culture*, New York: Harrington Park Press, 2001; (on Australia) Robert Reynolds, *From Camp to Queer: Remaking the Australian Homosexual*, Melbourne: University of Melbourne Press, 1998; Graham Willett, *Living Out Loud: A History of Gay and Lesbian Australia*, Melbourne: Allen and Unwin, 2000; (on New Zealand) Chris Brickell, *Mates and Lovers: A History of Gay New Zealand*, Auckland: Godwit for Random House, 2008; (on Canada) Gary Kinsman, *Regulation of Desire: Homo and Hetero Sexualities*, Montreal: Black Rose, 1995; (on Britain) Matt Cook (ed.) with Robert Mills, Randolph Trumbach and H. G. Cocks, *A Gay History of Britain: Love and Sex Between Men since the Middle Ages*, Oxford and Westport, CN: Greenwood, 2007; Rebecca Jennings, *A Lesbian History of Britain: Love and Sex between Women since 1500*, Oxford and Westport, CN: Greenwood, 2007. For the significance of shifts in the nineteenth century in Britain see Charles Upchurch, *Before Wilde: Sex between Men in Britain's Age of Reform*, Berkeley, Los Angeles and London: University of California Press, 2009; Sean Brady, *Masculinity and Male Homosexuality in Britain, 1861–1913*, Basingstoke and New York: Palgrave Macmillan. For important revisionist accounts of pre-Stonewall homophile politics see Julian Jackson, *Living in Arcadia: Homosexuality, Politics and Morality in France from the Liberation to AIDS*, Chicago: University of Chicago Press, 2009; Marc Stein, *Rethinking the Gay and Lesbian Movement*, New York: Routledge, 2012. On urban influences see David Higgs (ed.), *Queer Sites: Gay Urban Histories since 1600*, New York and London: Routledge, 1999; Matt Cook and Jennifer Evans, *Queer Cities, Queer Cultures: Europe since 1945*, London Bloomsbury, 2014; Chad Heap, *Homosexuality in the City: A Century of Research at the University of Chicago*, Chicago: University of Chicago Press, 2000; Frank Mort, *Capital Affairs: The Making of the Permissive Society*, London: Yale University Press, 2010.

On the impact of queer history see the special issue of *Social Text* 84–5, 23 (3–4), Fall/Winter 2005, edited by David L. Eng, Judith Halberstam and José Esteban Muñoz, and especially the introduction, pp. 1–17, 'What is Queer about Queer Studies Now?'; Brian Lewis (ed.), *British Queer History: New Approaches and Perspectives*, Manchester: Manchester University Press, 2013; and the special issue on the same theme of *Journal of British History* 51 (3), July 2012. See also articles in Donald Hall and Anne Marie Jagose (eds.), *The Routledge Queer Studies Reader*, New York and London: Routledge, 2012. For discussions of gender ambiguity and transgender in history see Esther Newton, *Mother Camp: Female Impersonators in America*, Chicago: University of Chicago Press, 1999; Julia Epstein and Kristina Straub (eds.), *Body Guards: The Cultural Politics of Gender Ambiguity*, New York and London: Routledge, 1991; Susan Stryker, *Transgender History*, Berkeley: Seal Press, 2008. For the history of the emergence of the perversions and non-normative sexualities generally see Julia Peakman, *The Pleasure's All Mine: A History of Perverse Sex*, London: Reaktion Books, 2013; Julia Peakman (ed.), *Sexual Perversions 1670–1890*, Basingstoke: Palgrave Macmillan, 2009; Vernon Rosario, *The Exotic Imagination: French History of Perversion*, Oxford: Oxford University Press, 1997. On sadomasochism see Alison Moore, *Sexual Myths of Modernity: Sadism, Masochism and Historical Teleology*, Lexington: Lanham, 2010.

4 Gender, Sexuality and Power

Key radical feminist works include: Robin Morgan (ed.), *Sisterhood is Powerful*, New York: Random House, 1973; Mary Daly, *Gyn/Ecology: The Metaethics of Radical Feminism*, London: Women's Press, 1979 (first published 1978); Kathleen Barry, *Female Sexual Slavery*, Englewood Cliffs, NJ: Prentice Hall, 1979; Laura Lederer (ed.), *Take Back the Night: Women on Pornography*, New York: William Morrow, 1980. Andrea Dworkin, though very much not a historian, had a powerful effect on some historians. See her *Pornography: Men Possessing Women*, London: Women's Press, 1981, and *Intercourse*, New York: Free Press, 1989. Sheila Jeffreys has extended the radical and revolutionary interpretation of male power in a series of studies: see her *Anticlimax: Feminist Perspectives on the Sexual Revolution*, London: Women's Press, 1990; *Unpacking Queer Politics: A Lesbian Feminist Perspective*, Cambridge: Polity, 2002; *Gender Hurts: A Feminist Analysis of the Politics of Transgenderism*, London: Routledge: 2014. Studies of violence from a different feminist perspective include Linda Gordon, *Heroes of their Own Lives: The Politics and History of Family Violence, Boston, 1880–1960*, New York and London: Virago, 1988. For British critiques of revolutionary feminism see Lynne Segal, *Is the Future Female? Troubled Thoughts on Contemporary Feminism*, London: Virago, 1987; Lynne Segal and Mary McIntosh (eds.), *Sex Exposed: Sexuality and the Pornography Debates*, London: Virago, 1992.

Two classic edited books by Martha Vicinus, *Suffer and be Still: Women in the Victorian Age*, London: Methuen, 1972, and *A Widening Sphere: Changing Roles of Victorian Women*, London: Methuen, 1980, bookend the first decade of feminist history. These brought together what were to become classic articles. Key texts on struggles over reproductive rights in the USA include James Mohr, *Abortion in America: The Origin and Evolution of National Policy, 1800–1900*, New York: Oxford University Press, 1978; James Reed, *From Private Vice to Public Virtue: The Birth Control Movement and American Society since 1830*, New York: Basic Books, 1978. Parallel studies on the UK include Angus McLaren, *Birth Control in Nineteenth-Century England: A Social and Intellectual History*, London: Croom Helm, 1978, and *Reproductive Rituals: Perceptions of Fertility in Britain from the 16th Century to the 19th Century*, London: Methuen, 1984; Kate Fisher, *Birth Control, Sex and Marriage in Britain 1918–1960*, Oxford: Oxford University Press, 2006.

Judith R. Walkowitz's *Nights Out: Life in Cosmopolitan London*, New Haven: Yale University Press, 2012, extends her analysis of city and sexual life into the twentieth century. Other works on feminism and social purity include: Edward Bristow, *Vice and Vigilance*, Dublin: Gill and Macmillan, 1977 (on Britain); David J. Pivar, *Purity Crusade: Sexual Morality and Social Control, 1868–1900*, Westport, CN:

Greenwood, 1973, and *Purity and Hygiene: Women, Prosti-tution and the 'American Plan', 1900–1930*, Westport, CN: Greenwood, 2002 (on the USA).

On the development of the category of gender in history see Joan Scott, *Gender and the Politics of History*, New York: Columbia University, 1988; Laura Lee Downs, *Writing Gender History*, 2nd edition, London: Bloomsbury, 2010; Sonya O. Rose, *What is Gender History?*, Cambridge: Polity, 2010; Judith Butler and Elizabeth Weed, *The Question of Gender: J. W. Scott's Critical Feminism*, Bloomington: Indiana University Press, 2011. The two defining essays by Gayle S. Rubin, 'The Traffic in Women: Notes on the "Political Economy" of Sex' and 'Thinking Sex: Notes for a Radical Theory of the Politics of Sexuality', are republished, together with various commentaries and modifications by the author, in her *Deviations: A Gayle Rubin Reader*, Durham, NC: Duke University Press, 2011. The impact of Rubin's essay 'Thinking Sex' is discussed in various contributions, includ-ing by Rubin herself, in a special edition of *GLQ: A Journal of Lesbian and Gay Studies* 17 (1), 2011. On the 'cultural turn' see Geoff Eley, *A Crooked Line: From Cultural History to the History of Society*, Ann Arbor: University of Michigan Press, 2005.

For a wide-ranging discussion of the difficulties of inter-sectional theories relating to sexuality, see Yvette Taylor, Sally Hines and Mark Casey (eds.), *Theorizing Intersectionality and Sexuality*, London: Palgrave, 2010. See also Jennifer C. Nash, 'Re-Thinking Intersectionality', *Feminist Review* 89, 2008, pp. 1–15. An important collection drawn from the *Journal of the History of Sexuality* is John Fout and Maura Shaw Tantillo (eds.), *American Sexual Politics: Sex, Gender and Race since the Civil War*, Chicago: Chicago University Press, 1993. On black feminist interventions see essays in Janet Price and Margaret Shildrick (eds.), *Feminist Theory and the Body: A Reader*, New York and London: Routledge, 1997. For a critically queer African-American perspective see Roderick A. Ferguson, *Aberrations in Black: Toward a Queer of Color Critique*, Minneapolis: University of Minnesota Press, 2004, and 'Of our Normative Strivings: African-American Studies and the Histories of Sexuality', in David L.

Eng, Judith Halberstam and José Esteban Muñoz (eds.), *Social Text* 84–5, 23 (3–4), Fall/Winter 2005, pp. 85–100.

On the history of masculinity as a distinctive field see Michael Roper and John Tosh (eds.), *Manful Assertions: Masculinities in Britain since 1800*, London: Routledge, 1991; Michael S. Kimmel, *The History of Men: Essays on the History of American and British Masculinities*, Albany: State University of New York Press, 2005, and *Manhood in America: A Cultural History*, 3rd edition, Oxford: Oxford University Press, 2012. See also J. A. Mangan and James Walvin (eds.), *Manliness and Morality: Middle-Class Masculinity in Britain and America 1800–1940*, Manchester: Manchester University Press, 1987; Angus McLaren, *The Trials of Masculinity: Policing Sexual Boundaries, 1830–1930*, Chicago: Chicago University Press, 1997, and *Impotence: A Cultural History*, Chicago: University of Chicago Press, 2007; George L. Mosse, *The Image of Man: The Creation of Modern Masculinity*, Oxford: Oxford University Press, 1996.

5 Mainstreaming Sexual History

For overviews of sexuality in Europe during this period see Anna Clark, *Desire: A History of European Sexuality*, London and New York: Routledge, 2008; and Dagmar Herzog, *Sexuality in Europe: A Twentieth-Century History*, Cambridge: Cambridge University Press, 2011.

A symposium on Thomas Laqueur's important work can be found in *Sexualities* 12, August 2009, including an essay by Laqueur himself, 'Sexuality and the Transformation of Culture: The Longue Durée', pp. 418–36. For a classic study of the making of the sexual order in Germany see Isabel V. Hull, *Sexuality, State and Civil Society in Germany, 1700–1815*, Ithaca, NY: Cornell University Press, 1997. For an influential anatomy of nineteenth-century modalities see Peter Gay, *The Bourgeois Experience: Victoria to Freud. Vol. 1: Education of the Senses* and *Vol. 2: The Tender Passion*, New York: Oxford University Press, 1984, 1986. On attitudes to children and childhood sexuality see Philip Jenkins, *Moral Panic: Changing Concepts of the Child Molester in*

Modern America, New Haven: Yale University Press, 1998; Louise A. Jackson, *Childhood Sexual Abuse in Victorian England*, London: Routledge, 2000; R. Danielle Egan and Gail Hawkes, *Theorizing the Sexual Child in Modernity*, New York: Palgrave Macmillan, 2010; and Hawkes and Egan, 'Sex, Popular Beliefs and Culture: Discourses on the Sexual Child', in Chiara Beccalossi and Ivan Crozier (eds.), *A Cultural History of Sexuality in the Age of Empire*, London: Bloomsbury, 2014, pp. 123–44; Stephen Angelides, 'Feminism, Child Sexual Abuse, and the Erasure of Child Sexuality', *GLQ: A Journal of Lesbian and Gay Studies* 10 (2), 2004, pp. 141–77, and 'Historicizing Affect, Psychoanalyzing History: Pedophilia and the Discourse of Child Sexuality', *Journal of Homosexuality* 46 (1–2), 2004, pp. 79–109; Linda Gordon, 'The Politics of Child Sex Abuse: Notes from American History', *Feminist Review* 28, 1988, pp. 56–64; James R. Kincaid, *Erotic Innocence: The Culture of Child Molesting*, Durham, NC: Duke University Press, 1998. On moral panics see Gilbert Herdt (ed.), *Moral Panics, Sex Panics: Fear and the Fight over Sexual Rights*, New York: New York University Press, 2009. On the role of religion see Lucy Delap and Sue Morgan (eds.), *Men, Masculinities and Religious Change in Twentieth-Century Britain*, London and Abingdon: Routledge, 2013; Heather White, *Reforming Sodom: Protestants and the Rise of Gay Rights*, Chapel Hill: University of North Carolina Press, 2015; Neil J. Young, *We Gather Together: The Religious Right and the Problem of Interfaith Politics*, New York: Oxford University Press, 2015.

On the ambiguities of twentieth-century sexual modernity see Dagmar Herzog (ed.), *Sexuality and German Fascism*, New York: Berghahn Books, 2005; and Dagmar Herzog, *Sex after Fascism: Memory and Morality in Twentieth-Century Germany*, Princeton, NJ: Princeton University Press, 2005. For acute feminist autobiographies which reflect on the male sexual revolution see Sheila Rowbotham, *Promise of a Dream: Remembering the Sixties*, London and New York: Verso, 2001; Lynne Segal, *Making Trouble: Life and Politics*, London: Serpent's Tail, 2007. See also Cas Wouters, *Sex and Manners: Female Emancipation in the West, 1890–2000*, London: Sage, 2004. For British perspectives on the sexual revolution, see Jeffrey Weeks, *The World We Have Won: The*

Remaking of Erotic and Intimate Life, London and New York: Routledge, 2007. A challenging focus on German sexual history, including the sexual revolution, can be found in Scott Spector, Helmut Puff and Dagmar Herzog (eds.), *After the History of Sexuality: German Genealogies with and beyond Foucault*, New York: Berghahn Books, 2012. See particularly Massimo Perinelli's chapter, 'Love, Lust, Violence, Liberation: Discourses on Sexuality on the Radical Left in West Germany, 1967–1972'. Dagmar Herzog explores the lessons from the sexual revolution learned by the American New Right in *Sex in Crisis: The New Sexual Revolution and the Future of America Politics*, New York: Basic Books, 2008. For pioneering studies of American fundamentalist perspectives see Didi Herman, *The Antigay Agenda: Orthodox Vision and the Christian Right*, Chicago: University of Chicago Press, 1997; Angelia Wilson, *Below the Belt: Sexuality and Politics in the Rural South*, New York: Continuum, 1999.

The multiple histories of the AIDS epidemic are dissected in Elizabeth Fee and Daniel M. Fox (eds.), *AIDS: The Burdens of History*, Berkeley: University of California Press, 1988, and *AIDS: The Making of a Chronic Disease*, Berkeley: University of California Press, 1992; Virginia Berridge and Philip Strong (eds.), *AIDS and Contemporary History*, Cambridge: Cambridge University Press, 1993. The implications of AIDS for social policy are discussed in Ronald Bayer, *AIDS in the Industrialized Democracies: Passions, Politics and Policies*, New Brunswick: Rutgers University Press, 1992; Ronald Bayer and Eric Feldman (eds.), *Blood Feuds: AIDS, Blood, and the Politics of Medical Disaster*, Oxford: Oxford University Press, 1999. Dennis Altman was a pioneer in stressing the extraordinary grassroots response to the epidemic. See his overview in *The End of the Homosexual?*, St Lucia, Queensland: University of Queensland Press, 2013. On British grassroots responses see the relevant chapters in my *Making Sexual History*, Cambridge: Polity, 2000. On different local and national activisms see Michael P. Brown, *RePlacing Citizenship: AIDS Activism and Radical Democracy*, New York: Guilford Press, 1997 (based on a study in Vancouver, British Columbia); Jennifer Power, *Movement, Knowledge, Emotion: Gay Activism and HIV/AIDS in*

Australia, Canberra: ANU Press, 2011; Deborah Gould, *Moving Politics: Emotions and ACT UP's Fight against AIDS*, Chicago: Chicago University Press, 2009; Daniel Defert, *Une Vie Politque*, Paris: Editions de Seuil, 2014.

On same-sex marriage, Kelly Kollman provides a detailed discussion of the contemporary policy background in *The Same-Sex Unions Revolution in Western Democracies: International Norms and Domestic Policy Change*, Manchester: Manchester University Press, 2013. On Scandinavia: Jens Rydström, *Odd Couples: A History of Gay Marriage in Scandinavia*, Amsterdam: Aksant, 2011. For France: Eric Fassin, 'Same Sex, Different Politics: "Gay Marriage" Debates in France and the United States', *Public Culture* 13 (2), 2001, pp. 215–32; C. Johnston, 'The PACS and (Post)Queer Citizenship in Contemporary Republican France', *Sexualities* 11 (6), December 2008, pp. 688–705. On Britain: Nicola Barker and Daniel Monk (eds.), *From Civil Partnerships to Same-Sex Marriage: Interdisciplinary Reflections*, London: Routledge, 2015. On the Netherlands: K. Waaldijk, 'Small Change: How the Road to Same-Sex Marriage Got Paved in the Netherlands', in Robert Wintermute and M. Andenaes (eds.), *Legal Recognition of Same-Sex Partnerships: A Study of National, European and International Law*, Oxford: Hart, 2001, pp. 437–64. On Southern Europe: Ana Cristina Santos, *Social Movements and Sexual Citizenship in Southern Europe*, London: Palgrave Macmillan, 2013. On the USA: George Chauncey, *Why Marriage? The History Shaping Today's Debate Over Gay Equality*, New York: Basic Books, 2004; M. J. Klarman, *From the Closet to the Altar: Courts, Backlash and the Struggle for Same-Sex Marriage*, Oxford: Oxford University Press, 2013; A. L. Brandzel, 'Queering Citizenship? Same-Sex Marriage and the State', *GLQ: A Journal of Lesbian and Gay Studies* 11 (2), 2005, pp. 171–204; P. Kandaswamy, 'State Austerity and the Racial Politics of Same-Sex Marriage in the United States', *Sexualities* 11 (6), December 2008, pp. 706–25.

On same-sex parenting see: Karen Griffin and Linda Mulholland (eds.), *Lesbian Mothers in Europe*, London: Cassell, 1997; Gillian Hanscombe and Jacqueline Forster, *Rocking the Cradle: Lesbian Mothers – A Challenge in Family Living*, London: Sheba Feminist Press, 1983; Ellen Lewin, *Lesbian*

Mothers: Accounts of Gender in American Culture, Ithaca, NY: Cornell University Press, 1993; Judith Stacey, *Unhitched: Love, Marriage, and Family Values from West Hollywood to Western China*, New York: New York University Press, 2011. On 'friends as family' see Kath Weston, *Families We Choose: Lesbians, Gays, Kinship*, New York: Columbia University Press, 1991; Peter Nardi, *Gay Men's Friendships: Invincible Communities*, Chicago: Chicago University Press, 1999; Jeffrey Weeks, Brian Heaphy and Catherine Donovan, *Same Sex Intimacies: Families of Choice and other Life Experiments*, London: Routledge, 2001.

On intimacy see Steven Seidman, *Romantic Longings: Love in America, 1830–1980*, New York: Routledge, 1991. and *Embattled Eros: Sexual Politics and Ethics in Contemporary America*, New York: Routledge, 1992. Some of the same ground is covered for Britain in Marcus Collins, *Modern Love: An Intimate History of Men and Women in Twentieth-Century Britain*, London: Atlantic Books, 2003. The developing debate on sexual or intimate citizenship has been a key vehicle for rethinking inclusion and exclusion, belonging and marginality. Ken Plummer has made a major contribution in *Telling Sexual Stories: Power, Change and Social Worlds*, London and New York: Routledge, 1995, and *Intimate Citizenship: Private Decisions and Public Dialogue*, Seattle: University of Washington Press, 2003. My own contribution can be found in 'The Sexual Citizen', *Theory, Culture and Society* 15 (3–4), 1998, pp. 35–52. Critical accounts of the concept can be found in David Bell and Jon Binnie, *The Sexual Citizen: Queer Politics and Beyond*, Cambridge: Polity, 2000; Laura Berlant, *The Queen of America Goes to Washington: Essays on Sex and Citizenship*, Durham, NC: Duke University Press, 1997; Shane Phelan, *Sexual Strangers: Gays, Lesbians and Dilemmas of Citizenship*, Philadelphia: Temple University Press, 2001.

6 The Globalization of Sexual History

The transnational turn is discussed in an American Historical Association Forum in the *American Historical Review* 114 (5), 2009. See Margot Canaday, 'Thinking Sex in the

Transnational Turn', pp. 1250–1, with further contributions on the USA, Africa, Asia, Europe, the Middle East and Latin America. Peter L. Stearns provides a succinct global history in *Sexuality in World History*, London and New York: Routledge, 2009. An earlier pioneering book is Vern L. Bullough, *Sexual Variance in Society and History*, Chicago: Chicago University Press, 1976. Angus McLaren provides a useful but largely Western focus in *Twentieth-Century Sexuality: A History*, Oxford: Blackwell, 1999. See also Peter Aggleton and Richard Parker (eds.), *Routledge Handbook of Sexuality, Health and Rights*, London and New York: Routledge, 2010. For discussion of transnational trends in relation to reproduction see Rosalind Petchesky and Karen Judd, *Negotiating Reproductive Rights: Women's Perspectives Across Countries and Cultures*, London: Zed Books, 1998; Carole H. Browner and Carolyn F. Sargent (eds.), *Reproduction, Globalization, and the State: New Theoretical and Ethnographic Perspectives*, Durham, NC, and London: Duke University Press, 2011; Michi Knecht, Maren Klitz and Stefan Bech (eds.), *Reproductive Technologies as Global Form: Ethnographies of Knowledges, Practices and Transnational Encounters*, Chicago: University of Chicago Press, 2012; Amy Lind (ed.), *Development, Sexual Rights and Global Governance*, London: Routledge, 2010. On global homosexualities and the rise of international LGBTQ movements see Barry D. Adam, Jan Willem Duyvendak and Andre Krouwel (eds.), *The Global Emergence of Gay and Lesbian Politics: National Imprints of a Worldwide Movement*, Philadelphia: Temple University Press, 1999; Manon Tremblay, David Paternotte and Carol Johnson (eds.), *The Lesbian and Gay Movement and the State: Comparative Insights into a Transformed Relationship*, Farnham: Ashgate, 2011.

For African sexual history see Marc Epprecht, *Sexuality and Sexual Justice in Africa: Rethinking Homophobia and Forging Resistance*, London and New York: Zed Books, 2013; S. N. Nyeck and Marc Epprecht (eds.), *Sexual Diversity in Africa: Politics, Theory and Citizenship*, Montreal: McGill-Queens University Press, 2013; Ruth Morgan and Saskia E. Wieringa (eds.), *Tommy Boys, Lesbian Men and Ancestral Wives: Female Same-Sex Experiences in Southern Africa*, Auckland Park, SA: Jacana Media, 2005; Saheed

Aderinto, *When Sex Threatened the State: Illicit Sexuality, Nationalism and Politics in Colonial Nigeria, 1900–1958*, Champaign: University of Illinois Press, 2015.

On China see Harriet Evans, *Women and Sexuality in China: Female Sexuality and Gender since 1949*, London: Continuum, 1997; Harriet Evans and Julia C. Strauss, *Gender in Flux: Agency and its Limits in Contemporary China*, Cambridge: Cambridge University Press, 2011; Elaine Jeffreys with Haiqing Yu, *Sex in China*, Cambridge: Polity, 2015. Travis S. K. Kong provides a well-researched study of same-sex practices in Hong Kong and China as a whole, *Chinese Male Homosexualities: Memba, Tongzhi and Golden Boy*, London: Routledge, 2011. Another Chinese-dominated island state is analysed in Audrey Yue and Jun Zubillaga-Pow (eds.), *Queer Singapore: Illiberal Citizenship and Mediated Cultures*, Hong Kong: Hong Kong University Press, 2012. On India see Mrinalini Sinha, *Colonial Masculinity: The 'Manly Englishman' and the 'Effeminate Bengali' in the late Nineteenth Century*, Manchester and New York: Manchester University Press, 1995, and *Specters of Mother India: The Global Restructuring of an Empire*, Durham, NC: Duke University Press, 2006. See also Gerard Sullivan and Peter A. Jackson (eds.), 'Gay and Lesbian Asia: Culture, Identity, Community', special issue of *Journal of Homosexuality* 40 (3/4), 2001. On the Philippines see Mark Johnson, *Beauty and Power: Transgendering and Cultural Transformations in the Southern Philippines*, Oxford and New York: Berg, 1997.

Joseph A. Massad has continued his analysis of Islam in *Islam in Liberalism*, Chicago: University of Chicago Press, 2015. On Latin America see Roger Lancaster, *Life is Hard: Machismo, Danger and Intimacy of Power in Nicaragua*, Berkeley and Los Angeles: University of California Press, 1992; Joseph Carrier, *De Los Otros: Intimacy and Homosexuality among Mexican Men*, New York: Columbia University Press, 1995; Richard Parker, *Beneath the Equator: Cultures of Desire, Male Homosexuality and Emerging Gay Communities in Brazil*, London: Routledge, 1999; Noelle M. Stout, *After Love: Queer Intimacy and Erotic Economies in Post-Soviet Cuba*, Durham, NC: Duke University Press, 2014.

On the remaking and queering of European sexualities see Lisa Downing and Robert Gillett (eds.), *Queer in Europe*, Farnham: Ashgate, 2011; Philip M. Ayoub and David Paternotte (eds.), *LGBT Activism and the Making of Europe: A Rainbow Europe?*, Basingstoke: Palgrave Macmillan, 2014; and Rober Kulpa and Joanna Mizielińska (eds.), *De-Centring Western Sexualities: Central and Eastern European Perspectives*, Farnham: Ashgate, 2011. On the biggest country in Europe, Russia, with a distinctive history, see Igor S. Kon, *The Sexual Revolution in Russia: From the Age of the Czars to Today*, New York, Free Press, 1995; Laurie Essig, *Queer in Russia: A Study of Sex, Self, and the Other*, Durham, NC: Duke University Press, 1999.

On human rights see Sonia Corrêa, Rosalind Petchesky and Richard Parker, *Sexuality, Health and Human Rights*, London and New York: Routledge, 2008. On LGBTQ human rights see the special issue of *Contemporary Politics* 15 (1), 2009. On humanism and posthumanism see 'Dossier: Theorizing Queer Inhumanisms', *GLQ: A Journal of Lesbian and Gay Studies* 114 (5), 2015, pp. 1273–86.

7 Memory, Community, Voice

For discussion of history in a postcolonial context see Michel-Rolph Trouillot, *Silencing the Past: Power and the Production of History*, Boston: Beacon Press, 2015. On the queer archive see the special edition of *Radical History Review* (120), Fall 2014, edited by Daniel Marshall, Kevin P. Murphy and Zeb Tortorici. As examples of specialist archives see R. D. Ridinger, 'Things Visible and Invisible: The Leather Archives and Museum', *Journal of Homosexuality* 43 (1), 2002, pp. 1–9; Aaron H. Devor, *The Transgender Archives: Foundations for the Future*, Victoria, BC: University of Victoria Libraries, 2014. On life histories see Ken Plummer's *Documents of Life 2*, London: Sage, 2002.

Notes

Introduction

1 Compare Vern L. Bullough, 'Sex in History: A Virgin Field', in *Sex, Society and History*, New York: Science History Publications, 1976, pp. 1–16.
2 This is an adaption of a schema first outlined in Jeffrey Weeks, *The World We Have Won: The Remaking of Erotic and Intimate Life*, London and New York: Routledge, 2007, pp. 4–7, and subsequently used in Jeffrey Weeks, 'What's History Got To Do With It? Researching Sexual Histories', in Jennifer Mason and Angela Dale (eds.), *Understanding Social Research: Thinking Creatively about Method*, Los Angeles, London and New Delhi: Sage, 2011, pp. 181–94.
3 Michel Foucault, *The History of Sexuality. Vol. 1: An Introduction*, London: Penguin, 1979.
4 Cas Wouters, *Informalization: Manners and Emotions since 1890*, London: Sage, 2007.
5 Lisa Duggan, *The Twilight of Equality? Neoliberalism, Cultural Politics, and the Attack on Democracy*, Boston: Beacon Press, 2003.

1 Framing Sexual History

1 See my account of identities as 'necessary fictions' in Jeffrey Weeks, *Invented Moralities: Sexual Values in an Age of Uncertainty*, Cambridge: Polity, 1995; and Scott Bravmann, *Queer*

Fictions of the Past: History, Culture, and Difference, Cambridge: Cambridge University Press, 1997.

2 See, for example, Laura Doan, *Disturbing Practices: History, Sexuality and Women's Experience of Modern War*, Chicago: University of Chicago Press, 2013.

3 On the sexual archive see Ann Cvetkovich, *An Archive of Feelings: Trauma, Sexuality, and Lesbian Public Culture*, Durham, NC: Duke University Press, 2003; and a further discussion in chapter 7.

4 James Procter, *Stuart Hall*, London: Routledge, 2004, p. 54.

5 Full references to these works are given in chapter 2, and in the suggestions for further reading.

6 Eve Kosofsky Sedgwick, *Epistemology of the Closet*, Berkeley: University of California Press, 1990; Adrienne Rich, 'Compulsory Heterosexuality and Lesbian Existence', *Signs* 5 (4), 1980, pp. 631–66. See chapters 3 and 4 for further discussion.

7 Carol S. Vance (ed.), *Pleasure and Danger: Exploring Female Sexuality*, New York: Routledge and Kegan Paul, 1984.

8 Elizabeth Grosz, *Volatile Bodies: Towards a Corporeal Feminism*, Bloomington: Indiana University Press, 1994.

9 Donna Haraway, *Simians, Cyborgs and Women: The Reinvention of Nature*, London: Free Association Books, 1991.

10 Alison Kafer, *Feminist, Queer, Crip*, Bloomington: Indiana University Press, 2013.

11 Anthony Giddens, *Modernity and Self-Identity: Self and Society in the Late Modern Age*, Cambridge: Polity, 1991.

12 Raewyn Connell, *Masculinities*, 2nd edition, Cambridge: Polity, 2005, p. 64.

13 John H. Gagnon and William Simon, *Sexual Conduct: The Social Sources of Human Sexuality*, London: Hutchinson, 1974; Ken Plummer, *Sexual Stigma: An Interactionist Account*, London: Routledge and Kegan Paul, 1975.

14 See Jeffrey Weeks, *Sex, Politics and Society: The Regulation of Sexuality since 1800*, 1st edition, Harlow: Longman, 1981, ch. 1, and *Making Sexual History*, Cambridge: Polity, 2000, pp. 86–105.

15 Henrietta L. Moore, *Still Life: Hopes, Desires and Satisfactions*, Cambridge: Polity, 2011, p. 158.

16 Heather Love, *Feeling Backward: Loss and the Politics of Queer History*, Cambridge, MA: Harvard University Press, 2007, p. 12. For a wider discussion of these themes see Margaret Wetherell, *Affect and Emotion: A New Social Science Understanding*, London: Sage, 2012; W. Reddy, *The*

Navigation of Feelings: A Framework for the History of Emotions, Cambridge: Cambridge University Press, 2001.

17 Eve Kosofsky Sedgwick, *Touching Feeling: Affect, Pedagogy, Performativity*, Durham, NC: Duke University Press, 2003, p. 97.

18 Ken Plummer, 'Generational Sexualities: Subterranean Traditions and the Hauntings of the Sexual World: Some Preliminary Research', *Social Interactions* 33 (2), 2010, pp. 163–91.

19 Chris Waters, 'Distance and Desire in the New British Queer History', *GLQ: A Journal of Gay and Lesbian Studies* 14 (1), 2008, pp. 139–55, discusses such a 'generational clash', citing as an example a radio discussion between myself and Matt Houlbrook.

20 Arnold I. Davidson, *The Emergence of Sexuality: Historical Epistemology and the Formation of Concepts*, Cambridge, MA: Harvard University Press, 2001, p. 53.

21 Mitchell Dean, *Critical and Effective Histories: Foucault's Methods and Historical Sociology*, London and New York: Routledge, 1994, p. 14.

22 Ken Plummer, 'Afterword: Liberating Generational Continuities and Change in the Radical Queer Western Era', in David Paternotte and Manon Tremblay (eds.), *The Ashgate Companion to Lesbian and Gay Activism*, Farnham: Ashgate, 2015, pp. 339–56.

23 Judith/Jack Halberstam, *In a Queer Time and Place: Transgender Bodies, Subcultural Lives*, New York: New York University Press, 2005.

2 The Invention of Sexual History

1 Sigmund Freud, *Introductory Lectures on Sexuality. Vol. 1*, Pelican Freud Library, Harmondsworth: Pelican Books, 1975, p. 41.

2 Arnold I. Davidson, *The Emergence of Sexuality: Historical Epistemology and the Formation of Concepts*, Cambridge, MA: Harvard University Press, 2001, p. 141.

3 For the emergence of the concepts of homosexuality and inversion see Judit Takács, 'The Double Life of Kertbeny', in Gert Hekma (ed.), *Past and Present of Radical Sexual Politics*, Amsterdam: UvA – Mosse Foundation, 2004, pp. 26–40; Herbert Kennedy, *Ulrichs: The Life and Works of Karl Heinrich Ulrichs, Pioneer of the Modern Gay Movement*, Boston: Alyson, 1988.

4   See discussion in Jeffrey Weeks, *Sexuality and its Discontents: Meanings, Myths and Modern Sexualities*, London: Routledge and Kegan Paul, 1985, pp. 64–72.

5   Thomas W. Laqueur, *Solitary Sex: A Cultural History of Masturbation*, London: Zone Books, 2003.

6   The outstanding study is Harry Oosterhuis, *Stepchildren of Nature: Krafft-Ebing, Psychiatry and the Making of Sexual Identity*, Chicago: University of Chicago Press, 2000.

7   On sexology see Lucy Bland and Laura Doan (eds.), *Sexology in Culture: Labelling Bodies and Desires* and *Sexuality Uncensored: The Documents of Sexual Science*, Cambridge: Polity, 1998.

8   Quoted in Davidson, *Emergence*, p. 63.

9   Oosterhuis shows this clearly in *Stepchildren*.

10 A summary of pre-sexology discussions of sex can be found in Chiara Beccalossi and Ivan Crozier (eds.), *A Cultural History of Sexuality in the Age of Empire*, London: Bloomsbury, 2014, pp. 6–7.

11 W. E. H. Lecky, *A History of European Morals from Augustus to Charlemagne*, 2 vols., London: Longmans, Green, 1869; Keith Thomas, 'The Double Standard', *Journal of the History of Ideas* 20 (2), April 1959, pp. 195–216.

12 Iwan Bloch, *The Sexual Life of Our Time in its Relation to Modern Civilization* (first published in German 1906), New York: Allied Books, 1908.

13 See the critical edition edited by Ivan Crozier: Havelock Ellis and John Addington Symonds, *Sexual Inversion (1897)*, London: Palgrave, 2008.

14 Edvard Westermarck, *The Origin and Development of the Moral Idea*, 2 vols., London: Macmillan, 1908; David Halperin, *One Hundred Years of Homosexuality, and Other Essays on Greek Love*, London: Routledge, 1990.

15 Hans Licht, *Sexual Life in Ancient Greece*, London: G. Routledge, 1931; Kenneth Dover, *Greek Homosexuality*, New York: Random House, 1980.

16 Max Hodann, *History of Modern Morals*, London: William Heinemann, 1937; Lesley A. Hall, *The Life and Times of Stella Browne: Feminist and Free Spirit*, London: I. B. Tauris, 2011.

17 See, for example, *Bernstein on Homosexuality*, Belfast: Atholl Books, n.d., and my discussion of the theme in Jeffrey Weeks, *Sex, Politics and Society: The Regulation of Sexuality since 1800*, 3rd edition, London: Routledge, 2012, pp. 214–20. The most sustained recent attempt at a Marxist reading of homo-

sexuality can be found in Peter Drucker, *Warped: Gay Normality and Queer Anti-Capitalism*, Leiden: Brill, 2015.

18 Gordon Rattray Taylor, *Sex in History*, London: Thames and Hudson, 1953, p. 13.

19 Steven Marcus, *The Other Victorians: A Study of Sexuality and Pornography in Mid-Nineteenth-Century England*, London: Weidenfeld and Nicolson, 1967.

20 Lawrence Stone, *The Family, Sex and Marriage in England 1500–1800*, London: Weidenfeld and Nicolson, 1977, p. 666.

21 Edward Shorter, *The Making of the Modern Family*, London: Fontana, 1977.

22 Peter Laslett, *The World We Have Lost*, London: Methuen, 1965. The family reconstitution and related demographic literature is discussed in Simon Szreter, *Fertility, Class and Gender in Britain, 1860–1940*, Cambridge: Cambridge University Press, 1996; Hera Cook, *The Long Sexual Revolution: English Women, Sex, and Contraception 1800–1975*, Oxford: Oxford University Press, 2004.

23 E. P. Thompson, *The Making of the English Working Class*, Harmondsworth: Penguin, 1967.

24 Robert A. Padgug, 'Sexual Matters: On Conceptualizing Sexuality in History', *Radical History Review* 20, Spring/Summer 1979, pp. 3–23 at p. 5.

25 John H. Gagnon and William Simon, *Sexual Conduct: The Social Sources of Human Sexuality*, London: Hutchinson, 1974.

26 See Peter L. Berger and Thomas Luckman, *The Social Construction of Reality: A Treatise in the Sociology of Knowledge*, Harmondsworth: Penguin, 1991. Chris Brickell has provided a clear overview of the implications of these approaches for historical work in 'A Symbolic Interactionist History of Sexuality?', *Rethinking History* 10 (3), 2010, pp. 415–32.

27 Ken Plummer, *Sexual Stigma: An Interactionist Account*, London: Routledge and Kegan Paul, 1975.

28 John Boswell, 'Revolutions, Universals and Sexual Categories', *Salmagundi* 59 (9), Fall 1982/Winter 1983, pp. 89–113.

29 Mary McIntosh, 'The Homosexual Role', *Social Problems* 16 (2), Fall 1968, pp. 182–92.

30 See my own *Coming Out: Homosexual Politics in Britain from the Nineteenth Century to the Present*, London: Quartet, 1977.

31 Michel Foucault, *The History of Sexuality. Vol. 1: An Introduction*, London: Allen Lane, 1979.

32 Carole S. Vance, 'Social Construction Theory: Problems in the History of Sexuality', in Dennis Altman et al., *Homosexuality, Which Homosexuality?*, Amsterdam: Schorer, and London: GMP, 1989, pp. 13–34.

33 Eve Kosofsky Sedgwick, *Epistemology of the Closet*, Berkeley: University of California Press, 1990; Judith Butler, *Gender Trouble: Feminism and the Subversion of Identity*, New York: Routledge, 1990.

34 Franz X. Eder, Lesley Hall and Gert Hekma (eds.), *Sexual Cultures in Europe: National Histories*, and *Sexual Cultures in Europe: Themes in Sexuality*, Manchester: Manchester University Press, 1999.

3 Querying and Queering Same-Sex History

1 Xavier Mayne (pseudonym of the American Edward I. Prime Stevenson), *The Intersexes: A History of Similisexualism as a Problem in Social Life* (originally 1907), New York: Arno Press, 1988; Didier Eribon, *Insult and the Making of the Gay Self*, Durham, NC: Duke University Press, 2004, part 1.

2 Christopher Nealon, *Foundlings: Lesbian and Gay Historical Emotion before Stonewall*, Durham, NC: Duke University Press, 2001.

3 See A. L. Rowse, *Homosexuals in History: A Study of Ambivalence in Society, Literature and the Arts*, London, Heinemann, 1977.

4 Chris Waters, 'The Homosexual as a Social Being in Britain, 1945–1968', *Journal of British Studies* 51 (3), July 2012, pp. 685–710.

5 Laura Doan, *Disturbing Practices: History, Sexuality and Women's Experience of Modern War*, Chicago and London: University of Chicago Press, 2013, introduction.

6 See Chiara Beccalossi, *Female Sexual Inversion: Same-Sex Desires in Italian and British Sexology, c. 1870–1920*, London: Palgrave Macmillan, 2012.

7 John Boswell, *Christianity, Social Tolerance, and Homosexuality: Gay People in Western Europe from the Beginning of the Christian Era to the Fourteenth Century*, Chicago: University of Chicago Press, 1980.

8 Note the title of the first major anthology: Martin Duberman, Martha B. Vicinus and George Chauncey (eds.), *Hidden from History: Reclaiming the Gay and Lesbian Past*, New York: NAL Library, 1989.

9   Jonathan Ned Katz, *Gay American History: Lesbians and Gay Men in the USA*, New York: Thomas Crowell, 1976, and *Gay/Lesbian Almanac*, New York: Harper & Row, 1983.

10 Katz, *Gay American History*, pp. 1–2. One aspect of recovery involved literally bring back to consciousness largely forgotten texts of the past. Katz was general editor of a multi-volume book series, 'Homosexuality: Lesbians and Gay Men in Society, History and Literature', published by Arno Press, New York, in the mid-1970s, which reprinted a wide range of books and pamphlets from the nineteenth and early twentieth centuries, as well as some original studies of that period, which richly documented the existence of a vibrant culture and of pioneering reform activities.

11 See Allan Bérubé, *My Desire for History: Essays in Gay, Community and Labor History*, edited with an introduction by John D'Emilio and Estelle Freedman, Chapel Hill, NC: University of North Carolina, 2011.

12 James D. Steakley, *The Homosexual Emancipation Movement in Germany*, New York: Arno Press, 1975; Jeffrey Weeks, *Coming Out: Homosexual Politics in Britain from the Nineteenth Century to the Present*, London: Quartet, 1977; Toby Marotta, *The Politics of Homosexuality*, Boston: Houghton Mifflin, 1981; John D'Emilio, *Sexual Politics, Sexual Communities: The Making of a Homosexual Minority in the United States*, Chicago: Chicago University Press, 1983.

13 Ken Plummer (ed.), *The Making of the Modern Homosexual*, London: Hutchinson, 1981. At about the same time there was a special double issue of the *Journal of Homosexuality* (Fall/Winter 1980/1) on 'Historical Perspectives on Homosexuality', which included a range of essays that raised unsettling questions about the unity of homosexuality.

14 Carroll Smith-Rosenberg, 'The Female World of Love and Ritual: Relations between Women in Nineteenth Century America', *Signs* 1, Autumn 1975, pp. 1–29, republished in Smith-Rosenberg, *Disorderly Conduct: Visions of Gender in Victorian America*, Oxford and New York: Oxford University Press, 1986; Lillian Faderman, *Surpassing the Love of Men: Romantic Friendship and Love between Women from the Renaissance to the Present*, London: Junction Books, 1980; Blanche Wiesen Cook, 'Female Support Networks and Political Activism: Lillian Wald, Crystal Eastman, Emma Goldman', in Nancy Cott and Elizabeth Pleck (eds.), *A Heritage of Her Own*, New York: Simon and Schuster, 1979, pp. 412–44; Blanche Wiesen Cook, ' "Women Alone Stir my Imagination":

Lesbianism and the Cultural Tradition', *Signs* 4 (4), 1979, pp. 718–39; Martha Vicinus (ed.), *Lesbian Subjects: A Feminist Studies Reader*, Bloomington and Indianapolis: Indiana University Press, 1996; Martha Vicinus, *Intimate Friends: Women who Loved Women, 1778–1928*, Chicago and London: Chicago University Press, 2004; Helena Whitbread (ed.), *The Secret Diaries of Miss Anne Lister*, London: Virago, 2010; Lorna Doan, *Fashioning Sapphism: The Origins of a Modern English Lesbian Culture*, New York and Chichester: Columbia University Press, 2001.

15   See Weeks, *Coming Out*, pp. 3–4; Randolph Trumbach, 'London's Sodomites: Homosexual Behavior and Western Culture in the 18th Century', *Journal of Social History* 11 (1), Fall 1977, pp. 1–33. For an assessment of McIntosh's work see Jeffrey Weeks, 'Mary McIntosh and the "Homosexual Role"', in *Making Sexual History*, Cambridge: Polity, 2000, pp. 53–74.

16   Didier Eribon, *Returning to Reims*, Los Angeles: Semiotext(e), 2013.

17   Michel Foucault, *The History of Sexuality. Vol. 1: An Introduction*, London: Penguin, 1979, p. 43.

18   Guido Ruggiero, *The Boundaries of Eros: Sex Crime and Sexuality in Renaissance Venice*, Oxford and New York: Oxford University Press, 1985; Michael Rocke, *Forbidden Friendships: Homosexuality and Male Culture in Renaissance Florence*, New York and Oxford: Oxford University Press, 1996; Alan Bray, *Homosexuality in Renaissance England*, London: Gay Men's Press, 1983; Kent Gerard and Gert Hekma (eds.), *The Pursuit of Sodomy: Male Homosexuality in Renaissance and Enlightenment Europe*, New York: Harrington Park Press, 1989; Randolph Trumbach, *Sex and the Gender Revolution. Vol. 1: Heterosexuality and the Third Gender in Enlightenment London*, Chicago: Chicago University Press, 1998; Kenneth Borris and G. S. Rousseau (eds.), *The Sciences of Homosexuality in Early Modern Europe*, London and New York: Routledge, 2008.

19   See the arguments presented in Edward Stein (ed.), *Forms of Desire: Sexual Orientation and the Social Constructionist Controversy*, New York: Routledge, 1992.

20   Carolyn Dinshaw, *Getting Medieval: Sexualities and Communities, Pre- and Postmodern*, Durham, NC, and London: Duke University Press, 1999, introduction.

21   Michel Foucault, *The History of Sexuality. Vol. 2: The Use of Pleasure*, London: Viking, 1985, and *The History of Sexuality.*

Vol. 3: The Care of the Self, London: Viking, 1985. See also Peter Brown, *The Body and Society: Men, Women, and Sexual Renunciation in Early Christianity*, New York: Columbia University Press, 1988; Bernadette Brooten, *Love Between Women: Early Christian Responses to Female Homoeroticism*, Chicago: University of Chicago Press, 1996.

22 Lewis Mumford, quoted in Ken Plummer, *Cosmopolitan Sexualities: Hope and the Humanist Imagination*, Cambridge: Polity, 2015, p. 62; Henning Bech, *Where Men Meet: Homosexuality and Modernity*, Cambridge: Polity, 1997. See also Chad Heap, 'The City as a Sexual Laboratory: The Queer Heritage of the Chicago School', *Qualitative Sociology* 26, Winter 2003, pp. 457–87.

23 George Chauncey, *Gay New York: Gender, Urban Culture, and the Making of the Gay Male World, 1890–1940*, New York: Basic Books, 1994, p. 3.

24 Matt Cook, *London and the Culture of Homosexuality, 1885–1914*, Cambridge: Cambridge University Press, 2003.

25 Morris B. Kaplan, *Sodom on the Thames: Sex, Love and Scandal in Wilde Times*, Ithaca, NY: Cornell University Press, 2005.

26 Matt Houlbrook, *Queer London: Perils and Pleasures in the Sexual Metropolis, 1918–1957*, Chicago: Chicago University Press, 2005.

27 H. G. Cocks, *Nameless Offences: Homosexual Desire in the 19th Century*, London: I. B. Tauris, 2003; Helen Smith, *Masculinity, Class and Same-Sex Desire in Industrial England, 1895–1951*, London: Palgrave Macmillan, 2015; John Howard, *Men Like That: A Southern Queer History*, Chicago: Chicago University Press, 1999; Colin R. Johnson, *Just Queer Folk: Gender and Sexuality in Rural America*, Philadelphia: Temple University Press, 2013.

28 David M. Halperin, 'The Normalization of Queer Theory', in Gust A. Yep, Karen E. Lovaas and John P. Elia (eds.), 'Queer Theory and Communication: From Disciplinary Queers to Queering the Discipline', special issue of *Journal of Homosexuality* 45 (2/3/4), 2003, pp. 339–43 at p. 339.

29 David M. Halperin, *Saint Foucault: Towards a Gay Hagiography*, Oxford: Oxford University Press, 1996, p. 62.

30 Eve Kosofsky Sedgwick, *Epistemology of the Closet*, Berkeley: University of California Press 1990; also Eve Kosofsky Sedgwick, *Between Men: English Literature and Male Homosexual Desire*, New York: Columbia University Press, 1985. On the binary and heteronormativity see Michael Warner, *The Trouble*

with Normal: Sex, Politics and the Ethics of Queer Life, Cambridge, MA: Harvard University Press, 1999; and Jonathan Dollimore, *Sexual Dissidence: Augustine to Wilde, Freud to Foucault*, Oxford: Oxford University Press, 1991.

31 Judith Butler, *Gender Trouble: Feminism and the Subversion of Identity*, New York: Routledge, 1990, p. ix.

32 Marjorie Garber, *Vested Interests: Cross-Dressing and Cultural Anxiety*, New York: Routledge, 1992, p. 17.

33 Susan Stryker, *Transgender History*, Berkeley: Seal Press, 2008.

34 Michel Foucault, *Herculine Barbin, Being the Recently Discovered Memoirs of a Nineteenth-Century French Hermaphrodite*, New York: Pantheon Books, 1980.

35 See, for example, Joanne Meyerowitz, *How Sex Changed: A History of Transsexuality in the United States*, Cambridge, MA: Harvard University Press, 2004; Judith Halberstam, *Female Masculinity*, Durham, NC: Duke University Press, 1998; Alison Oram, *Her Husband Was a Woman! Women's Gender-Crossing in Modern British Popular Culture*, London: Routledge, 2007.

36 See Gayle Rubin, 'Thinking Sex: Notes for a Radical Theory of the Politics of Sexuality', in Carole S. Vance (ed.), *Pleasure and Danger: Exploring Female Sexuality*, London: Routledge and Kegan Paul, 1984, pp. 267–319. See suggestions for further reading for more detailed references.

37 José Esteban Muñoz, *Cruising Utopias: The Then and There of Queer Futurity*, New York: New York University Press, 2009, p. 1; Heather Love, *Feeling Backward: Loss and the Politics of Queer History*, Cambridge, MA: Harvard University Press, 2007, p. 3.

38 Biddy Martin, *Femininity Played Straight: The Significance of Being Lesbian*, New York and London: Routledge, 1996; Muñoz, *Cruising Utopias*, p. 42.

39 David Halperin and Valerie Traub (eds.), *Gay Shame*, Chicago: University of Chicago Press, 2009.

40 George Chauncey, 'The Trouble with Shame', in Halperin and Traub, *Gay Shame*, pp. 277–82.

41 Leo Bersani, *Homos*, Cambridge, MA: Harvard University Press, 1995; Leo Bersani and Adam Phillips, *Intimacies*, Chicago: University of Chicago Press, 2008; Lee Edelman, *No Future: Queer Theory and the Death Drive*, Durham, NC: Duke University Press, 2004.

42 Henrietta L. Moore, *Still Life: Hopes, Desires and Satisfactions*, Cambridge: Polity, 2011, pp. 168–9.

43 Doan, *Disturbing Practices*, ch. 1. See Doan, *Fashioning Sapphism*.
44 Brian Lewis (ed.), *British Queer History: New Approaches and Perspectives*, Manchester and New York: Manchester University Press, 2013, p. 4.
45 David M. Halperin, *How to Do the History of Homosexuality*, Chicago: Chicago University Press, 2002. See also David M. Halperin, *How to Be Gay*, Cambridge, MA: Harvard University Press, 2012.
46 Valerie Traub, *The Renaissance of Lesbianism in Early Modern England*, Cambridge: Cambridge University Press, 2002.
47 Dinshaw, *Getting Medieval*. See also her *How Soon is Now? Medieval Texts, Amateur Readers, and the Queerness of Time*, Durham, NC: Duke University Press, 2012.
48 Louise Fradenberg and Carla Freccaro (eds.), *Premodern Sexualities*, New York: Routledge, 1996, preface.

4 Gender, Sexuality and Power

1 Lisa Duggan and Nan D. Hunter, *Sex Wars: Sexual Dissent and Political Culture*, New York: Routledge, 1995. See also Janice M. Irvine, *Talk about Sex: The Battles over Sex Education in the United States*, Berkeley: University of California Press, 2004.
2 Andrea Dworkin and Catharine MacKinnon, *Pornography and Civil Rights: A New Day for Women's Equality*, Minneapolis, MN: Organizing Against Pornography, 1988.
3 Joanna Bourke, *Rape: A History from 1860 to the Present*, London: Virago, 2008, p. 435.
4 Carole S. Vance (ed.), *Pleasure and Danger: Exploring Female Sexuality*, London: Routledge and Kegan Paul, 1984; Ann Snitow, Christine Stansell and Sharon Thompson (eds.), *The Powers of Desire: The Politics of Sexuality*, New York: Monthly Review Press, 1983, published in the UK under the title *Desire: The Politics of Sexuality*, London: Virago, 1984.
5 Ellen DuBois and Linda Gordon, 'Seeking Ecstasy on the Battlefield: Danger and Pleasure in Nineteenth-Century Feminist Sexual Thought', in Vance, *Pleasure and Danger*, pp. 31–49.
6 Susan Brownmiller, *Against our Will: Men, Women and Rape* (originally 1978), New York: Open Road, 2013.
7 Alice Echols, 'The New Feminism of Yin and Yang', in Snitow et al., *Powers of Desire*, pp. 62–81; and 'The Yang of the Id:

Feminist Sexual Politics 1968–83', in Vance, *Pleasure and Danger*, pp. 50–72. The articles reference Morgan, Barry and Daly.

8   Catharine A. MacKinnon, 'Does Sexuality have a History?', in Domna C. Stanton (ed.), *Discourses of Sexuality: From Aristotle to AIDS*, Ann Arbor: University of Michigan Press, 1992, pp. 117–36 at pp. 125, 117. See also Catharine A. MacKinnon, *Feminism Unmodified: Discourses on Life and Law*, Cambridge, MA: Harvard University Press, 1987.

9   Sheila Jeffreys, *The Spinster and Her Enemies: Feminism and Sexuality 1880–1930*, London: Pandora, 1985. See suggestions for further reading for full references.

10   Bourke, *Rape*, p. 6; Janie L. Leatherman, *Sexual Violence and Armed Conflict*, Cambridge: Polity, 2011; Estelle B. Freedman, *Redefining Rape: Sexual Violence in the Era of Suffrage and Segregation*, Cambridge, MA: Harvard University Press, 2013; Bourke, *Rape*, p. viii.

11   Judith R. Walkowitz, *City of Dreadful Delight: Narratives of Sexual Danger in Late-Victorian London*, London: Virago, 1992, p. 245.

12   See Judith Newton, Mary P. Ryan and Judith R. Walkowitz (eds.), *Sex and Class in Women's History*, London: Routledge and Kegan Paul, 1983, editors' introduction, p. 3: 'A theory of gender and of male domination is central to the study of capitalism itself.'

13   Walkowitz, *City*, p. 243.

14   Linda Gordon, *Woman's Body, Woman's Right: Birth Control in America*, Harmondsworth: Penguin, 1977. The book was republished in a revised and updated edition as *The Moral Property of Women: A History of Birth Control Politics in America*, Urbana and Chicago: University of Chicago Press, 2007.

15   Rosalind P. Petchesky, *Abortion and Woman's Choice: The State, Sexuality, and Reproductive Freedom*, New York: Longman, 1984. Studies on the UK include Angus McLaren, *Birth Control in Nineteenth-Century England: A Social and Intellectual History*, London: Croom Helm, 1978.

16   Judith R. Walkowitz, *Prostitution and Victorian Society: Women, Class and the State*, Cambridge: Cambridge University Press, 1980, p. 9.

17   Judith R. Walkowitz, 'Male Vice and Female Virtue: Feminism and the Politics of Prostitution in Nineteenth-Century Britain', in Snitow et al., *Powers of Desire*, pp. 43–61; Walkowitz, *City*, pp. 10, 243. See also Lucy Bland, *Banishing the Beast:*

Feminism, Sex and Morality, 2nd edition, London: I. B. Tauris, 2002.

18 Domna C. Stanton, 'Introduction: The Subject of Sexuality', in *Discourses of Sexuality*, pp. 1–46 at p. 17. See also Hester Eistenstein and Alice Jardine (eds.), *The Future of Difference*, New York: Columbia University Press, 1980.

19 Catherine Gallagher and Thomas Laqueur (eds.), *The Making of the Modern Body: Sexuality and Society in the Nineteenth Century*, published first as a special issue of the journal *Representations* 14, Spring 1986, then Berkeley: University of California Press, 1987; Thomas Laqueur, *Making Sex: Body and Gender from the Greeks to Freud*, Cambridge, MA: Harvard University Press, 1990.

20 Juliet Mitchell, *Psychoanalysis and Feminism*, London: Allen Lane, 1974; Sally Alexander and Barbara Taylor (eds.), *History and Psyche: Culture, Psychoanalysis, and the Past*, Basingstoke: Palgrave Macmillan, 2012; Michael Roper, 'Slipping out of View: Subjectivity and Emotion in Gender History', *History Workshop Journal* 52, Spring 2005, pp. 57–72; Joy Damousi and Robert Reynolds (eds.), *History on the Couch: Essays in History and Psychoanalysis*, Carlton, Victoria: Melbourne University Press, 2003.

21 In Joan W. Scott, *Gender and the Politics of History*, New York: Columbia University Press, 1988.

22 Gayle Rubin, 'The Traffic in Women: Notes on the "Political Economy" of Sex', in Rayner R. Reitter (ed.), *Towards an Anthropology of Women*, New York: Monthly Review Press, 1974, pp. 157–210 at p. 165.

23 Raewyn Connell, *Gender*, 2nd edition, Cambridge: Polity, 2009. See also Connell, *Gender and Power: Society, the Person and Sexual Politics*, Cambridge: Polity, 2013.

24 Laqueur, *Making Sex*. Other historians queried the timescale, suggesting that the classical view had co-existed with a 'modern' view since the Greeks: see Katharine Park and Robert A. Nye, 'Destiny is Anatomy', *New Republic* 204, 18 February 1991, pp. 53–7. See further discussion in chapter 5.

25 Gayle Rubin, 'Thinking Sex: Notes for a Radical Theory of the Politics of Sexuality', in Vance, *Pleasure and Danger*, pp. 267–319 at p. 275.

26 Anna Marie Jagose and Don Kulick, 'Introduction', and David Valentine, 'The Categories Themselves', contributions to a symposium on 'Thinking Sex/ Thinking Gender', in *GLQ: A Journal of Lesbian and Gay Studies* 10 (2), 2004, pp. 211–12 and 215–20.

27 Vance, 'Pleasure and Danger', pp. 16–17.

28 John D'Emilio and Estelle B. Freedman, *Intimate Matters: A History of Sexuality in America*, 1st edition, New York: Harper & Row, 1988; 2nd edition, Chicago: University of Chicago Press, 1997, ch. 5.

29 Combahee River Collective, 'A Black Feminist Statement', in G. T. Hull, P. B. Scott and B. Smith (eds.), *All the Women are White, All the Blacks are Men, But Some of Us are Brave*, New York: Feminist Press, 1982, pp. 13–22 at p. 14. The concept of intersectionality is often attributed to Crenshaw, but as this brief discussion shows it was widely used before her key article: Kimberlé W. Crenshaw, 'De-Marginalizing the Intersections of Race and Class: A Black Feminist Critique of Antidiscrimination Doctrine, Feminist Theory, and Anti-racist Politics', *University of Chicago Legal Forum* 1989, pp. 139–67.

30 Jacqueline Jones, *Labor of Love, Labor of Sorrow: Black Women, Work and the Family from Slavery to the Present*, New York: Basic Books, 1985.

31 Gwyn Campbell and Elizabeth Elbourne (eds.), *Sex, Power and Slavery*, Athens: Ohio University Press, 2014, introduction.

32 Abdul R. JanMohamed, 'Sexuality on/of the Racial Border: Foucault, Wright, and the Articulation of "Racialized Sexuality"', in Stanton, *Discourses of Sexuality*, pp. 94–116 at p. 97.

33 Evelynn M. Hammonds, 'Towards a Genealogy of Black Female Sexuality: The Problematic Silence', in Janet Price and Margaret Shildrick (eds.), *Feminist Theory and the Body: A Reader*, New York and London: Routledge, 1997, pp. 249–59.

34 Lisa Duggan, *Sapphic Slashers: Sex, Violence and American Modernity*, Durham, NC: Duke University Press, 2000; Julian B. Carter, *The Heart of Whiteness: Normal Sexuality and Race in America, 1880–1940*, Durham, NC: Duke University Press, 2007.

35 Gail Bederman, *Manliness and Civilization: A Cultural History of Gender and Race in the US, 1880–1917*, Chicago: Chicago University Press, 1995.

36 Rickie Solinger, *Wake up Little Susie: Single Pregnancy and Race before Roe v. Wade*, New York: Routledge, 1992.

37 Steven Selden, *Inheriting Shame: The Story of Eugenics and Racism in America*, New York: Teachers College Press, 1999; Jessie M. Rodrique, 'The Black Community and the Birth

Control Movement', in Kathy Peiss and Christina Simmons (eds.), *Passion and Power: Sexuality in History*, Philadelphia: Temple University Press, 1989, pp. 138–56; Rennie Simson, 'The Afro-American Female: The Historical Context of the Construction of Sexual Identity', in Snitow et al., *Powers of Desire*, pp. 243–9 at p. 247.

38 Ann Laura Stoler, *Race and the Education of Desire: Foucault's History of Sexuality and the Colonial Order of Things*, Durham, NC: Duke University Press, 2012, and *Carnal Knowledge and Imperial Power: Race and the Intimate in Colonial Rule*, 2nd edition, Berkeley: University of California Press, 2010.

39 See Louise Jackson, 'Sex, Religion and the Law: The Regulation of Sexual Behaviour, 1820–1920', and Raeline Frances, 'Prostitution: The Age of Empire', both in Chiara Beccalossi and Ivan Crozier (eds.), *A Cultural History of Sexuality in the Age of Empire*, London: Bloomsbury, 2014, pp. 83–100, 145–70, respectively; Philippa Levine, *Gender and Empire*, Oxford: Oxford University Press, 2004, and *Prostitution, Race and Politics: Policing Venereal Disease in the British Empire*, London: Routledge, 2014.

40 Sean Brady, 'Homosexuality: European and Colonial Encounters', in Beccalossi and Crozier, *Cultural History*, pp. 43–62; Robert Aldrich, *Colonialism and Homosexuality*, London: Routledge, 2008; Siobhan B. Somerville, 'Scientific Racism and the Invention of the Homosexual Body', in Lucy Bland and Laura Doan (eds.), *Sexology in Culture: Labelling Bodies and Desires* and *Sexuality Uncensored: The Documents of Sexual Science*, Cambridge: Polity, 1998, and *Queering the Color Line: Race and the Invention of Homosexuality in American Culture*, Durham, NC: Duke University Press, 2000.

41 Leonore Davidoff, 'Class and Gender in Victorian England', in Newton et al., *Sex and Class*, pp. 17–71 at p. 44.

42 John Tosh, *Manliness and Masculinities in Nineteenth-Century Britain: Essays on Gender, Family and Empire*, Harlow: Pearson, 2005, p. 1; Michael S. Kimmel, *The History of Men: Essays on the History of American and British Masculinities*, Albany: State University of New York, 2005, p. 3.

43 Raewyn Connell, *Masculinities*, Cambridge: Polity, 2005.

44 Raewyn Connell, 'The Big Picture: Masculinities in Recent World History', *Theory and Society* 22 (5), October 1993, pp. 597–623; George L. Mosse, *The Image of Man: The Creation of Modern Masculinity*, Oxford and New York: Oxford

University Press, 1996, and *Nationalism and Sexuality: Respectability and Abnormal Sexuality in Modern Europe*, New York: Howard Fertig, 1997.

45 Tosh, *Manliness and Masculinities*, p. 7.

46 John Tosh, *A Man's Place: Masculinity in the Middle-Class Home in Victorian England*, New Haven and London: Yale University Press, 1999.

47 Lesley A. Hall, *Hidden Anxieties: Male Sexuality, 1900–1950*, Cambridge: Polity, 1991; Simon Szreter and Kate Fisher, *Sex before the Sexual Revolution: Intimate Life in England 1918–1963*, Cambridge: Cambridge University Press, 2010. More dramatically, on Germany post-World War I see Klaus Theweleit, *Male Fantasies: Women, Floods, Bodies, History. Vol. 1*, Cambridge: Polity, 1987.

48 Tosh, *Manliness and Masculinities*, p. 8.

5   Mainstreaming Sexual History

1 David M. Halperin, 'The Normalization of Queer Theory', in Gust A. Yep, Karen E. Lovaas and John P. Elia (eds.), 'Queer Theory and Communication: From Disciplinary Queers to Queering the Discipline', special issue of *Journal of Homosexuality* 45 (2/3/4), 2003, pp. 339–43; Laura Doan, *Disturbing Practices: History, Sexuality and Women's Experience of Modern War*, Chicago: University of Chicago Press, 2013.

2 Jeffrey Weeks, *Sex, Politics and Society: The Regulation of Sexuality from 1800*, 1st edition, Harlow: Longman, 1981; 3rd edition, London: Routledge, 2012.

3 John D'Emilio and Estelle B. Freedman, *Intimate Matters: A History of Sexuality in America*, 1st edition, New York: Harper & Row, 1988; 2nd edition, Chicago: Chicago University Press, 1997.

4 Lesley A. Hall, *Sex, Gender and Social Change in Britain from 1880*, London: Palgrave Macmillan, 2012. See also Thomas Laqueur, 'Sexuality and the Transformation of Culture: The Longue Durée', *Sexualities* 12, August 2009, pp. 418–36.

5 Kim M. Phillips and Barry Reay, *Sex before Sexuality: A Premodern History*, Cambridge: Polity, 2011, p. 13.

6 See Jeffrey Weeks, *Sexuality*, 3rd edition, London: Routledge, 2010, p. 3.

7 Phillips and Reay's *Sex before Sexuality* provides a concise and well-argued survey of these debates.

8   Faramerz Dabhoiwala, *The Origins of Sex: A History of the First Sexual Revolution*, London: Allen Lane, 2012.

9   Weeks, *Sex, Politics and Society*, 3rd edition, ch. 2.

10   Thomas W. Laqueur, 'Sexual Desire and the Market Economy during the Industrial Revolution', in Domna C. Stanton (ed.), *Discourses of Sexuality: From Aristotle to AIDS*, Ann Arbor: University of Michigan Press, 1992, pp. 185–215 at p. 186. See also Henry Abelove, 'Some Speculations on the History of "Sexual Intercourse" during the "Long Eighteenth Century"', in Andrew Parker, Mary Russo, Doris Summer and Patricia Yaeger (eds.), *Nationalisms and Sexualities*, New York: Routledge, 1992, pp. 335–42 at p. 337.

11   Thomas Laqueur, *Making Sex: Body and Gender from the Greeks to Freud*, Cambridge, MA: Harvard University Press, 1990, and *Solitary Sex: A Cultural History of Masturbation*, London: Zone Books, 2003. Compare Hera Cook, *The Long Sexual Revolution: English Women, Sex, and Contraception 1800–1975*, Oxford: Oxford University Press, 2004, p. 13, where she suggests that men's freedom from the economic consequences of pregnancy was likely to be a major reason for societal fear of uncontrolled male lust, including masturbation and homosexuality.

12   For a clear summary of his mature views see Randolph Trumbach, 'From Age to Gender, c. 1500–1750: From the Adolescent Male to the Adult Effeminate Body', in Sarah Toulalan and Kate Fisher (eds.), *Sex and the Body: 1500 to the Present*, London: Routledge, 2013, pp. 123–41.

13   Karen Harvey, 'The Century of Sex? Gender, Bodies, and Sexuality', *Historical Journal* 45 (4), 2002, pp. 899–916; Jennifer Jordan, '"That ere with Age, his strength Is utterly decay'd": Understanding the Male Body in Early Modern Manhood', in Kate Fisher and Sarah Toulalan (eds.), *Bodies, Sex and Desire from the Renaissance to the Present*, Basingstoke: Palgrave Macmillan, 2011, pp. 27–48.

14   Randolph Trumbach, *Sex and the Gender Revolution. Vol. 1: Heterosexuality and the Third Gender in Enlightenment London*, Chicago and London: Chicago University Press, 1998, p. 322; Shani De'Cruze, 'Sex Violence since 1750', in Toulalan and Fisher, *Sex and the Body*, pp. 444–59; Tim Hitchcock, *English Sexualities, 1700–1800*, Basingstoke: Macmillan, 1997; Anna Clark, *Women's Silence, Men's Violence: Sexual Assaults in England*, London: Pandora, 1987.

15   Anna Clark, *Desire: A History of European Sexuality*, New York and London: Routledge, 2008, p. 2.

16   Louis-Georges Tin, *The Invention of Heterosexual Culture*, Boston, MA: MIT Press, 2012.

17   Jonathan Ned Katz, *The Invention of Heterosexuality*, New York: NAL/ Dutton, 1995.

18   David M. Halperin, *Saint Foucault: Towards a Gay Hagiography*, Oxford: Oxford University Press, 1996, p. 44.

19   Phillips and Reay, *Sex before Sexuality*, pp. 40–59.

20   John R. Gillis, *For Better, For Worse: British Marriages, 1600 to the Present*, Oxford: Oxford University Press, 1985; Nancy F. Cott, *Public Vows: A History of Marriage and the Nation*, Cambridge, MA: Harvard University Press, 2002; Sharon Marcus, *Between Women: Friendship, Desire and Marriage in Victorian England*, Princeton, NJ: Princeton University Press, 2007.

21   See, for example, Lynda Nead, *Victorian Babylon: People, Streets and Images in Nineteenth-Century London*, New Haven: Yale University Press, 2005; Lisa Z. Sigel, *Governing Pleasure: Pornography and Social Change in England, 1815–1914*, New Brunswick, NJ: Rutgers University Press, 2002; Chad Heap, *Slumming: Sexual and Racial Encounters in American Nightlife 1885–1940*, Chicago: Chicago University Press, 2008; H. G. Cocks, *Classified: The Secret History of the Personal Column*, London: Random House, 2009.

22   Cas Wouters, *Informalization: Manners and Emotion since 1890*, London: Sage, 2007.

23   Doan, *Disturbing Practices*, ch. 4.

24   Christina Simmons, *Making Marriage Modern: Women's Sexuality from the Progressive Era to World War II*, Oxford: Oxford University Press, 2009; Alison Mackinnon, *Love and Freedom: Professional Women and the Reshaping of Personal Life*, Cambridge: Cambridge University Press, 1997; Kevin White, *Sexual Liberation as Sexual Licence? The American Revolt against Victorianism*, Chicago: Ivan R. Dee, 2000; Marcus Collins, *Modern Love: An Intimate History of Men and Women in Twentieth-Century Britain*, London: Atlantic Books, 2003; Lisa Z. Sigel, *Making Modern Love: Sexual Narratives and Identities in Inter-War Britain*, Philadelphia: Temple University Press, 2012.

25   Simon Szreter, *Fertility, Class and Gender in Britain, 1860–1940*, Cambridge: Cambridge University Press, 1996, p. 573; Simon Szreter and Kate Fisher, *Sex before the Sexual Revolution: Intimate Life in England 1918–1963*, Cambridge: Cambridge University Press, 2010.

26 Cook, *Long Sexual Revolution*; Lucy Bland, *Modern Women on Trial: Sexual Transgression in the Age of the Flapper*, Manchester: Manchester University Press, 2013; Alana Harris and Timothy Jones (eds.), *Love and Romance in Britain, 1918–1970*, London: Palgrave Macmillan, 2014.

27 Dagmar Herzog, *Sexuality in Europe: A Twentieth-Century History*, Cambridge: Cambridge University Press, 2011, p. 45. Herzog's book was the subject of a forum in *Contemporary European History* 22 (2), May 2013, with contributions from: Jeffrey Weeks, 'Pleasure and Duty' (pp. 277–82); Franz X. Eder, 'The Politics of Discourse' (pp. 283–8); Dan Healey, 'Sex and Socialism' (pp. 289–93); Victoria Harris, 'Histories of "Sex", Histories of "Sexuality"' (pp. 295–301); and a response from Dagmar Herzog, 'What Incredible Yearnings Human Beings Have' (pp. 303–17).

28 Herzog, *Sexuality in Europe*, p. 85.

29 Margot Canaday, *The Straight State: Sexuality and Citizenship in Twentieth-Century America*, Princeton, NJ: Princeton University Press, 2009; Jennifer Terry, *An American Obsession: Science, Medicine, and the Place of Homosexuality in Modern Society*, Chicago: University of Chicago Press, 2009. For early manifestations of the links between anti-communism and sexual conservatism see Erica Ryan, *Red War on the Family: Sex, Gender and Americanism in the First Red Scare*, Philadelphia: Temple University Press, 2014.

30 Heike Bauer and Matt Cook (eds.), *Queer 1950s: Rethinking Sexuality in the Postwar Years*, London: Palgrave Macmillan, 2012.

31 Jeffrey Weeks, *The World We Have Won: The Remaking of Erotic and Intimate Life*, London and New York: Routledge, 2007, chs. 3 and 4.

32 Gert Hekma and Alain Giami (eds.), *Sexual Revolutions*, London: Palgrave Macmillan, 2014.

33 Gertrude Himmelfarb, *The De-Moralization of Society: From Victorian Values to Modern Values*, London: Institute of Economic Affairs, 1995; Daniel Bell, *The Cultural Contradictions of Capitalism*, New York: Basic Books, 1996; Francis Fukuyama, *The Great Disruption: Human Nature and the Reconstitution of Social Order*, London: Profile Books, 1999.

34 Dagmar Herzog, 'Postscript: Tomorrow Sex will be Good Again', in Scott Spector, Helmut Puff and Dagmar Herzog (eds.), *After the History of Sexuality: German Genealogies*, New York: Berghahn Books, 2012, pp. 282–6.

35   Arthur Marwick, *The Sixties: Cultural Revolution in Britain, France, Italy, and the United States, c.1958–c.1974*, Oxford: Oxford University Press, 1998, p. 15.
36   Himmelfarb, *De-Moralization*, pp. 217–18.
37   Jeffrey Escoffier, 'Pornography, Perversity and the Sexual Revolution', in Hekma and Giami, *Sexual Revolutions*, pp. 203–18; Wouters, *Informalization*, p. 9.
38   Anthony Giddens, *Modernity and Self-Identity*, Cambridge: Polity, 1991, and *The Transformation of Intimacy: Sexuality, Love and Eroticism in Modern Societies*, Cambridge: Polity, 1992.
39   Paula A. Treichler, 'AIDS, Homophobia, and Biomedical Discourse: An Epidemic of Signification', *October* 43, Winter 1987, pp. 31–70; Elizabeth Fee and Daniel Fox (eds.), *AIDS: The Burdens of History*, Berkeley: University of California Press, 1988.
40   Jeffrey Weeks, 'AIDS and the Regulation of Sexuality', in Virginia Berridge and Philip Strong (eds.), *AIDS and Contemporary History*, Cambridge: Cambridge University Press, 1993, pp. 17–36. This is also included in Jeffrey Weeks, *Making Sexual History*, Cambridge: Polity, 2000.
41   Martin P. Levine, 'The Implications of Constructionist Theory for Social Research on the AIDS Epidemic amongst Gay Men', in Gilbert Herdt and Shirley Lindenbaum (eds.), *The Time of AIDS: Social Analysis, Theory, and Method*, London: Sage, 1992, pp. 185–98. See also Robert A. Padgug, 'Gay Villain, Gay Hero: Homosexuality and the Social Construction of AIDS', in Kathy Peiss and Christina Simmons (eds.), *Passion and Power: Sexuality in History*, Philadelphia: Temple University Press, 1989, pp. 293–310.
42   Alain Giami, 'Sex, Medicine and Disease', in Gert Hekma (ed.), *A Cultural History of Sexuality in the Modern Age*, London: Bloomsbury, 2014, pp. 127–48.
43   Allan M. Brandt, *No Magic Bullet: A Social History of Venereal Disease in the United States since 1880*, New York: Oxford University Press, 1987, p. 5; Frank Mort, *Dangerous Sexualities: Medico-Moral Politics in England since 1830*, London and New York: Routledge and Kegan Paul, 1987, p. 2; Ronald Bayer, *Private Acts, Social Consequences: AIDS and the Politics of Public Health*, New York: Free Press, 1989.
44   Dennis Altman, *Power and Community: Organizational and Cultural Responses to AIDS*, London: Taylor and Francis, 1994. On British grassroots responses see Weeks, *Making Sexual History*.

45   On Britain see Virginia Berridge, *AIDS in the UK: The Making of Policy, 1981–1994*, Oxford: Oxford University Press, 1996.

46   Steven Epstein, *Impure Science: AIDS, Activism, and the Politics of Knowledge*, Berkeley: University of California Press, 1996, p. 17.

47   George Chauncey, *Why Marriage? The History Shaping Today's Debate over Gay Equality*, New York: Basic Books, 2004.

48   Jens Rydström, *Odd Couples: A History of Gay Marriage in Scandinavia*, Amsterdam: Aksant, 2011.

49   Jeffrey Weeks, 'Liberalism by Stealth? The Civil Partnership Act and the New Equalities Agenda in Perspective', in Nicola Barker and Daniel Monk (eds.), *From Civil Partnerships to Same-Sex Marriage: Interdisciplinary Reflections*, London: New York, 2015, pp. 29–44.

50   Daniel Winunwe Rivers, *Radical Relations: Lesbian Mothers, Gay Fathers, and Their Children in the United States since World War II*, Chapel Hill, NC: University of North Carolina Press, 2013.

51   John Boswell, *Same-Sex Unions in Premodern Europe*, New York: Villard Books, 1994.

52   Alan Bray, *The Friend*, Chicago and London: University of Chicago Press, 2003, p. 240. For Anne Lister see chapter 3.

53   Helmut Puff, 'After the History of (Male) Homosexuality', in Spector et al., *After the History of Sexuality*, ch. 1; Valerie Traub, 'Friendship's Loss: Alan Bray's Making of History', in Jody Greene (ed.). 'The Work of Friendship: In Memoriam Alan Bray', special issue of *GLQ: A Journal of Lesbian and Gay Studies*, 10 (3), 2004, pp. 339–66.

54   Deborah Cohen, *Family Secrets: Living with Shame from the Victorians to the Present Day*, London: Viking, 2013; Matt Cook, *Queer Domesticities: Homosexuality and Home Life in Twentieth-Century London*, Basingstoke: Palgrave Macmillan, 2014.

55   Alan Frank, Patricia Ticinato Clough and Steven Seidman (eds.), *Intimacies: A New World of Relational Life*, New York: Routledge, 2013, p. 2.

56   Ken Plummer, *Telling Sexual Stories: Power, Change and Social Worlds*, London: Routledge, 1995, and *Intimate Citizenship: Private Decisions and Public Dialogue*, Seattle: University of Washington Press, 2003.

57   Lisa Duggan, *The Twilight of Equality? Neoliberalism, Cultural Politics and the Attack on Democracy*, Boston: Beacon Press, 2012; Suzanna Danuta Walters, *The Tolerance Trap*:

How God, Genes, and Good Intentions are Sabotaging Gay Equality, New York: New York University Press, 2014; Jasbir K. Puar, *Terrorist Assemblages: Homonationalism in Queer Times*, Durham, NC: Duke University Press, 2007.

58 Gert Hekma, 'Introduction', in Hekma, *Cultural History*, pp. 1–26.

59 Brian Heaphy, Carol Smart and Anna Einarsdottir, *Same Sex Marriages: New Generations, New Relationships*, London: Palgrave Macmillan, 2012.

6 The Globalization of Sexual History

1 Marc Epprecht, 'Transnationalism in Sexuality Studies: An "Africanist" Perspective', in Peter Aggleton, Paul Boyce, Henrietta L. Moore and Richard Parker (eds.), *Understanding Global Sexualities: New Frontiers*, London: Routledge, 2012, pp. 186–202 at p. 193.

2 Elizabeth A. Povinelli and George Chauncey, 'Thinking Sexuality Transnationally', *GLQ: A Journal of Lesbian and Gay Studies* 5(4), 1999, pp. 439–50; Dennis Altman, *Global Sex*, Chicago: Chicago University Press, 2000.

3 D. Held, A. McGrew, D. Goldblatt and J. Perraton, 'Rethinking Globalization', in D. Held and A. McGrew (eds.), *The Global Transformations Reader*, Cambridge: Polity, 2000, pp. 54–60 at pp. 54–5.

4 Adapted from Jeffrey Weeks, *The World We Have Won: The Remaking of Erotic and Intimate Life*, London and New York: Routledge, 2007, pp. 206–8.

5 For critical analyses see Rosemary Hennessy, *Profit and Pleasure: Sexual Identities in Late Capitalism*, New York: Routledge, 2000; Jon Binnie, *The Globalization of Sexuality*, London: Sage, 2004.

6 Ken Plummer, *Cosmopolitan Sexualities*, Cambridge: Polity, 2015, p. 4.

7 Saskia Wieringa and Horacio Sívori (eds.), *The Sexual History of the Global South: Sexual Politics in Africa, Asia, and Latin America*, London: Zed Books, 2013.

8 Susan L. Mann, *Gender and Sexuality in Modern China*, Cambridge: Cambridge University Press, 2011.

9 S. N. Nyeck and Marc Epprecht (eds.), *Sexual Diversity in Africa: Politics, Theory and Citizenship*, Montreal: McGill-Queens University Press, 2013; Neville Hoad, *African Intimacies: Race, Homosexuality, and Globalization*, Minneapolis:

University of Minnesota Press, 2007; Sylvia Tamale (ed.), *African Sexualities: A Reader*, Cape Town: Pambauka Press, 2011.

10 Anjali Arondekar, *For the Record: On Sexuality and the Colonial Archive in India*, Durham, NC: Duke University Press, 2009. See also Ann Laura Stoler, *Along the Archival Grain: Epistemic Anxieties and Colonial Common Sense*, Princeton, NJ: Princeton University Press, 2010.

11 For example, the contributors to Arnaldo Cruz-Malavé and Martin F. Manalansan IV (eds.), *Queer Globalizations: Citizenship and the Afterlife of Colonialism*, New York: New York University Press, 2002.

12 Marc Epprecht, *Heterosexual Africa? The History of an Idea from the Age of Explorations to the Age of AIDS*, Athens: Ohio University Press; Scottsville, SA: University of Kwa-Zulu-Natal, 2008, ch. 1.

13 Mann, *Gender and Sexuality*, introduction.

14 Epprecht, 'Transnationalim', pp. 186–7. On the conversation between different sexual cultures, especially in relation to sexology, see Heike Bauer (ed.), *Sexology and Translation: Cultural and Scientific Encounters across the Modern World*, Philadelphia: Temple University Press, 2015.

15 See Ann Laura Stoler, *Race and the Education of Desire: Foucault's History of Sexuality and the Colonial Order of Things*, Durham, NC: Duke University Press, 2012.

16 Mitchell Dean, *Critical and Effective Histories: Foucault's Methods and Historical Sociology*, London and New York: Routledge, 1994, p. 95.

17 Discussion of Burton and his impact can be found in Marc Epprecht, *Heterosexual Africa?*, and *Hungochani: The History of a Dissident Sexuality in Southern Africa*, 2nd edition, Montreal: McGill-Queens University Press, 2013; and in Joseph A. Massad, *Desiring Arabs*, Chicago: Chicago University Press, 2007.

18 See Hoad, *African Intimacies*, ch. 5 for a subtle critical account.

19 Rudi C. Bleys, *The Geography of Perversion: Male-to-Male Sexual Behaviour outside the West and the Ethnographic Imagination, 1750–1918*, London: Cassell, 1996.

20 Göran Therborn, *Between Sex and Power*, London: Routledge, 2004; Plummer, *Cosmopolitan Sexualities*, p. 147.

21 Peter A. Jackson, 'Pre-Gay, Post-Queer: Thai Perspectives on Proliferating Gender/Sex Diversity in Asia', in Gerard Sullivan and Peter A. Jackson (eds.), 'Gay and Lesbian Asia: Culture,

Identity, Community', special issue of *Journal of Homosexuality* 40 (3/4), 2000, pp. 1–26 at p. 4.

22 Tom Boellstorff, 'Some Notes on the Frontiers of Sexuality and Globalization', in Aggleton et al., *Understanding Global Sexualities*, pp. 171–85 at p. 176.

23 Anne McClintock, *Imperial Leather: Race, Gender and Sexuality in the Colonial Context*, New York: Routledge, 1995.

24 Mrinalini Sinha, *Colonial Masculinity: The 'Manly Englishman' and the 'Effeminate Bengali' in the late Nineteenth Century*, Manchester: Manchester University Press, 1995, and *Specters of Mother India: The Global Restructuring of an Empire*, Durham, NC: Duke University Press, 2006; Mann, *Gender and Sexuality*.

25 Corinne Lennox and Matthew Waites (eds.), *Human Rights, Sexual Orientation and Gender Identity in the Commonwealth*, London: Institute of Commonwealth Studies and Human Rights Consortium, 2012, available online at http://commonwealth.sas.ac.uk/publications/house-publications/lgbt-rights-commonwealth

26 Massad, *Desiring Arabs*. I should declare an interest, as I am one of the Western authors criticized for careless words about Islamic attitudes.

27 Jasbir K. Puar, *Terrorist Assemblages: Homonationalism in Queer Times*, Durham, NC: Duke University Press, 2007, p. xi. See also Jinthana Haritaworn, *The Biopolitics of Mixing: Thai Multiracialities and Haunted Ascendencies*, Farnham: Ashgate, 2012.

28 Khaled El-Rouayheb, *Before Homosexuality in the Arab-Islamic World, 1500–1800*, Chicago: University of Chicago Press, 2005.

29 Abdelwahab Bouhdiba, *Sexuality in Islam*, London: Routledge and Kegan Paul, 1985.

30 Dror Ze'evi, *Producing Desire: Changing Sexual Discourse in the Ottoman Middle East, 1500–1900*, Berkeley: University of California Press, 2006. See also Jarrod Hayes, *Queer Nation: Marginal Sexualities in the Maghreb*, Chicago: University of Chicago Press, 2000.

31 For example, Pardis Mahdavi, *Passionate Uprisings: Iran's Sexual Revolution*, Stanford: Stanford University Press, 2009; and Shereen El Feki, *Sex and the Citadel: Intimate Life in a Changing Arab World*, London: Chatto and Windus, 2013.

32 Dan Healey, *Homosexual Desire in Revolutionary Russia: The Regulation of Sexual and Gender Dissent*, Chicago: University of Chicago Press, 2001.

33   Mann, *Gender and Sexuality.*
34   Carrie Hamilton, *Sexual Revolution in Cuba: Passion, Politics and Memory*, Chapel Hill: University of North Carolina Press, 2012; Noelle M. Stout, *After Love: Queer Intimacy and Erotic Economies in Post-Soviet Cuba*, Durham, NC: Duke University Press, 2014.
35   See Ian Lumsden, *Machos, Maricones and Gays: Cuba and Homosexuality*, Philadelphia: Temple University Press, 1996.
36   Peter L. Stearns, *Sexuality in World History*, London: Routledge, 2009, ch. 7; S. Frühstück, *Colonizing Sex: Sexology and Social Control in Modern Japan*, Berkeley: University of California Press, 2003.
37   Peter A. Jackson and N. M. Cook (eds.), *Genders and Sexualities in Modern Thailand*, Chiang Mai: Silkworm Books, 1999, esp. N. M. Cook and P. A. Jackson, 'Desiring Constructs: Transforming Sex/Gender Orders in Twentieth Century Thailand', pp. 1–27.
38   Sean Patrick Larvie, 'Queerness and the Specter of Brazilian National Ruin', *GLQ: A Journal of Gay and Lesbian Studies* 5 (4), 1999, pp. 527–57 at p. 528.
39   Meredith L. Weiss and Michael J. Bosia (eds.), *Global Homophobia: States, Movements, and the Politics of Oppression*, Urbana: University of Illinois Press, 2013. On women particularly see Evelyn Blackwood and Saskia E. Wieringa (eds.), *Female Desires: Same-Sex Relations and Transgender Practices across Cultures*, New York: Columbia University Press, 1999; Leila J. Rupp, *Sapphistries: A Global History of Love between Women*, New York: New York University Press, 2009.
40   Katarzyna Korycki and Abouzar Nasirzadeh, 'Homophobia as a Tool of Statecraft: Iran and its Queers', in Weiss and Bosia, *Global Homophobia*, ch. 8.
41   Kapya J. Kaoma, 'The Marriage of Convenience: The U.S. Christian Right, African Christianity, and Postcolonial Politics of Sexual Identity', in Weiss and Bosia, *Global Homophobia*, ch. 2.
42   Tom Boellstorff, *The Gay Archipelago: Sexuality and Nation in Indonesia*, Princeton, NJ: Princeton University Press, 2005.
43   Epprecht, *Hungochani.*
44   A point made by Leila J. Rupp, 'Outing the Past: US Queer History in Global Perspective', in Leila J. Rupp and Susan K. Freeman (eds.), *Understanding and Teaching U.S. Lesbian, Gay, Bisexual and Transgender History*, Madison: University of Wisconsin Press, 2014, pp. 17–30.

45   Lynn Hunt, *Inventing Human Rights: A History*, New York: W. W. Norton, 2007, p. 20; Joanna Bourke, *What it Means to Be Human: Reflections from 1791 to the Present*, London: Virago, 2011, pp. 135–7.

46   Rosalind Petchesky, 'Sexual Rights: Inventing a Concept, Mapping an International Practice', in Richard Parker, Peter Aggleton and R. M. Barbosa (eds.), *Framing the Sexual Subject: The Politics of Gender, Sexuality and Power*, Berkeley: University of California Press, 2000, pp. 81–103; Plummer, *Cosmopolitan Sexualities*, pp. 90–4.

47   Rosalind Pollock Petchesky and Karen Judd, *Negotiating Reproductive Rights: Women's Perspectives Across Countries and Cultures*, London: Zed Books, 1998.

48   Kerry Kollman and Matthew Waites, 'The Global Politics of Lesbian, Gay, Bisexual and Transgender Human Rights: An Introduction', in 'The Global Politics of LGBT Human Rights', special issue of *Contemporary Politics* 15 (1), 2009, pp. 1–17.

49   Joke Swiebel, 'Lesbian, Gay, Bisexual and Transgender Human Rights: The Search for an International Strategy', *Contemporary Politics* 15 (1), 2009, pp. 19–35.

50   Petchesky, 'Sexual Rights'.

51   Corinne Lennox and Matthew Waites, 'Human Rights and Gender Identity in the Commonwealth: From History and Law to Developing Activism and Transnational Dialogue', in Lennox and Waites (eds.), *Human Rights*, pp. 1–59 at p. 44.

52   Bourke, *What it Means to be Human*, p. 159.

53   Dean, *Critical and Effective Histories*, p. 136.

54   See Rosi Braidotti, *Transpositions: On Nomadic Ethics*, Cambridge: Polity, 2006, p. 15, and *The Posthuman*, Cambridge: Polity, 2013.

55   See Frida Beckman (ed.), *Deleuze and Sex*, Edinburgh: Edinburgh University Press, 2011.

56   Plummer, *Cosmopolitan Sexualities*, p. 100.

57   Tom Boellstorff, *Coming of Age in Second Life: An Anthropologist Explores the Virtually Human*, Princeton, NJ, and London: Princeton University Press, 2008.

58   Carol Gilligan, *Joining the Opposition*, Cambridge: Polity, 2013, p. 167.

7   Memory, Community, Voice

1   Peter Scott-Presland, *Amiable Warriors: A History of the Campaign for Homosexual Equality and its Times. Vol. 1: A*

Space to Breathe 1954–1973, London: Paradise Press, 2015, pp. xv, xix.

2   Raphael Samuel, *Theatres of Memory: Past and Present in Contemporary Culture*, revised edition (first published 1994), London and New York: Verso, 2012.

3   Bill Schwarz, 'Foreword', in Samuel, *Theatres of Memory*, pp. vii–xix. See also discussion in Susannah Radstone, *The Sexual Politics of Time: Confession, Nostalgia, Memory*, London and New York: Routledge, 2007.

4   Laura Lee Downs, *Writing Gender History*, 2nd edition, London: Bloomsbury, 2010, p. 31.

5   Graham Willett, 'Making an Exhibition of Ourselves: GLQ History as Public History', *La Trobe Journal* 87, May 2011, pp. 4–18 at p. 4.

6   Allan Bérubé, *Coming Out Under Fire: The History of Gay Men and Women in World War II*, New York: Free Press, 1990. See John D'Emilio and Estelle Freedman, 'Introduction', in Allan Bérubé, *My Desire for History: Essays in Gay, Community and Labor History*, edited by D'Emilio and Freedman, Chapel Hill, NC: University of North Carolina, 2011, pp. 1–40. See also Nan Alamilla Boyd and Horacio N. Roque Ramirez (eds.), *Bodies of Evidence: The Practices of Queer Oral History*, Oxford and New York: York University Press, 2012, introduction, pp. 1–22.

7   Joan Nestle, 'The Will to Remember: The Lesbian Herstory Archives of New York', *Journal of Homosexuality* 34 (3/4), 1998, pp. 225–35 at p. 228, and *A Restricted Country*, Berkeley: Cleiss Press, 2003.

8   Nestle, 'Will to Remember', p. 229.

9   Paul Thompson, *The Voice of the Past: Oral History*, 3rd edition, Oxford: Oxford University Press, 2000, p. 4.

10   Michel Foucault, *Archaeology of Knowledge*, London: Tavistock, 1978.

11   Nan Alamilla Boyd, 'History as Social Change: Queer Archives and Oral History Projects', in Leila J. Rupp and Susan K. Freeman (eds.), *Understanding and Teaching U.S. Lesbian, Gay, Bisexual and Transgender History*, Madison: University of Wisconsin Press, 2014, pp. 311–19.

12   Judith Halberstam, 'Reflections on Queer Studies in Pedagogy', in Gust A. Yep, Karen E. Lovaas and John P. Elia (eds.), 'Queer Theory and Communication: From Disciplinary Queers to Queering the Discipline', special issue of *Journal of Homosexuality* 45 (2/3/4), 2003, pp. 361–4 at p. 364.

13   Ann Cvetkovich, *An Archive of Feelings: Trauma, Sexuality, and Lesbian Public Culture*, Durham, NC: Duke University Press, 2003.

14   Daniel Marshall, Kevin P. Murphy and Zeb Tortorici, 'Editors' Introduction: Queering Archives: Historical Unravelings', *Radical History Review* (120), Fall 2014, pp. 1–11 at pp. 1–2.

15   Alison Flood, 'Women's Library Campaign Gathers Steam', *Guardian*, 11 April 2012.

16   Willett, 'Making an Exhibition'.

17   For example, a guide to gay and lesbian sources by Matt Houlbrook is available online at the National Archives: http://www.nationalarchives.gov.uk/help-with-your-research/research-guides/gay-lesbian-history

18   Thompson, *Voice of the Past*, p. 25.

19   Ken Plummer, *Telling Sexual Stories: Power, Change and Social Worlds*, London: Routledge, 1995, p. 5.

20   Radstone, *Sexual Politics of Time*.

21   Cvetkovich, *Archive of Feelings*, ch. 4.

22   Notably Jacques Derrida, *Archive Fever: A Freudian Impression. Religion and Postmodernism*, Chicago: Chicago University Press, 1996.

23   Mike Savage, *Identities and Social Change in Britain since 1940: The Politics of Method*, Oxford: Oxford University Press, 2010, p. 186.

24   Thompson, *Voice of the Past*, pp. 8, 15–16, 113–14.

25   Esther Newton, *Cherry Grove, Fire Island: Sixty Years in America's First Gay and Lesbian Town*, Boston: Beacon Books, 1993; Elizabeth L. Kennedy and Madeline D. Davis, *Boots of Leather, Slippers of Gold: The History of a Lesbian Community*, New York: Routledge, 1993.

26   Carrie Hamilton, 'Sex, "Silence", and Audio-Tape', in Boyd and Roque Ramirez (eds.), *Bodies of Evidence*, pp. 23–40; and Carrie Hamilton, *Sexual Revolution in Cuba: Passion, Politics and Memory*, Chapel Hill: University of North Carolina Press, 2012. The foreword, 'Cuban Voices' by Elizabeth Dore, pp. vii–xii, summarizes the difficulties confronted by the project.

Index

9/11 106

abortion 62, 84, 108, 126
abstinence 83
activism 2, 53, 90, 119, 123,
    126
    LGBTQ activism 41–2, 106,
    111, 117
    see also social movements
adolescence 126
adult education 118
affect 17–19, 53, 66
Africa 96, 99, 100, 102, 103,
    105, 110–11, 123–4
African-American
    experience 76
AIDS see HIV/AIDS
AIDS generation 20
Albany Trust 123
Alexander, Sally 66
Althusser, Louis 65
Altman, Dennis 90, 97
America, pre-Columbian 111
American Psychiatric
    Association 52
American Revolution 112
Americanization 97

Amsterdam 40
'ancestral history' 54
Animism 103
Annales school 31
anorexia nervosa 16
anthropology 28, 33, 64
anti-capitalism 7–8, 97
anti-essentialism 60, 61
anti-globalization 7–8, 97
anti-humanism 84, 114
anti-social turn 53
antiviral drug therapies 90
Apartheid 111
Arab world 99, 102, 106, 107
Arcadie organization 38
archives 124
Arondekar, Anjali 99
ars erotica 101
Asia 103
'assemblages' 18
Australia 41, 124
Australian Lesbian and Gay
    Archives 123
Australian Women's Liberation
    and Lesbian Feminist
    Archives 123
Austria 40

baby-boomers 19–20, 31, 85
Barbin, Herculine 51
Barnard conference 57
Barry, Kathleen 59
Bell, Daniel 85
Bengali people 105
Berger, Peter 33
Berlin 40, 46
Bersani, Leo 53
Bérubé, Allan 41, 51, 118–19
binary divide 36, 37, 50–1, 81,
    95, 106
biology 17, 25, 27, 44
biopower 16, 35
birth control 35, 62, 71, 83,
    87, 113, 126
bisexuality 12, 81
Bloch, Iwan 27–8
bodies 15–17, 65, 67, 81
Boellstorff, Tom 104, 111, 115
borders, national 96
Bosia, Michael J. 110
Boswell, John 34, 40, 44–5, 92
Bouhdiba, Abdelwahab 107
Bourdieu, Pierre 18
Bourke, Joanna 58, 61, 114
Braidotti, Rosi 114
Brandt, Allan M. 89
Bray, Alan 45, 92–3
Brazil 109, 111
Britain 18, 27, 65, 72, 83, 88
    and archives 122–3, 124
    and feminism 59, 122–3
    and homosexuality 14, 38,
        41–2, 71–2, 73–4, 91,
        95, 105
    and London 45–7, 92, 93
British Library 124
British National Archives 124
Brooten, Bernadette 45
Brown, Peter 45
Browne, Stella 29
Brownmiller, Susan 59, 60, 61
Buddhism 103
Buffalo, New York 127

Burton, Richard 102
butch–femme relations 41, 57,
    127
Butler, Judith 36, 50, 51, 104

Caesar, Julius 39
Campaign for Homosexual
    Equality 116, 123
Canada 41, 124
capital punishment 110
capitalism 7–8, 66, 77, 97
Caribbean 105
Carpenter, Edward 28, 38, 48,
    71
Carter, Julian B. 70
Castro, Mariela 109, 128
categorization 35, 37, 39, 45,
    54, 102, 103
Catholicism 45, 92–3, 109
change, sexual 5, 79, 80–1
change, social 76, 77, 127
Chaucer, Geoffrey 55
Chauncey, George 46, 47, 53,
    91, 92
children 6, 35, 79, 98
China 92, 99, 101, 102, 103,
    105, 108
Christianity 45, 78, 82, 92–3,
    102, 103, 106, 107,
    109, 110
Christina, queen of Sweden 39
Civil Partnership Act 91
'civilizing process' 14, 104
Cixous, Hélène 64
Clark, Anna 81
climate 102
COC organization 38
Cohen, Deborah 93
Cold War 84
colonialism 76, 96–7, 101,
    102, 104–7, 109, 111,
    113, 119
    postcolonialism 85, 107–8,
        110, 111
Combahee River Collective 69

commercialization 7, 76
community 118–20
'compulsory
    heterosexuality' 15
confession 125
Confucianism 103, 109
Connell, Raewyn 16–17, 72–3
conservatism, religious 102,
    104, 110
conservatism, sexual 48, 57–8,
    84, 94, 108–9
conservatism, social 7, 18, 19,
    20, 22, 31, 49, 129
consumerism 83, 85, 86, 97
Contagious Diseases Acts 59,
    63, 71
continuism 7, 8
Cook, Matt 46, 47, 93
counter-history 116–19
'crip' liberation 16
Cuba 108, 128
Cullwick, Hannah 72
cultural history 61, 64, 65
cultural studies 75, 118
cultures, sexual 4, 22, 33, 37,
    83
    and globalization 96, 100–3,
        106–7, 108, 109, 110,
        111, 113
    urban sexual subcultures 14,
        46
Cvetkovich, Ann 121–2, 126
cyborgs 16

Dabhoiwala, Faramerz 78–9
Daly, Mary 59
Darwinism 19, 25
Daughters of Bilitis 38
Davidoff, Leonore 72
Davidson, Arnold 21
Davis, Madeline D. 127
Dean, Mitchell 101
Declaration of Montreal 113
declinism 6–7, 8, 21
deconstructionism 33, 36, 49

'Deep South' 48
Deleuze, Gilles 17, 18, 49, 114
D'Emilio, John 41, 42, 68, 76,
    119
democratic history 2, 10, 117
Denmark 91
dependence, female 59
Derrida, Jacques 49
desire 33, 55, 118
'desiring machines' 18, 49
detraditionalization 87
deviance 33, 86, 93, 111
digital revolution 16
Dinshaw, Carolyn 55
disabled people 16
diversity 5, 19, 46, 130
    sexual 7, 25, 58, 82, 96, 99,
        112, 124
divorce reform 108
Doan, Laura 39, 54, 75, 83
domesticity 73, 76, 88, 93
double standards 27
Dover, Kenneth 29
drugs 98
DuBois, Ellen 58
Duggan, Lisa 70
Durkheim, Emile 24
Dworkin, Andrea 57, 59
dystopianism 53

East Asia 103
Echols, Alice 59
economics 8, 97, 103
Edel, Deborah 121
Edeleman, Lee 53
education studies 118
effeminization 105
eighteenth century 31, 34, 46,
    67, 70, 78, 80–1, 82, 92
Elias, Norbert 18
Ellis, Havelock 25, 26, 28, 29,
    60, 72, 104
embodiment 5, 17, 19
emotion 4, 7, 17, 18, 33, 53,
    66–7, 87, 122, 127

empowerment, personal 16
England 45, 65, 71
English-speaking countries 27
Enlightenment 78, 114
ephemera 121–2
Epprecht, Marc 96, 99, 100, 101, 102
Epstein, Steven 90
Eribon, Didier 38, 43
Escoffier, Jeffrey 86
essentialism 20, 32, 44–5, 49, 60, 61, 89
ethnicity 46, 112
eugenics 71, 72, 109
Europe 71, 73, 92, 94, 103–4, 106
European Union 104
everyday life 82, 108, 128
exploitation 8, 86, 102

Faderman, Lillian 42
family life 31, 62, 103, 108, 109, 112, 126
Fanon, Frantz 110
fascism 83–4
'female corporeality' 16
female identity 17–18, 62
'female principle' 59
female sexuality 58, 61–4
femininity 12, 72
feminism 7, 9–10, 14, 18, 59, 79, 83, 118, 122–3
feminism, black 68–70
feminism, first-wave 58
feminism, second-wave 15–16, 32, 57, 66, 86
fertility 80
Fisher, Kate 83
'formalization'/'informalizat ion' 7, 14, 82, 83
Foucault, Michel 14, 21, 22, 30, 101–2, 114
  and homosexuality 43–4, 45, 48–9, 50, 51, 54

and memory 120, 125
and modern sexuality 77, 78, 84
and social constructionism 9, 34–5, 36, 37
and structures of power 7, 16, 63, 64, 68, 120
France 18, 38, 91
Freedman, Estelle 61, 68, 76, 119
freedom of speech 58
French Revolution 79, 112
'French theory, new' 64
French-speaking countries 27
Freud, Sigmund 17, 23, 25, 27–8
  and Marxism 29–30, 43
Frontiers: A Journal of Women's Studies 126
Fukuyama, Francis 85

Gagnon, John H. 17, 32–3, 35
GALA (Gay and Lesbian Memory in Action) 123–4
Gallagher, Catherine 65
Garber, Marjorie 51
gay communities 40
'Gay International' 106
Gay Liberation Front 123
gay liberation movement 2, 20, 32, 35, 41, 43, 51, 125
gay politics 18, 49, 51
gay rights *see* LGBTQ rights
Gay Shame conference 53
Geertz, Clifford 65
geisha houses 109
gender 5, 112, 120
  and globalization 103, 109
  and identity 17–18, 62, 66, 108
  and sexuality 3, 12, 25, 51, 57–74, 78, 79

gender absolutism 16
gender order 51, 67, 73, 74
gender studies 121
gender theory 72
generations 19–20, 87
'geography of perversions' 14, 102
German-speaking countries 27
Germany 14, 29, 83
Giami, Alain 85
Gibbon, Edward 26–7
Giddens, Anthony 16, 87
Gide, André 38, 71
Gilligan, Carol 115
GLBT Historical Society of North California 122, 123
GLBT History Museum 123
global North 2, 87, 98
global South 2, 10, 85, 87, 99, 101, 109, 113, 129
globalization 7–8, 96–115
Goffman, Erving 36
Gordon, Linda 58, 62–3, 64
governmentality 7, 35
'Great Transition' 31, 85
Greater London Council 123
Greeks, ancient 28–9
Greenblatt, Stephen 65
Greenwich Village, New York 83
gross indecency 105
Grosz, Elizabeth 16
Guattari, Félix 17, 18, 114

'habitus' 18
Halberstam, Judith/Jack 21, 121
Hall, Lesley 74, 76
Hall, Stuart 13–14
Hall-Carpenter Archives 123
Halperin, David 28, 48, 49, 53, 54, 75
Hamilton, Carrie 108, 127–8

Hammonds, Evelynn M. 69–70
happiness 76
Haraway, Donna 16
health needs 112
Heaphy, Brian 95
hedonism 85
Hekma, Gert 85, 94
Herzog, Dagmar 83, 84, 86
heterosexuality 12, 24, 79–80
  and globalization 107, 110
  heteronormativity 15, 50, 70, 81–4, 100
  and marriage 35, 70, 82–3, 88, 108, 109
  and parenting 35, 88
  and reproduction 27, 35
  writings on 36, 39
heterosexualization 10, 81, 82
Himmelfarb, Gertrude 85, 86
Hinduism 103
Hirschfeld, Magnus 1–2, 25, 26, 28, 29, 38, 104
history, additive/ transformative 75
history groups 118, 123
History Workshop Journal 32
History Workshop movement 32, 117
HIV/AIDS 20, 70, 87, 88–90
  and 1990s 18, 21, 90
  and archives 122, 123
  and globalization 99, 102, 104, 110
  and homosexuality 48, 49, 57, 88, 89, 90, 91–2
Hoad, Neville 99
Hodann, Max 29
homogenization, global 103–4
'homonationalism' 94, 106, 113
'homonormativity' 94
homophobia 10, 68, 106, 110–11

homoeroticism 45, 107
Homosexual Law Reform
    Society 38, 123
homosexual rights 8, 10, 87,
    105, 106, 110, 111, 113
homosexual roles 14, 34, 43, 92
homosexuality 12, 24, 28–30,
    36–56, 78, 126–7,
    153n10, 163n11
  and 1970s 28, 39, 40–2, 50,
    56, 86
  and Britain 14, 38, 41–2,
    71–2, 73–4, 91, 95, 105
  and London 45–7, 92, 93
  and globalization 99–100,
    102, 105–8, 109–11
  and HIV/AIDS 48, 49, 57,
    88, 89, 90, 91–2
  and identity 35–6, 42–8, 49,
    50, 52, 54, 55, 89
  and legitimization 38–9, 40,
    105
  and Netherlands 38, 91
  and nineteenth century 34,
    47, 49, 79, 82, 93, 107
  and race 46, 89, 106
  and regulation 105–8,
    109–11, 128
  and social
    constructionism 34–6,
    37, 43, 44–6, 49–50
  and United States 38, 41–2,
    55, 84, 89, 105
  and HIV/AIDs 48, 49, 57,
    88
  and New York 45, 46
  and same-sex marriage 91,
    92, 94
Houlbrook, Matt 47
human rights 10, 98, 107,
    111, 112–15
  see also LGBTQ rights;
    reproductive rights;
    sexual rights; women's
    rights

humanism 84, 114–15
humanities studies 15
Hunt, Lynn 112
hygiene, social 109
hysteria 16, 24

identity, sexual 3, 5, 12,
    17–18, 23, 113, 120
  and gender 17–18, 62, 66,
    108
  and globalization 98, 128
  and homosexuality 35–6,
    42–8, 49, 50, 52, 54,
    55, 89
  and self 37, 76, 128
ILGA (International Gay and
    Lesbian
    Association) 113
illegality 47, 109
illegitimacy 31
IMF (International Monetary
    Fund) 8
imperialism 71, 73, 100, 105,
    113
inclusivity 94
India 99, 102, 105, 111
Indian Penal Code 105
Indianapolis 58
individualism 85, 114
individuality 16, 25
Indonesia 110, 111
industrialization 31, 79, 80
inequalities 98, 101, 120
interactionism 17, 33, 36
interconnectedness 101
International Conference on
    LGBT Human
    Rights 113
International Gay and Lesbian
    Human Rights
    Commission 113
intersectionality 10, 19, 68–72
interwar years 83
Iran 102, 110
Iraq 105

Irigaray, Luce 64
Islam 99, 103, 105–6, 107, 110
Islamophobia 102, 106
Israel 106

Jack the Ripper 65–6
Japan 109
Jeffreys, Sheila 60, 64
Jesus 39
Jim Crow laws 69
Johannesburg 123–4
Journal of Homosexuality 153n13
Journal of Social History 32
Journal of the History of Sexuality 39
justice, sexual 1–2, 12, 26, 98, 111, 124

Kafer, Alison 16
Kaoma, Kapya J. 111
Kaplan, Morris B. 47
Katz, Jonathan Ned 41, 81–2, 153n10
Kemp, Margery 55
Kennedy, Elizabeth L. 127
Kertbeny, Karl-Maria (Karoly-Maria Benkert) 24, 28, 38, 81
Kimmel, Michael 72
Kinsey, Alfred 20, 33
knowledge, sexual 14
knowledge, unofficial 116–19
Krafft-Ebing, Richard von 24, 25, 26, 52
Kristeva, Julia 64

labelling, social 35
Lacanian 'recovery of Freud' 17, 43
language 3, 18, 23–6, 33, 81–2
Laqueur, Thomas 65, 67, 80
Larvie, Sean Patrick 109

Laslett, Peter 31
Latin America 99
Leather Archives, Chicago 124
Leatherman, Janie 61
Lecky, W. E. H. 27
legislation 71, 90, 91, 105
legitimization of homosexuality 38–9, 40, 105
Lennox, Corinne 113
Lesbian Herstory Archive 118, 119, 121
lesbianism 40, 80, 92, 111
and identity 42–3, 55
and memory 119, 121, 128
lesbianism, black 68–70
Lewis, Brian 54
LGBT History Month 2
LGBTQ people 9, 14, 104
and activism 41–2, 106, 111, 117
and memory 117, 121–2, 123, 127
LGBTQ Oral History Digital Collaboratory 124
LGBTQ rights 8, 10, 87, 105, 106, 110, 111, 113
liberalization 19, 86, 87, 124, 129
liberationism 6, 19, 20, 43
see also gay liberation movement; women's movement
Liberia 110
libraries 124
Licht, Hans 29
Lister, Anne 43, 93
London 34, 40, 45–7, 65, 92, 93
London Metropolitan Archives 124
London Metropolitan University 122
London School of Economics 122–3

loss 18, 53, 109, 122, 126
Love, Heather 18, 52

McIntosh, Mary 34, 35, 37, 43, 92
MacKinnon, Catharine 57, 59–60
McLaren, Angus 62
magic 23–6
mainstreaming 75–95, 124, 129
Malawi 110
male sexuality 59, 60, 80
Malthus, Thomas 79
Mann, Susan 99, 100–1, 105, 108
Marcus, Steven 30, 31
Marcuse, Herbert 30, 85
Marotta, Toby 41
marriage 52, 76, 88
marriage, forced/arranged 113
marriage, heterosexual 35, 70, 82–3, 88, 108, 109
marriage, mixed race 70
marriage, same-sex 10, 88, 91–5, 110
marriage reforms 108
Martin, Biddy 52
Marxist Social Democratic Party 29
Marx/Marxism 7, 24, 29–30, 43, 65, 125
masculinity 12, 72–3, 110
Massad, Joseph 102, 105–6, 113
masturbation 12, 24, 27, 80, 163n11
materialism 29, 114
Mattachine Society 38
Mayne, Xavier (Edward I. Prime Stevenson) 38
Mbeki, Thabo 102
Mead, George Herbert 17
meaning, symbolic 33

medicalization of sexuality 89–90
Mediterranean 102
melancholia 18, 53, 125–6
Melbourne 123
memory 10, 18, 41, 116–30
men 72–4, 80, 163n11
men, black 69
metaphor, spatial 14
Michigan 53
Middle East 92, 102
migration 32, 84, 103
Minneapolis 58
misery, sexual 83
Mitchell, Alice 70
Mitchell, Juliet 66
mobility, social 83
modernity 83, 84, 87
modernization, sexual 6, 107–10
Mollies Clubs 92
Money, John 51
Moore, Henrietta 53
morality 8, 27, 29, 62
    Victorian 20, 70, 71, 81
    Western 79, 102
Morgan, Robin 59
Mort, Frank 89
multiculturalism 113
Munby, A. J. 72
Muñoz, José Esteban 52
myth 118, 120

nationalism 94, 102, 107
    'homonationalism' 94, 106, 113
Native Americans 92
Nealon, Christopher 38
neocolonialism 101
neoliberalism 7–8, 94, 97
Nestle, Joan 118, 119, 121
Netherlands 14, 38, 91
New British Queer History 46, 54

'New Deal' 84
New Right 57
New York 40, 45, 46, 83
New York Public Library 124
Newton, Esther 127
nineteenth century 6, 19–20,
    29, 35, 63
    and globalization 102,
        104–5, 107
    and homosexuality 34, 47,
        49, 79, 82, 93, 107
    and marriage 76, 82, 93
    pornography 30, 82
    and structures of power 59,
        60, 65, 72, 73–4
non-governmental
    organizations (NGOs) 4
normalization 52, 81–4, 90,
    120
North Africa 103
North America 103
nostalgia 21–2, 120, 125–6
Nussbaum, Martha 114
Nyeck, S. N. 99

One Institute 123
one-child policy 108
oppression 67, 69, 86
oral history 41, 74, 83, 109,
    120, 124, 125–9
ordinariness 52
organization, social 33, 103
Ottoman Empire 107
outcast groups 63
Outspoken: Oral History from
    LGBTQ Pioneers 124

PACS (*pacte civil de
    solidarité*) 91
Padgug, Robert A. 32
parenthood 35, 80, 87, 88,
    163n11
parenting, same-sex 88, 92
parents, single 88, 126

Paris 46
pathologies, sexual 25
patriarchy 59, 66, 69, 73, 107
performance 33, 36, 50
permissiveness 31
perversion 12, 25, 28, 29,
    36–7, 52, 60
perversity 29
Petchesky, Rosalind 62, 113
'phet' 109
Philippines 111
Phillips, Kim M. 78
pleasure 60, 84, 86, 120
Pleasure and Danger
    conference papers 58,
    60, 68
Plummer, Ken 17, 19, 21, 33,
    42, 94, 98, 103,
    114–15, 125
politics 4, 5, 83–4, 88, 89
    gay politics 18, 49, 51
population growth 26, 79
pornography 30, 57, 59, 82,
    97–8
Portsmouth 63
postcolonialism 85, 107–8,
    110, 111
posthumanism 114
postmodernity 125
poststructuralism 33, 36, 49,
    64, 65, 72, 114
poverty 8, 103
power 57–74, 76
power, political 108
power, structures of 3, 7, 8,
    13, 50, 119–20
power, technologies of 16, 63,
    84, 105
power relations 8, 30, 61, 67,
    75, 76, 102, 113
    and memory 120, 125,
    127–8
power-knowledge 35
Powers of Desire 58, 60

Pride History Group 124
priests 55
privacy 112
progressive narrative 6, 7
proletarianization 31
prostitution 27, 55, 58, 63,
    71, 82, 89, 126
psychoanalysis 17, 66, 126
psychology 14, 17, 27, 33, 44
Puar, Jasbir 18, 94, 106, 113
public health 90
Pulp Fiction film 55
Puritanism 85
purity, social 63–4, 71, 83, 122

'queer', meaning 48
queer archives 121
queer challenge 48–50
'queer futurity' 53
queer studies 36, 52, 53, 117,
    121
queer theory 15, 18, 20, 36–7,
    46, 49
queer time 21

race 10, 19, 46, 61, 68–72,
    89, 106, 112, 127
racism 61, 113
Radical History Review 32,
    122
Radstone, Susannah 125
Rainbow Jews 124
rape 59, 60–1
rationalism 114
Reay, Barry 78
records, unofficial 120
Reformation, Protestant 78, 82
regionalism 103–4
regulation 76, 79, 84, 105–8
Reich, Wilhelm 30
religion 79, 98, 103
    Christianity 45, 102, 103,
        106, 107, 110
    Catholicism 45, 92–3, 109
    Protestantism 78, 82

Hinduism 103
and human rights 112
Islam 99, 102, 103, 105–6,
    107, 110
religious fundamentalism 102,
    104, 106, 110
Renaissance 45
repression 6, 30–1, 34, 58, 73,
    76, 81, 86, 105, 126
reproduction 25, 76, 80, 87,
    163n11
reproduction policies 108
reproductive freedom 57,
    62–3, 98
reproductive rights 104,
    112–13
reproductive technologies 98
resistance 16, 35, 63, 76, 111,
    120
    and homosexuality 41, 47,
        48
    and race 69, 70, 71
revolution, cultural 19, 85, 86
revolution, sexual 6, 31, 78–9,
    82, 86–7, 107
Rich, Adrienne 15
Rivers, Daniel 92
Rome, ancient 26, 40
Roper, Michael 66
Rubin, Gayle 52, 67
Rukus! Black LGBT
    Archive 124
Russia 108, 110

sadomasochism 57
Said, Edward 106
same-sex marriage 10, 88,
    91–5, 110
same-sex parenting 88, 92
Samuel, Raphael 32, 117,
    119
San Francisco 40, 45, 122,
    123
Sanger, Margaret 62
Sappho 39

Savage, Mike 126
Scandinavia 91
'Scholar and the Feminist IX'
    conference 57
Schwarz, Bill 118
scientia sexualis 101
scientific approach 26, 90, 97
Scott, Joan 65, 66
Scott-Presland, Peter 116–17
secrecy 119
secularization 79
Sedgwick, Eve Kosofsky 15,
    18, 36, 49–50, 53, 67–8
seventeenth century 78
sex change operations 16, 110
sex education 7, 57
sex reform 6, 29, 81
sex wars 9, 18, 57, 68
sexologists, pioneering 1–2,
    17, 20, 23, 24–6, 47,
    118, 125
sexology 1, 17, 24–6
sexual abuse of children 57
sexual histories,
    non-academic 116–19
sexual instinct 24, 25, 27, 29,
    30
sexual life 31, 71, 76
sexual orientation 37, 44, 113
sexual rights 62–3, 102, 104,
    105, 112–15
sexuality, commercialization
    of 76
sexuality, female 58, 61–4
'sexuality', meaning of 23
sexuality, modern 10, 77–81,
    125
sexuality, racialized 69–70
sexuality, science of 1, 25, 26,
    37
sexuality, white 70
sexuality and gender 12, 25,
    51, 57–74, 78, 79
sexualization 6, 35, 42, 59,
    72, 82

heterosexualization 10, 81,
    82
sexually transmitted
    infections 63, 89, 97
Shakespeare, William 39
shame 18, 19, 53, 119, 120
Shorter, Edward 31
Signs journal 64
Simon, William 17, 32–3, 35
Simson, Rennie 71
Sinha, Mrinalini 105
Sívori, Horacio 99
sixteenth century 80
slavery 69, 104
slide shows 51, 118–19, 121
Smith-Rosenberg, Carroll 42
social class 10, 19, 46, 61,
    68–72, 78, 127
  middle class 47, 63
  working class 32, 41, 63, 72
social constructionism 32–7,
    61–2
  1970s 11, 20, 34
  deconstructionism 33, 36, 49
  and Foucault 9, 34–5, 36,
    37
  and homosexuality 34–6,
    37, 43, 44–6, 49–50
social control 34, 37
social factors 44
social history 10, 32, 54, 64,
    75
Social History journal 32
social movements 4, 89–90,
    98, 104, 122, 127
    see also activism
social policy studies 118
social psychology 14, 33
social science literature 39
society, human 28, 112
sociology 14, 17, 24, 28, 33,
    118
sodomy 44, 55, 105
'Sotadic Zone' 102
South Africa 111

South America 73, 92, 102
South Asia 103
South Sea Islands 102
Southampton 63
South-East Asia 105
Soviet Union 83–4, 108
Spanish conquistadors 73
Spivak, Gayatri 49
Stalinism 108
state regulation 58
Steakley, James 41
sterilization 71
stigma, sexual 14, 35–6, 39, 40, 53
Stoler, Ann 71
Stoller, Robert 51
Stone, Lawrence 30, 31
Stonewall 51, 119
Stopes, Marie 74, 83
'Straight State' 84
subjectivity 17–19, 35, 66, 129
subjugation 59, 120
sublimation 86
subordination 10, 58, 61, 66
suffering 120
suffrage 122
Symonds, John Addington 28, 29, 38
Szreter, Simon 83

talks 118–19, 121
Tamale, Sylvia 99
Taylor, Barbara 66
Taylor, Gordon Rattray 30
technology 16, 98
Tennessee 70
Thailand 109
theory 13–15, 20, 64, 72
  queer theory 15, 18, 20, 36–7, 46, 49
Therborn, Göran 103
Thomas, Keith 27
Thompson, E. P. 32
Thompson, Paul 119–20, 125
time 20–2, 130

Tin, Louis-Georges 81
Tissot, Samuel 24
tolerance 26, 45, 78, 94
Tomkins, Silvan 18
Tosh, John 72, 73
tourism, sex 98, 101
trafficking 104
transgender 16, 50–2, 87, 109, 112, 113
Transgender Archives 124
transnationalism 2, 4, 10, 97, 98–101, 102, 111
transvestites 12, 51
Traub, Valerie 53, 54–5
Treichler, Paula 88
Trumbach, Randolph 45, 80
truth 21, 24, 120
Turkey 107
Turner, Victor 65
'turns' 15
twentieth century 6, 49, 71, 72, 82–3, 100

Uganda 110
Ulrichs, Karl Heinrich 24, 28, 38
United Nations Declaration on the Elimination of Violence against Women 112
United Nations General Assembly 112
United States 14, 18, 20, 57–8, 65, 76–7, 88, 106
  and homosexuality 38, 41–2, 55, 84, 89, 105
  and HIV/AIDs 48, 49, 57, 88
  and New York 45, 46
  and same-sex marriage 91, 92, 94
  and marriage 83, 91, 92, 94
  and memory 41, 118, 120–2, 123, 124, 126
  and race 69–71, 89

Universal Declaration of
  Human Rights 112
universalism 66, 106, 115
university courses 2
University of California 121
University of Southern
  California 123
University of Victoria 124
urban life 14, 46–7
urbanization 31
US service personnel 118–19
utopianism 52–3, 58, 101

Vance, Carole S. 15, 36, 58,
  60, 68
variability, sexual 33
veils 113
Vicinus, Martha 42
victimization 53, 61
Victorian morality 20, 70, 71,
  81
Vienna Conference on Human
  Rights 112
violence, sexual 58–61, 64, 69,
  81, 120, 126

Waites, Matthew 113
Walkowitz, Judith 61, 62, 63,
  64, 65
war 61, 84, 127
Ward, Freda 70
wealth 103
Weber, Max 24
Weeks, Jeffrey 41–2, 76
Weiss, Meredith L. 110
Wells, Ida B. 70

West Asia 103
Westermarck, Edvard 28
Western concepts 13, 101
Western scholarship 100
Western sexuality 10, 33, 76,
  78, 81, 84, 101, 106
Western values 85, 89, 110,
  125–6
Westphal, Carl 24
Whig interpretation 53
'white slave trade' 104
Whitman, Walt 47
Wieringa, Saskia 98–9
Wilde, Oscar 29, 39, 47, 71
Willett, Graham 118
Williams, Raymond 18, 65
women 83, 104
  exploitation of 8, 102
  and memory 109, 122
  subordination/subjugation
    of 58, 59, 61, 66
women, black 70, 71
women, hysterical 35
women's bodies 15–16, 67, 81
women's centres 118
Women's Library 122–3
women's movement 2, 61, 125
women's rights 8, 15–16, 87,
  112, 113
words 23–6
World Bank 8
Wouters, Cas 87

Yogyakarta Principles 113

Ze'evi, Dror 107